Contributions to Economics

Lei Delsen • Frank Bauer • Gilbert Cette
Mark Smith
Editors

Comparative Analyses of Operating Hours and Working Times in the European Union

Physica-Verlag
A Springer Company

Editors

Dr. Lei Delsen
Department of Economics
Institute for Management Research
Nijmegen School of Management
Radboud University Nijmegen
Thomas van Aquinostraat 5
6500 HK Nijmegen
Netherlands
l.delsen@fm.ru.nl

Dr. Frank Bauer
IAB Regional Nordrhein-Westfalen
Josef-Gockeln-Straße 7
D-40474 Düsseldorf
Germany
frank.bauer6@iab.de

Prof. Gilbert Cette
Banque de France
46-2400 DEMS
31, rue Croix des Petits Champs
75049 Paris Cedex 01
France
gilbert.cette@banque-france.fr

Dr. Mark Smith
Grenoble Ecole de Management
12, rue Pierre Sémard, BP 127
38003 Grenoble CX
France
mark.smith@grenoble-em.com

ISSN 1431-1933
ISBN 978-3-7908-2184-0 e-ISBN 978-3-7908-2185-7
DOI 10.1007/978-3-7908-2185-7
Springer Dordrecht Heidelberg London New York

Library of Congress Control Number: 2009926889

Cover design: SPi Publisher Services

Printed on acid-free paper

Springer is part of Springer Science+Business Media (www.springer.com)

Contents

1 Topics for Comparative Research on Operating Hours in the EU

Lei Delsen, Frank Bauer, Gilbert Cette and Mark Smith

1.1 Introduction

This volume is the second book based on comparative and comprehensive data from the 2003 representative European Union Company survey of Operating hours, Working times and Employment (EUCOWE) in France, Germany, the Netherlands, Portugal, Spain and the United Kingdom. This publication complements and builds on the first book published in 2007 in which the methodology and the descriptive national findings, as well as some first comparative analytical results, of the EUCOWE project were presented.[1] In several of the countries studied the survey represented one of the first dedicated studies on the operating time. The EUCOWE survey was the first attempt to collect cross-national comparative data on operating hours and opening times and as such represents an innovative source of information of working patterns, establishment behaviour and competitiveness in the EU.

At the firm and industry level, as well as the macroeconomic level, operating hours are one of the essential determinants of productivity and competitiveness not to mention the standard of living of the wider population.[2] In essence operating hours, opening times and service hours can be considered as central to the behaviour of establishments in relation to their clients and, as a result, the organisation of employment and working time

1 Delsen, L., D. Bosworth, H. Groß and R. Muñoz de Bustillo y Llorente (eds.) (2007) *Operating Hours and Working Times. A Survey of Capacity Utilisation and Employment in the European Union*, Heidelberg: Physica Verlag.

2 Pioneering work on the measurement of the rate of capital utilisation in relation to industrial efficiency and productivity is by Foss (1963) on US manufacturing firms and by Marris (1964) on UK manufacturing firms.

L. Delsen et al., *Comparative Analyses of Operating Hours and Working Times in the European Union*,
DOI: 10.1007/978-3-7908-2185-7_1,

of their employees. The extent to which organisations are required to serve clients within and outside "normal" working hours will also help shape the duration and intensity of utilisation of capital. While establishments will have some freedom in determining how they deal with their specific operating time requirements, and any fluctuations within those hours, they will also be subject to regulation and policy at the national and pan-national level. Thus operating hours are central to policy debates at both the European and national level. Concerns over the competitiveness of European firms and the reconciliation of work and family life are all impacted upon by operating hours of the establishments where employees work.

The EUCOWE survey also explored differences between economic sectors and establishment size in the use of part-time work, shift work, staggered working times, Saturday and Sunday work, overtime, agency workers and fixed-term employees and on-call labour (employees without an agreed number of hours). Additionally another highly relevant topic considered was the flexibility of operating hours. We were able to explore the extent to which opening and operating hours management has to react to fluctuations in business activity and how organisations cope with these fluctuations. In turn the survey includes information on what certain types of operating hours management means for working time and employment (for more details see Box 1).

In the first book based on the EUCOWE survey, operating times in the six countries covered by the investigation were explored. As shown in previous studies, these analyses confirmed the huge differences between European countries along a number of different dimensions of operating hours. Within countries Delsen *et al.* (2007) showed how daily, weekly and annual operating hours at the establishment level are effected by workplace size, sector and an array of other characteristics. Here we build on this work by analysing these establishment characteristics across countries with each chapter containing a strong comparative element.

In this second book the EUCOWE research team presents in-depth cross-country analyses of the relationship between operating hours, working time and employment in the European Union. To date comparative research on the relationship between operating hours, working time and employment has been limited; it has only covered certain sectors of economic activity, notably manufacturing, and, when considering the extension of operating hours, shift work has been the main focus. Moreover, small establishments have often been excluded (see for example Foss, 1963; 1981; 1997; Marris, 1964; Bautista *et al.*, 1981; Betancourt and Clague, 1981; Anxo *et al.*, 1995; EC, 1991; 1995; Lehndorff, 2000; Bauer,

Box 1: The EUCOWE project

The main objective of the EUCOWE project was the collection and analysis of comparative and representative data on the relationship between operating hours and working-time arrangements, and their consequences for employment in six EU member countries: Germany, France, the UK, the Netherlands, Portugal and Spain. The central component of the project was an establishment survey in 2003 in each of the participating countries. The survey was administered to around ten thousand establishments in each country and produced net national samples of between 1,400 to 3,000 establishments.

This innovative project was funded by the European Commission as part of its Fifth Framework Programme and began on October 1st, 2001. The EUCOWE project was conducted by ISO (Institute for Research on Social Opportunities) in Cologne (Frank Bauer, Hermann Groß, Lisgret Militzer-Schwenger, Georg Sieglen), the Institute for Work and Technology in Gelsenkirchen (Gerhard Bosch, Steffen Lehndorff, Sebastian Schief), the University of Marseille (Gilbert Cette, Yusuf Kocoglu, Arnaud Sylvain), the Radboud University Nijmegen (Lei Delsen, Jeroen Smits), the Catholic University of Porto (Alberto Castro, José Varejão), the University of Salamanca (Rafael Muñoz de Bustillo y Llorente, Enrique Fernández Macías) and the University of Manchester (Derek Bosworth, Mark Smith, Marilyn Carroll). This project was coordinated by Frank Bauer and Hermann Groß.

The EUCOWE survey and the data generated from it address methodical and methodological shortcomings of previous European surveys on operating hours (Bauer, Groß and Sieglen, 2002; 2007). All data were harmonised *ex ante*, the questionnaire was the same in all countries, data cleaning and computing was done collectively, and importantly the weighting procedures and the direct and indirect calculation of operating hours were kept identical in all national and comparative descriptions and analyses.

The innovation of the EUCOWE survey is not only the fact that it covers all economic sectors and all establishment sizes in the six countries, but also that in addition to shift work, staggered working times and actual individual working time (contractual working times and overtime hours) are included and taken into account for the calculation of operating hours. This methodological advance permits the calculation of the *indirect* measure of operating hours more correctly than in earlier studies (see Bauer, Groß and Sieglen, 2007). On this basis, operating hours in all sectors of economy can be calculated adequately, because the "shift bias" of former studies is avoided (see Box 2). A copy of the standardised EUCOWE questionnaire developed for the project is included in the appendix of this volume.

Groß and Sieglen, 2002). The EUCOWE data permit the comparison of operating hours management within national economies by sector and establishment size as well as a range of other detailed characteristics of the workplace (see Box 1). Thus the focus here is on international differences in operating hours and between national working-time patterns in the six EU countries, between and within small and medium sized establishments (SMEs) and larger establishments, and foreign owned establishments, *i.e.* multinational enterprises (MNEs), and between and within service sector and industrial sector establishments. In addition to the duration of operating times we also seek to explore international differences in the flexibility of operating hours and working time.

The duration of operating hours indicates the duration of capital equipment or capital utilisation. Since the basic interest of the EUCOWE project is in the utilisation of capital, the ideal weighting factors would be proportional to "capital values". The choice of the weighting factors based upon "capital values" is very complicated to implement in practical research, for there are several quite different "capital values" such as original cost, book value, replacement value, insurance value due to the vagaries of technical progress, obsolescence and other market forces and it can be very hard to choose the best values (Anxo, 2002: 183). In the EUCOWE project two different procedures to measure operating hours are used: the *direct* measure and the *indirect* measure. Each measure has its own limitations (see Box 2).

Box 2: Different measurements of operating hours

The EUCOWE questionnaire allows the calculation of operating hours using a *direct* and an *indirect* measure (see Bauer, Groß and Sieglen, 2007). The direct measurement is calculated from the answer given by the respondents to the question "How long does your establishment operate in a usual week?". Operating hours are defined as the weekly business hours, including preparation times and times for maintenance. This is an easy way to measure operating hours, but this measure does not capture the different levels of work intensity in different departments of the establishment. Moreover, answering this question may give rise to a risk of over or under estimation of the average. The indirect measurement of operating hours is a more objective measure that takes into consideration the length and the intensity of operating hours. The indirect measure of operating hours is calculated using three working-time arrangements:

- effective working time of employees working neither in staggered working time nor in shift work;
- effective duration of staggered working time;
- effective duration of shift work.

The adjective "effective" refers to the consideration of overtime hours in the formula for the calculation of the working-time arrangements. On the basis of the assumption that overtime hours can be taken into account for the calculation of the extension of operating hours, reported overtime hours per employee were added to the three working-time arrangements for cases in which the sum of this addition is less than or equal to 24 hours per day. For the calculation of the total operating hours of an establishment the assumption has to be made that the assignment of employees to these three working-time arrangements is not overlapping. The total operating hours of an establishment is an employee weighted average of these three working time arrangements. With this procedure it is also possible to aggregate to the (establishment or employee weighted) average of operating hours of a sector or of the economy as a whole.

At the macro level, aggregate operating hours depend very much on the openness of the economy, the composition and structure of sectors, and the size of establishments in a country. Apart from these characteristics, other important determinants include the phase of the business cycle, the production techniques, institutions and culture; these are core determinants of the choices around how to achieve the desired flexibility, i.e. the mix of duration and flexibility of operating time, labour contract structure and working-time options. Not only do individual firms' organisational choices play a crucial role but labour supply behaviours also impact upon operating hours. In this respect individuals strive to match employment, time and income with their personal preferences and circumstances. Here organisational flexibility can be defined as the degree to which an organisation is capable of continually adapting the deployment of people and resources to the ever changing demands of the environment and difference in work processes. Operating hours and working-time management can be considered to be crucial for economic competitiveness and organisational performance and are also closely linked to job security, job creation and thus social welfare as well. Longer operating hours, long working weeks and the flexibilisation of working time, resulting from the decoupling of business operating hours and individual working time, affect the quality of life outside the establishment. Thus the different implications of operating hours and working-time management for work-life balance within countries are an important component of the analyses in this volume.

In neoclassical economic theory of operating time production costs occupy centre stage. The traditional neoclassical theory typically neglects the presence of *transaction costs*. An increase in the working week of capital means that the equipment will be operated longer: earlier in the morning, later in the evening, at night, and/or at weekends. Operating capital longer may essentially be achieved by either having everybody working longer hours or by adding new shifts, both routes may be accompanied by higher labour costs, overtime and shift premia (Betancourt and Clague, 1981; Anxo *et al.*, 1995; Dupaigne, 2000; 2001; Heiler, 1998). However, as a result of biological and social factors, such a change in work and leisure patterns generally diminishes the welfare of leisure and raises the wage rate for unsocial working time (see Hamermesh, 1996; 1998). Thus management must weigh the extra costs of premia against the flexibility gained and the avoidance of the hiring costs of additional labour (Blyton *et al.*, 1989: 114). In empirical research it is often assumed that the disutility of work is higher during early morning, late evening and night, than during the main period of the day or during weekends. Labour at unsocial schedules is thus a different good to labour during standard hours, hence its equilibrium price is different; this helps explain the use of premia (Bautista *et al.*, 1981).

Apart from these production costs, transaction costs also have to be taken into account. Institutional economic theory emphasises these transaction costs, the costs required to keep the firm afloat given certain duration of operating hours or opening times, *i.e.* the administrative, negotiating and monitoring costs associated with the decoupling of working hours and operating hours. Within a firm, the divergence between (individual) working hours and operating hours or days per week or per year increasingly creates a demand on organisational and logistical procedures; more attention has to be paid to the information and communication systems within the firm. For instance, more rosters and timetables are needed; opportunities for job rotation have to be created or increased, part-time jobs are introduced or extended; also more time is needed to transfer duties, and employees are expected to work on irregular days and times, for instance working on Saturday and/or Sunday, mini shifts, compressed working week or shift work. Thus the extent of decoupling, measuring the divergence between working hours of full-time employees and operating hours, indicates the extent to which organisational, communication and logistic procedures are needed and hence can be considered a proxy for transaction costs. These transaction costs are partly fixed. This helps to explain why, other things being equal, shift work is more common in bigger firms.

Active time management will imply time flexibility both on the working hours side for the employees and on the business hours side of the workplace and, as there is some discretion, the ultimate choice may differ between countries, sectors of activity as well as establishments.

The cross-national EUCOWE data only partly confirm conclusions from the earlier literature (see Delsen *et al.*, 2007). In 2003 operating hours, working time and employment contracts indeed varied considerably between the EU countries. In all countries operating hours increase with establishment size, due to the fact that shift work is still the most powerful means of lengthening operating hours and at the same time mostly a large enterprise phenomenon. From an overall perspective, weekly operating hours are clearly longer in the producing industries than in the service sector, but at national level this is only true for France, Germany, Portugal and the UK, while is Spain and the Netherlands the figures for the service sector are actually higher than in the producing sector. Moreover, there are very significant differences within sectors, especially within the subdivisions of the service sector. Also the developments in operating hours and in the use of the various working-time arrangements and their contribution to operating hours differ substantially between the six EU member states. Based on the developments in operating hours and employment between 1998 and 2003, Delsen *et al.* (2007) conclude that there is neither a straightforward positive or negative relationship between operating hours and employment, nor between the business cycle and operating time and employment. Furthermore part-time work has an ambiguous relationship with operating time and, according to the EUCOWE data, is not widely used as a means for extending operating hours in any country. However, we cannot exclude the possibility that part-time work could be used in this way in some sectors, such as the retail sector (see Bauer and Groß, Chapter 4, this volume). In some countries those establishments which have to cope with the greatest demands for flexibility – those which operate and compete on the international market – also have the longest operating hours. Nevertheless, in all countries varying working time is the most important instrument used to cope with fluctuations, particularly in the service sector.

1.2 Topics for further cross-country analyses of operating hours

The innovative nature of the project and the unique data present an ideal opportunity for the further analyses presented in the following chapters of this book. In particular a number of new areas of research are opened up by the EUCOWE data, including analysis of the service sector, smaller firms and the public sector not to mention a more detailed analysis of working patterns than has been possible in previous studies.

As already mentioned, operating hours in the service sector have never been subject of international comparative research before. For the first time, the EUCOWE data allow us to assess operating hours and the management of working time in the service sector. Are there differences between countries and how can these differences be explained? To what extent does the service sector differ from other sectors, compared to, for example, the manufacturing sector? What are the main differences between subdivisions of the service sector? Are there cross-country trends to be identified or do operating hours within the subdivisions of the service sector vary internationally? Another relevant research question in this respect is: how does the organisational form of the enterprise influence operating hours? Are they longer in market-based enterprises; are the working times of employees shorter and less “unsocial” in the public sector bodies?

A question which has not been addressed empirically before relates to operating hours and operating hours management in public or not for profit organisations. These organisations often have to guarantee public health, security and order, *etc*., and many of these services have to be delivered or at least be available for 24 hours a day on every day of the year. The question of how public services influence operating hours management in the service sector is an important one.

Up until now, the majority of research has only considered shift work as a key component of the extension of operating hours, however, the analyses presented in this book show other forms of working time, particularly staggered working times, are important constituents of extended operating hours in the service sector, and overtime work is very important for the flexibility of operating hours. Since surveys from an employees' perspective are usually the main source of information for studies on working time and operating hours, the findings for overtime is a well known finding. Overtime hours are a traditional instrument used to lengthen operating hours, particularly for small and medium enterprises. In Europe, the level of use of overtime is relatively stable but the share of overtime compensated by time in lieu instead of premia is increasing. In recent years legislation has been introduced in, for example, Greece, France and Ireland to allow time in lieu to reduce overtime pay, and to create employment. In Germany there also is a strong shift from paid overtime to time in lieu. This shift is linked to the development of individual working-time accounts (Bauer *et al*., 2004; Pannenberg, 2005). To reduce overtime costs, European employers use alternatives, including variation of working time around an average, time accounts, part-time work, and the greater use of workers without employment contracts (see Freyssinet and Michon, 2003). On the other hand, in 2007, to stimulate economic growth, the French government abolished the payroll taxes and income tax on overtime and supplementary hours (Loi TEPA). This TEPA law lowers the cost of overtime for employers and increases the gain for the employee.

In contrast to the focus on overtime, information on staggered working time has been scarce until now since it can only be gained from employer based surveys rather than those on employees. An employee does not necessarily know that he or she is working in a staggered working-time pattern as long as duration and location of his or her individual working time does not vary. The richness of the EUCOWE dataset allows us to highlight the previously unrecognised importance of staggered working times; for example a very interesting finding shows the extent to which Portuguese enterprises utilise staggered working times, while elsewhere, particularly in Spain, this instrument of operating hours management is practically unknown.

For the first time data on the linkages between operating hours, working time and employment in small establishments are also available (those with less than twenty employees). The EUCOWE data allow access to information about the operating hours management in SMEs. A number of important factors have remained under researched in SMEs. For example the extent to which small units can achieve long and flexible operating hours, when, for example, shift work may not be an instrument available to them. The data also allow the analysis of the way that SMEs cope with fluctuations since we have a more precise picture of SMEs' operating hours and working-time management. The analysis of the employment policies of SMEs also enables us to consider whether SMEs really are the driving factor of securing and creating employment.

Another important policy question that will be addressed in this book concerns the impact of operating hours and working-time management on employees' social lives and on work-life balance. If the operating hours management of the firm allows the establishment of cost efficient and flexible working time this needs to be set against the guarantee of sufficient income and working time sovereignty for the employees. It is important to consider whether operating hours and resulting working-time patterns hamper or improve the work-life balance.

Another crucial aspect of operating hours flexibility is how the establishment copes with fluctuations in demand and/or production. To answer this question this book investigates the coping strategies of establishments and analyses differentiated types of coping strategies, *i.e.* variation of personnel staff, of working time and variation of technological equipment.

An important factor for the assessment of fluctuations and the strategies of coping with fluctuations is the extent to which the establishments operate and compete on local, national or global markets. The analysis of the specific conditions of competition is a precursor for clarifying the requirements for the coping strategies for fluctuations, *i.e.* the requirements for the flexibility of operating hours. These analyses link to the question of what kind of operating hours and working-time management multinational enterprises (MNEs) have. The working-time management in MNEs may be influenced by national models of the country of origin or may be relatively independent of such national influence.

In the face of stronger international and global competition and increased customer orientation, the flexibility of operating hours gains in importance beyond their mere duration. To what extent does "globalisation" affect operating hours management? What are the specific features of enterprises, which are affected by international competition? How does globalisation affect working-time patterns? Which working-time patterns are being utilised to gain flexibility?

There is a strong relationship between the pressures of globalisation/internationalisation, fluctuations and costs pressure of business activity. The distinction between fluctuations which are foreseeable, and those which are not, enabling an organisation to assign coping strategies to the problem. The latter makes it possible to tell, where and which type of fluctuations are dealt with by changing the working time of permanent personnel or where other policies, such as "hire and fire", dominate. How does globalisation – or more generally, competition at different levels – influence the type and scope of working-time flexibility and the relationship with employment?

1.3 The structure of this book

In the next six empirical chapters in this volume detailed comparative analyses of the determinants and consequences of the duration and flexibility of opening hours and operating times in Europe are presented.

In Chapter 2 Gilbert Cette, Yusuf Kocoglu and Arnaud Sylvain compare the use of flexible working patterns in four European countries. In particular, working patterns that lead to a decoupling of working time and operating time are considered. The analysis is based on logistic regressions performed on individual data from the 2003 European Union Company survey of Operating hours, Working times and Employment (EUCOWE) survey. The comparison covers France, Germany, the United Kingdom and the Netherlands. Logistic regressions by country confirm previous conclusions on the main determinants of the decoupling of working time and operating time. The fact that the significant determinants of flexible working patterns are the same in every country strengthens these results. An analysis based on a single model encompassing all of the countries leads to an original result: all other things being equal, the use of flexible working patterns differs greatly between countries. Germany and the United Kingdom appear to have more flexibility in this sense than France and the Netherlands. In these latter countries, this may highlight the need to reduce rigidities in the labour market so as to make the decoupling of working time and operating time easier.

In Chapter 3 Lei Delsen and Jeroen Smits explain differences in weekly operating hours between countries from differences in working-time strategies, establishment characteristics and the economic and institutional context. The point of departure is that the weekly operating hours and working-time arrangements used are the result of both demand and supply factors. The research results indicate that in Europe weekly operating hours are largely determined by the use of certain working-time options, including shift work, staggered work, weekend work and overtime hours and by the contractual weekly working hours. The use of these options results from a compromise that reflects differences in preferences and the relative bargaining power of employers and employees. This compromise is again influenced by economic conditions as well as by the institutional environment of the establishment. Although establishment size is an important determinant, internal characteristics of the establishment play a lesser role in explaining differences in weekly operating hours in the EU, while the economic and institutional context in which the establishment operates plays the smallest determining role.

In Chapter 4 Frank Bauer and Hermann Groß present results on the duration and the constitution of operating hours in the service sector in an internationally comparative way for the first time. Against a theoretical background, two stylised models of production and service work are contrasted and the specific structures of service work are elaborated. On the basis of descriptive statistics and multivariate analyses the authors show the effect of establishment size, country variables and working-time patterns on the duration and constitution of operating hours in the different service sub-sectors. In this context it is of great interest to analyse the different patterns of operating hours and working-time management in the public sector, on the one hand, and in services in the private sector, on the other hand. The chapter closes with reflections on future research given the development of instruments to capture and measure operating hours management.

In Chapter 5 Mark Smith, Stefan Zagelmeyer and Georg Sieglen explore the relationship between operating hours and working patterns in establishments of different sizes in six European countries. They analyse the extent to which the operating times of small and medium-sized establishments are explained by their different utilisation of working arrangements and the particular constraints or flexibilities that smaller organisations may face in relation to larger establishments. These authors show

how operating hours are positively related to establishment size and the use of various working-time patterns. However, at the same time, the operating hours of SMEs can benefit from the adoption of working-time practices likely to extend operating hours.

In Chapter 6 Sebastian Schief investigates the flexibility patterns adopted by domestic and foreign-owned companies. Firstly, he determines whether foreign-owned establishments use different flexibility patterns to those adopted by domestic companies. Secondly, the influence of the country of origin on flexibility patterns is examined. In addition, he examines the influence of local conditions on companies. The results confirm the existence of the country of origin, transnational and local environment effects. Specific flexibility patterns for the five countries under investigation are detected. The results indicate that the basic shape of flexibility patterns is determined by the local environment. However, it can be argued that ownership does play a role and that a company's country of origin is also influential. Nevertheless, the key factors determining work organisation still seem to be located in the local environment in which companies operate.

In Chapter 7 Enrique Fernández-Macías and Rafael Muñoz de Bustillo Llorente study the impact of capacity utilisation at the establishment level on the quality of work and work-life balance of employees in six EU countries. The analysis is based on two European surveys, one carried out at the establishment level (European Union Company survey of Operating hours, Working times and Employment, EUCOWE) and the other based on responses from individual workers (European Working Conditions Survey, EWCS). The link between the establishment and the individual worker is made through an analytical model in which working-time organisation plays the pivotal role. The results show that the working-time instruments commonly used in Europe for increasing capacity utilisation do have a negative impact both on the quality of work and on work-life balance, although there are, in many cases, ameliorating factors (both intrinsic rewards and external compensation, such as pay) that seem to alleviate this negative impact.

References

Anxo, D., G. Bosch, D. Bosworth and G. Cette (1995) *Work Patterns and Capital Utilisation – An International Comparative Study*, Dordrecht: Kluwer Academic Publishers.

Anxo, D. (2002) Capital operating time in Swedish manufacturing: Recent developments, in: F. Bauer, H. Groß and G. Sieglen (eds.) *Operating hours in Europe*, Berichte des ISO 66, Köln: Institut zur Erforschung sozialer Chancen: 181-196.

Bauer, F., H. Groß, K. Lehmann and E. Munz (2004) Arbeitszeit 2003. *Arbeitszeitgestaltung. Arbeitsorganisation und Tätigkeitsprofile*, Berichte des ISO 70, Köln: Institut zur Erforschung sozialer Chancen.

Bauer, F., H. Groβ and G. Sieglen (eds.) (2002) *Operating hours in Europe*, Berichte des ISO 66, Köln: Institut zur Erforschung sozialer Chancen.

Bauer, F., H. Groß and G. Sieglen (2007) Methodology of the EUCOWE Project, in: L. Delsen, D. Bosworth, H. Groß and R. Muñoz de Bustillo y Llorente (eds.) *Operating Hours and Working Times. A Survey of Capacity Utilisation and Employment in the European Union*, Heidelberg: Physica Verlag, 21-40

Bautista, R. M., Hughes, H., Lim, D. Morawetz and F. Thoumi (1981) *Capital Utilization in Manufacturing: Colombia, Israel, Malaysia and the Philippines*, New York: Oxford University Press.

Betancourt, R. R. and C. K. Clague (1981) *Capital Utilization: A Theoretical and Empirical Analysis*, Cambridge: Cambridge University Press.

Blyton, P., J. Hassard, S. Hill and K. Starkey (1989) *Time, work and organization*, London: Routledge.

Delsen, L., D. Bosworth, H. Groß and R. Muñoz de Bustillo y Llorente (eds.) (2007) *Operating Hours and Working Times. A Survey of Capacity Utilisation and Employment in the European Union*, Heidelberg: Physica Verlag.

Dupaigne, M. (2000) *Capital utilization and the willingness to rest: A general equilibrium analysis*, Econometric Society World Congress 2000 Contributed Papers 0391, Econometric Society, August 11-16, Seattle.

Dupaigne, M. (2001) Capital utilization and work schedules: the welfare costs of shiftworking, *Economics Letters*, (73): 195-200.

EC (1991) Developments on the Labour Market in the Community. Results of a Survey Covering Employers and Employees, *European Economy*, 47, Brussels/Luxembourg: European Commission, Directorate-General for Economic and Financial Affairs.

EC (1995) Performance of the European Union labour market. Results of an ad hoc labour market survey covering employers and employees, *European Economy*, Reports and Studies No. 3, Brussels/Luxembourg: European Commission, Directorate-General for Economic and Financial Affairs.

Foss, M. (1963) The utilization of capital equipment. Postwar compared with prewar, *Survey of Current Business*, June, 43 (6): 8-16.

Foss, M. (1981) *Changes in the Workweek of Fixed Capital: U.S. Manufacturing, 1929 to 1976*, Washington: American Enterprise Institute.

Foss, M. (1997) *Shiftwork, Capital Hours and Productivity Change*, Dordrecht: Kluwer Academic Publishers.

Freyssinet, J. and F. Michon (2003) *Overtime in Europe*, EIROnline, February, Dublin: European Foundation for the Improvement of Living and Working Conditions.

Heiler, K. (1998) The "Petty Pilfering of Minutes" or What has Happened to the Length of the Working Day in Australia?, *International Journal of Manpower*, 19 (4): 266-280.

Hamermesh, D. S. (1996) *Who works when? Evidence from the US and Germany*, NBER Working Papers 5855, Cambridge: National Bureau of Economic Research.

Hamermesh, D. S. (1998) When we work, *American Economic Review*, 88 (2): 321-325.

Lehndorff, S. (2000) *Working time and operating hours in the European automotive industry*, Gelsenkirchen: Institut Arbeit und Technik.

Marris, R. (1964) *The Economics of Capital Utilization*, Cambridge: Cambridge University Press.

Pannenberg, M. (2005) Long-term effects of unpaid overtime. Evidence for West Germany, *Scottish Journal of Political Economy*, 52 (2): 177-193.

2 Flexible Working Patterns and Factor Utilisation: A Cross-country Comparison

Gilbert Cette, Yusuf Kocoglu and Arnaud Sylvain

2.1 Introduction

Rigidities in the labour and products markets are often considered to adversely affect the economic equilibrium and to be one of the causes of the variation in employment rates across the industrialised economies (OECD, 2006). Empirical analyses of the labour market have essentially focused on rigidities caused by strict employment protection legislation (OECD, 2004). They conclude that these rigidities have a direct effect on the labour market equilibrium but also an indirect impact because they affect investment behaviour and lead to the search for higher productivity gains (OECD, 2003). However, to our knowledge, very few studies have aimed at comparing rigidities in working patterns among countries. Yet these rigidities have a direct effect on the so-called productive efficiency, i.e. the utilisation of production factors capital and labour.

This chapter proposes a cross-country analysis of flexible working patterns. We compare and analyse the use of different flexibility patterns that enable the decoupling of working time and operating time, such as shift (work) or staggered working times.[1] In this chapter, a flexible working pattern is defined as a working pattern where working hours and operating hours are decoupled.

Previous comparisons among countries or economic sectors based on aggregated or establishment data (Anxo *et al.*, 1995a; 1995b; Foss, 1997;

---

1 Shift work is defined as the succession of different teams on the same workstation. In companies using staggered working time, there are different teams but they do not necessarily work on the same workstation; they can also work at the same or at different times. See Appendix 1.

L. Delsen et al., *Comparative Analyses of Operating Hours and Working Times in the European Union*,
DOI: 10.1007/978-3-7908-2185-7_2,

Bauer, Groß and Sieglen, 2002; Delsen *et al.*, 2007) highlight great and significant differences in the use of shift work and in the level of capital operating time. But they do not provide any clear information about the reasons for these differences. Whether they arise from differences in the structure of production or stem from differences in regulation that may favour or restrict flexible working patterns is not clear.

Studies on decoupling mainly deal with shift work and industry. They generally distinguish between structural and cyclical determinants of shift work (see Cette, 2002 for a detailed review of the literature):

- The first structural determinant of shift work is the cost structure of companies. All other things being equal, the use of shift work makes it possible to increase capital operating time and therefore to save productive capital. The more production techniques are capital intensive, the more the impact on cost is potentially significant. Using company data, Cette (1989) and Heyer (1998) have shown a strong and significant positive correlation between the use of shift work and capital intensity. Another structural determinant is company size. Developing shift work may be complex and entails very high fixed costs. Cette (1989) and Heyer (1998) have also found a positive correlation between the use of shift work and company size. The final determinant of shift work is its specific cost. The latter can be financial and due to night work, weekend work, or specific bonuses associated with shift work (Lanfranchi, Ohlsson and Skalli, 2004); the cost may also be impacted upon by regulatory measures;
- The use of shift work also depends on cyclical factors. For instance, as shown by previous studies on aggregated data (Anxo *et al.*, 1995a; 1995b; Cette and Taddei, 1995; Foss, 1997 or Bauer, Groß and Sieglen, 2002) or individual data (Heyer, 1998), the capital utilisation rate is positively correlated with the cost incentive to develop shift work. Furthermore, given the short term immobility of productive capital, increasing capital operating time and the use of shift work are means for companies to cope with unexpected demand shocks (Shapiro, 1993; Heyer, 1998).

Theoretical approaches to the use of shift work and the relationship between decoupling and economic fluctuations have also been proposed by Dupaigne (1998; 2002) who shows that, if decoupling can be considered as a buffer between volatile demand and rigid supply and hence as a flexibility option, it can also increase output volatility in response to aggregate shocks and the persistence of these shocks.

Our cross-country comparison of flexible working patterns uses individual data from the 2003 EUCOWE survey. This survey covers thousands of companies from different economic sectors and different countries (see Delsen *et al.*, Chapter 1, this volume). The countries considered in our analysis are France, Germany, the Netherlands and the United Kingdom.

The analysis of decoupling uses cross-section regressions based on the year 2003 and solely concerns structural flexibility. The study of flexible working patterns to address fluctuations in the business cycle does not come within the scope of this chapter. Nonetheless, we need to ensure that the business cycles in the different countries under review are synchronised or at least that there is no significant difference in their cyclical positions. Otherwise, these differences may incorrectly be assumed to be structural in the regressions.

The cyclical positions of France, Germany, the United Kingdom and the Netherlands for the years 2002 and 2003 are compared using different indicators: two output gap indicators from the OECD and the European Commission and capacity utilisation rates from Eurostat (Table 2.1).

Table 2.1 Cyclical positions of France, Germany, the United Kingdom and the Netherlands. Year 2002 and 2003

	Output gap (%) OECD		**Output gap (%) European Commission**		**Capacity utilisation rate (%)**	
	2002	2003	2002	2003	2002	2003
France	-0.3	-1.3	1.2	-0.1	85.3	84.8
Germany	0.2	-1.4	-0.1	-1.2	83.6	83.4
Netherlands	-0.2	-2.2	-0.1	-1.9	84.5	83.4
United Kingdom	-0.1	-0.1	0.2	0.1	82.7	82.0

Sources: (i) Output gap, OECD: Economic Outlook, June 2006; (ii) Output Gap, European Commission: Spring 2006 forecasts; (iii) Capacity utilisation rates: Eurostat. To be compared, capacity utilisation rates are mean centred rates over the period 2002-2005. Capacity utilisation rates refer only to Industry.

In 2002, cyclical positions in the four countries were similar except for France which was closer to a cyclical peak according to the European Commission's output gap indicator. In 2003, cyclical positions worsened except for the United Kingdom where it stabilised. Over the two years 2002-2003 there is no clear sign of significant divergence between any of the four countries' cyclical positions. Therefore, cyclical positions should not bias cross-section regressions.

The chapter is divided into four sections. Section 2.2 discusses our use of the EUCOWE dataset and describes the variables used in regression analyses. Section 2.3 outlines the regression methodology. Estimation results of country models and of the overall model are presented in Section 2.4 together with a specific focus on the existence of structural differences among countries. Since they may have a negative impact on the macroeconomic equilibrium, it may prove efficient to reduce such differences. Conclusions are drawn in Section 2.5.

2.2 The EUCOWE survey and the indicators used in regression analyses

A detailed description of this survey can be found in Delsen *et al.* (2007) (see also Delsen *et al.*, Chapter 1, this volume). The indicators to be explained (the dependent variables in regressions) summarise the use of flexible working patterns.[2] Six binary indicators are computed at company level:

- The use of shift work (yes/no): indicator is set to 1 if the company uses shift work; it is 0 if there is no shift;
- The use of staggered working times (yes/no): indicator is set to 1 if the company uses staggered working times; it is 0 if there is no staggered working times;
- The existence of a decoupling of working time and operating time through shift work and/or staggered working times (yes/no): the indicator is 1 if the company uses shift work and/or staggered working times. It is set to 0 if there is neither shift work nor staggered working times;
- Daily operating time,[3] weekly operating time and annual operating time. These indicators are set to 1 if corresponding operating times are higher than the sample median. They are set to 0 if operating times are below or equal to the median sample.

These six indicators do not entirely summarise flexible working patterns. By focusing on the relationship between (capital) operating time or opening hours and working time, they cover the different dimensions of decoupling. While incomplete, the analysis of decoupling alone is however crucial since it may enable better equipment efficiency and adjustment to consumer needs.

Table 2.2 shows the distribution of the first three indicators. The proportions of establishments using decoupling through staggered working

2 See Appendix 1 for more details on the definition of the variables.

3 Operating time is also used to mean opening hours.

times or shift work are fairly similar across the selected countries. Whatever the indicator, proportions are higher in Germany and lower in the Netherlands. France and the UK lie in-between with similar proportions (see Delsen *et al.* (2007) for an extensive descriptive analysis of decoupling).

Table 2.2 Distribution of dependant variables (% of establishments)

	Germany	France	Netherlands	United Kingdom
Shift work	38.2	28.8	18.5	27.6
Staggered working time	39.6	26.8	22.0	28.4
Decoupling	59.3	47.0	33.0	45.2

It is important to ensure that the selected indicators are all useful and not redundant. To do so, concordance indices are computed for every pair of indicators. Given any pair of indicators within a country, the concordant index corresponds to the percentage of establishments for which both indicators share the same value. In the case of no redundancy, the index indicator equals 0.5. Detailed results of the comparison of indicators by pairs are presented in Cette, Kocoglu, Sylvain (2006). These results, which tend to justify the use of six different indicators, can be summarised as follow:

- Shift work and staggered working times are two distinct aspects of decoupling: in every country, the concordance index is below 0.6 except for the Netherlands where it reaches 0.75;
- Concordance indices for the decoupling indicator and each of the three operating time indicators lie between 0.55 and 0.65. They exceed 0.7 only in three cases;
- Concordance indices for either the shift work indicator or the staggered working times indicator and each of the three operating time indicators are close to 0.7. However, they never exceed 0.76. Redundancy is thus limited;
- Concordant indexes based on the three operating time indicators are between 0.8 and 0.9 except for the Netherlands where they are close to 0.75. While it is not complete, the redundancy between these indicators is high.

2.3 A "*ceteris paribus*" analysis

Since regressions are not intended to describe average behaviours, they are performed on gross samples. Regressions based on logistical models enable us to highlight the statistical relationship between numerous independent variables and the dependant variable, "all other things being equal". As previously mentioned, the explained (or dependant) variable is one of the following:

1. Use of shift work;
2. Use of staggered working times;
3. Decoupling of working time and operating time;
4. Daily operating time;
5. Weekly operating time;
6. Annual operating time.

The explanatory variables are divided into five groups:

1. Establishment-related variables: type of establishment (enterprise, non-profit organisation, public institution, other) and economic sector;
2. Variables related to employment: number of employees and structure of employment (share of women, share of part-time employees, share of "managerial staff");
3. Degree of competition: local, national, international;
4. A variable indicating whether or not the establishment is covered by a collective agreement on working time and/or operating hours;
5. Variables reflecting fluctuations in activity: daily, weekly and annual fluctuations are distinguished.

One category of each explanatory variable has to be defined as the reference category. Since variables in groups 1, 3, 4 and 5 are discrete, the choice of a reference category is straightforward. To define a reference category for continuous variables in group 2, these variables are transformed into discrete variables. The reference modality is the lowest one.

The capital/labour ratio has previously been highlighted as a major determinant of shift work and the decoupling of working time and operating hours. Unfortunately, there is no such variable in the survey. This determinant is therefore taken into account using sectoral dummy variables which may be considered as proxies for the average sectoral capital/labour ratio in competitive sectors (under the restrictive assumption that competition leads to a convergence in production techniques within sectors of economic activity). In non-competitive sectors, sectoral dummies may capture the need for continuity in public services. To make these sectoral dummies as precise as possible, establishments are grouped into 21 sectors of economic activities in country regressions and 39 sectors are distinguished in estimations based on the overall sample.

2.4 Estimation results

First, logistic regressions are computed considering six dependant variables and four countries. These country analyses are aimed at (1) defining the significant determinants of flexible working patterns in each country and (2) comparing the relative influence of these determinants among countries.

Second, logistical regressions are performed on the overall sample. In this instance, an additional country dummy is added as explanatory variable (the reference category is France). Regressions on the overall sample allow us to assess the existence of country specific effects that may represent national rigidities.

The variables are described in the Appendix. For an overview of logistic regression, see Appendix 4 in Cette, Kocoglu and Sylvain (2006). Our results are globally consistent with those of Zagelmeyer and Smith (2005) who used the EUCOWE survey to explore the relationship between operating hours, working patterns and pay bonuses.

2.4.1 Country regressions

Table 2.3 summarises country regression results of the binary model explaining the impact of different variables on the use of flexible working patterns. Detailed results are in Appendix 2.4. Country regressions lead to the following common results:

- Compared to other legal forms of organisation, flexible working patterns are more frequent in enterprises compared to non-profit organisation or public institutions. Operating time is on average also greater in enterprises;
- Decoupling increases with the size of the establishment. This relationship is strongly significant and consistent with previous results from Cette (1989) and Heyer (1998). In our specific case, this relationship may indicate that flexible working patterns are associated with fixed costs that are easier to handle in larger establishments;

Table 2.3 Country regression results (summary)

<table>
<tr><th rowspan="2">Independent variables</th><th colspan="2">Impact of independent variables on flexibility indicators</th></tr>
<tr><th>All flexibility indicators except staggered working hours</th><th>Staggered working hours</th></tr>
<tr><td>Legal form of organisation: enterprise</td><td colspan="2">+</td></tr>
<tr><td>Size of establishment</td><td colspan="2">+++</td></tr>
<tr><td>Share of women in employment</td><td>--</td><td>--</td></tr>
<tr><td>Share of "managerial staff" in employment[a]</td><td>SME: + +; LF: --</td><td>SME: + +; LF: --</td></tr>
<tr><td>Share of part-timers in employment</td><td colspan="2">+</td></tr>
<tr><td>Competitive environment</td><td>+</td><td>+</td></tr>
<tr><td>Intensity of competition[b]</td><td>++</td><td>++</td></tr>
<tr><td>Collective agreement on working time or capital operating time</td><td>+</td><td>+</td></tr>
<tr><td>Fluctuations in demand</td><td>++</td><td>++</td></tr>
<tr><td>Medium term fluctuations[c]</td><td>+</td><td>+</td></tr>
<tr><td>Foreseeable fluctuations</td><td></td><td></td></tr>
<tr><td>Capital intensity[d]</td><td>+++</td><td>+++</td></tr>
<tr><td>Need for long opening hours[e]</td><td>+++</td><td>+++</td></tr>
<tr><td>Retail or wholesale trade</td><td>++</td><td>++</td></tr>
</table>

– + and – signs indicate significant positive and negative effects. ++ and -- indicate strong significancy of the variables. +++ and --- indicate very strong significancy.

a: SME are small and medium establishments; LF: Large firms; b: National rather than local competition and international rather than national competition; c: Weekly rather than daily fluctuations and annual rather than weekly fluctuations; d: Sectors of economic activity with higher capital intensity are "manufacture of refined petroleum products", "manufacture of chemical and chemical products", "manufacture of basic metal" and "manufacture of fabricated metal products"; e: Sectors particularly concerned are health care, hotels and restaurants and transport equipment.

– Details on the model can be found in Appendix 4 of Cette, Kocoglu and Sylvain (2006).

– Table 2.3 summarises country regression results of the binary models explaining the impact of different variables on the use of flexible working patterns. Detailed results are in the Appendix 2.4.

Note: all other things being equal, the use of different types of flexible working patterns increases with the size of the establishment.

- With the exception for staggered working hours, decoupling of working time and operating time is more frequent in economic sectors where capital intensity is high. This result is statistically significant and consistent with previous studies (Cette, 1989; Heyer, 1998). It may indicate that the reduction in cost associated with an increase in (capital) operating time rises with capital intensity. On the other hand, the rise of staggered working is independent from the sector of economic activity. Flexible working patterns are also widespread in sectors where long opening hours (at least above average working time) are needed;
- The relationship between the share of women in employment and flexible working patterns differs according to the dependant variable:

- The share of women in employment is negatively linked with the use of shift work. Women may be more reluctant to work unsocial hours because of the need to reconcile private and professional life. There may also be the legacy of legal restrictions;
- But the share of women in employment is positively linked with the use of staggered working hours. The fact that staggered working hours do not necessarily involve working unsocial hours might explain that result. It is also possible that staggered working hours are associated with part-time work (the majority of part-time employees are women).

- The relationship between flexible working patterns and the share of "managerial staff" is complex: with the exception of staggered working hours, flexible working patterns are more developed when the proportion of "managerial staff" is around the median proportion and less developed when this share is high. This might be explained by the fact that flexibility requires a certain level of management which would represent a sort of a fixed cost. On the other hand, where the proportion of managerial, technical or administrative staff is high the white-collar nature of the work may not require shift working. Staggered working hours are weakly linked to the proportion of "managerial staff".
- Flexible working patterns increase with the share of part-time employees. Two types of explanations can be provided to interpret this result:
  - Combined with decoupling, part-time work allows greater flexibility, *i.e.* better adjustment to opening hours or operating time.
  - Part-time work may also be a corollary to the unsocial hours entailed by flexibility. Furthermore, it has to be remembered that part-time work is defined as a weekly working time below 35 hours so this definition may include some short hours full-timers.
- With the exception of staggered working hours, flexibility is more developed when establishments face competition. Flexibility is more frequent where the establishment experiences international competition than when it is at domestic or local level. This is an important result: competition could require flexibility in working time to increase efficiency. On the other hand, staggered working times are more frequent when competition is local.
- Flexible working patterns are more frequent when there is a collective agreement on working time or capital operating time: the corollaries of the unsocial hours entailed by flexibility (in financial terms or in terms of working time reduction) may require a collective agreement. The use of staggered working is independent from this variable;

- Flexible working patterns are more frequent when establishments face fluctuations in demand. This relationship is stronger with staggered working hours. Concerning the five other indicators this relationship is more significant when fluctuations are monthly or annual, which can be explained by the reorganisation costs implied by these types of flexibility. Whether or not these fluctuations are foreseeable has no impact on the use of flexible working patterns.

2.4.2 Regressions on the overall sample

These estimations are aimed at comparing the use of flexible working patterns among countries. If we assume that the impact of variables are identical and that the differences among countries can be simply summarised through a country dummy, the grouping of national samples allows us to increase the number of sectoral dummies (39 in the overall estimations, 21 in country regressions).

Detailed results are set out in Appendix 2.4b. Regressions results on the overall sample are consistent with those on national samples. Focusing on country dummies, (Table 2.4), it appears that the use of flexible working patterns is significantly greater in Germany and the UK than in the Netherlands and France. Germany has the highest score on five of the six indicators for flexibility. In every case, Germany and the UK are the first two countries in terms of development of flexibility. This may suggest that rigidities on the goods and labour markets would prevent companies from using some flexible working patterns in the Netherlands and France more than in Germany and the UK.

Table 2.4 Regression results, overall sample (summary). Country dummies: country ranking

	Shift work	Staggered hours	Decoupling	Daily operating time	Weekly operating time	Annual operating time	Mean
Germany	2	1	1	1	1	1	1.1
United Kingdom	1	2	2	2	2	2	1.8
France	3	2	3	2	3	3	2.6
Netherlands	4	3	4	3	4	4	3.6

Table 2.4 summarises regression results of binary models (on the overall sample) explaining the impact of different variables on the use of flexible working patterns. Detailed results are presented in Appendix 2.4b.

Note: The figures give each country's ranking with regard to the dependant variable. All other things being equal, shift work is more frequent in the UK than in Germany, France and the Netherlands.

2.5 Conclusions

Our analysis corroborates previous studies regarding the main determinants of decoupling of working time and operating time. It shows that these determinants are identical across the four countries considered. Nonetheless, all other things being equal, the extent of decoupling differs greatly between these four countries. Irrespective of the indicator considered, the ranking of the four countries in terms of the development of flexible working patterns is very similar, which may strengthen our results. Germany and the UK are the countries in which flexible working patterns are most frequent; these types of flexibility are less widespread in the Netherlands; France lies between these two groups. In France and the Netherlands, these results highlight the need for reforms aimed at promoting of flexible working patterns.

Differences between countries may imply differences in rigidities on their respective goods and labour markets which would limit the use of flexible working patterns. However, this conclusion is based on the radical assumption that country dummies only reflect institutional (and not economic) rigidities. This finding should therefore be treated with caution and needs to be substantiated by further research.

References

Anxo D., G. Bosch, D. Bosworth, G. Cette, T. Sterner and D. Taddei (eds.) (1995a) *Work Patterns and Capital Utilisation: An International Comparative Study*, Dordrecht: Kluwer Academic Publishers.

A French version has also been published in 1995: Utilisation des équipements et horaires de travail: Comparaison internationale, INSEE Méthodes, 49-50-51.

Anxo, D., G. Bosch, D. Bosworth, G. Cette, T. Sterner and D. Taddei (1995b) Horaires de travail et durée d'utilisation des équipements: quelques aspects théoriques, *Economie et Statistique*, 287: 37-43.

Bauer, F., H. Groß and G. Sieglen (eds.) (2002) *Operating Hours in Europe*, Berichte des ISO 66, Köln: Institut zur Erforschung sozialer Chancen.

Cette, G. (1989) Recours au travail posté et caractéristiques des entreprises, *Economie et Prévision*, 87: 43-48.

Cette, G. (2002) Capital Operating Time and Shiftwork in France, in: F. Bauer, H. Groß and G. Sieglen (eds.) (2002) *Operating Hours in Europe*, Berichte des ISO 66, Köln: Institut zur Erforschung sozialer Chancen: 31-46.

Cette, G., Y. Kocoglu and A. Sylvain (2006) *Flexibilité organisationnelle par le découplage entre temps de travail et durée d'utilisation des équipements: Une comparaison empirique entre la France, l'Allemagne, le Royaume-Uni et les Pays-Bas*, unpublished paper.

Cette, G. and D. Taddei (1995) Durée d'utilisation des équipements industriels: mesure et éléments de comparaison internationale, *Economie et Statistique*, 287: 27-36.

Delsen, L., D. Bosworth, H. Groß and R. Muñoz de Bustillo y Llorente (eds.) (2007) *Operating Hours, Capacity Utilisation, Working Times and Employment in the European Union*, Heidelberg: Physica Verlag.

Dupaigne, M. (1998) Capital operating time and economic fluctuations, *Recherches Économiques de Louvain*, 64 (3): 243-267.

Dupaigne, M. (2002) Travail posté et durée d'utilisation des équipements dans les fluctuations économiques, *Annales d'Économie et de Statistiques*, 66: 235-256.

Foss, M. (1997) *Shiftwork, Capital Hours and Productivity Change*, Dordrecht: Kluwer Academic Publishers.

Heyer, E. (1998) *Rigidités de l'offre et degrés d'utilisation des facteurs de production,* PhD thesis, University of Aix-Marseille II, March.

Lanfranchi, J., H. Ohlssin and A. Skalli (2004) Action collective et différences compensatrices: le cas des travailleurs masculins à horaires atypiques, *Economie et Prévision*, 164-165 (3-4): 57-79.

OECD (2003) *The Sources of Economic Growth in OECD Countries*, Paris: Organisation for Economic Co-Operation and Development.

OECD (2004) *Employment Outlook*, Paris: Organisation for Economic Co-Operation and Development.

OECD (2005) *Economic Outlook*, December, Paris: Organisation for Economic Co-Operation and Development.

OECD (2006) *Economic Policy Reforms – Going for Growth*, Paris: Organisation for Economic Co-Operation and Development.

Shapiro, M. D. (1993) Cyclical Productivity and the Workweek of Capital, *American Economic Review*, 83 (2): 229-233.

Zagelmeyer, S. and M. Smith (2005) *SMEs in Europe: Operating Hours, Working Patterns and Pay Premia*, Performance and Reward Conference, Manchester Metropolitan University Business School, UK, April.

Appendix 2.1 The variables

All variables are based on the EUCOWE survey.

2.1.1 The flexibility indicators

Each of the six flexibility indicators highlights a specific aspect of the decoupling of working hours and operating hours. Flexibility is understood as a decoupling between working hours and operating hours.

Shift work is defined as different shifts working successively on *the same piece of equipment* whatever the number of shifts. This variable is taken directly from the EUCOWE survey. This binary variable is 1 if the establishment reports shift work.

Staggered working hours are defined as a working organisation whereby different teams work at different overlapping periods (which involves working on different piece of equipment). For instance, some employees may work from 8 am to 4 pm and others from 11 am to 7 pm with operating time from 8 am to 7 pm. This variable is also directly taken from the EUCOWE survey. It is 1 if establishment declares staggered working hours.

Decoupling of working time and operating time: this variable is based on the shift work variable and the staggered working hours variable. It is a binary variable which equals 1 if the establishment reports staggered working hours or/and shift work *i.e.* if there is a decoupling of working time and operating time.

Daily operating time: the EUCOWE survey provides information on daily operating time. This variable is continuous and converted into a binary variable using the following conversion: it is 1 if daily operating time is above the sample median (national sample).

Weekly operating time is the product of daily operating time and the number of operating days in a week. These two variables come directly from the EUCOWE survey. This continuous variable is then converted into a binary variable as in the case of daily operating time.

Annual operating time is the product of daily operating time and the average number of operating days across the year (EUCOWE survey variable). It is converted into a binary variable in the same way as daily and weekly operating times.

2.2.2 The explanatory variables

The explanatory variables are the following:

Legal form of organisation is a four category variable: enterprise, public institution, non-profit organisation, other. The reference category is "enterprise".

Employment: the number of establishment employees comes directly from the EUCOWE survey. It is transformed into a 5 categories variable: 1 to 9 employees;

10 to 19 employees; 20 to 49 employees; 50 to 249 employees; 250 and more employees. The reference category is "1 to 9 employees".

The ***Share of women in employment*** is an EUCOWE survey question. The four modality variable used in the estimations is based on quartiles of the corresponding distribution: share of women below the first quartile; equal or above the first quartile and below the median; equal or above the median and below the third quartile; above the third quartile. The reference category is "share of women below the first quartile".

The ***Share of "managerial staff" in employment*** is also an EUCOWE survey question. The variable used in estimation is constructed as for the share of women in employment.

The ***Share of part-time workers in employment*** is an EUCOWE survey question. Part-time is defined as a weekly working time below 34/35 hours. Variable used in estimations is a five category variable. First category is "no part-time work" and the four others are based on quartiles. The reference category is "no part-time work".

Competition: EUCOWE survey distinguishes three degrees of competition: local, national and international. Each degree is used in estimations through binary variables. Another binary variable concerning the relevance of any degree of competition is also used.

Collective agreement on working hours or operating time: this binary variable corresponds to the survey question on the existence of a collective agreement on working time and/or operating hours. The reference category is "no collective agreement".

Fluctuations in demand: the EUCOWE survey identifies three kinds of fluctuations: daily, weekly and annual. Each kind of fluctuation is transformed into a binary variable (fluctuations/no fluctuations). Reference category is "no fluctuations".

Sector of economic activity: based on available data, the largest number of sectors is distinguished in the estimations. In national estimations, samples are divided into 21 economic sectors (see appendix 2.3a). Estimations based on the overall sample uses 39 sectors of economic activity (see appendix 2.3b). The reference category is "primary sector".

Appendix 2.2 Distribution of variables

Table A2.2 Distribution of variables (% of national establishments)

	Germany	France	Netherlands	UK
Flexibility indicators				
Shift work	38.2	28.8	18.5	27.6
Staggered working times	39.6	26.8	22.0	28.4
Decoupling	59.3	47.0	33.0	45.2
Daily operating time	54.4	57.1	49.3	49.2
Weekly operating time	58.8	49.6	53.9	50.2
Annual operating time	49.4	42.9	49.9	37.1
Legal form of organisation				
Enterprise	69.5	76.6	72.4	62.2
Public institution	13.8	13.4	9.7	6.3
Non-profit organisation	9.5	7.8	13.3	20.0
Other	7.2	2.2	4.6	11.5
Company size (number of employees)				
1-9	17.5	20.5	27.8	26.0
10-19	6.6	8.8	11.4	15.4
20-49	20.2	24.8	22.6	26.9
50-249	17.3	19.6	17.0	19.0
>= 250s	38.4	26.3	21.2	12.7
Share of women in employment				
<Q1	28.5	26.8	30.7	25.7
Q1<= share of women <Q2	24.1	24.8	23.2	25.1
Q2<= share of women <Q3	23.8	24.5	23.9	25.4
>= Q3	23.6	23.9	22.2	23.8
Share of "managerial staff" in employment				
<Q1	37.6	32.1	36.6	37.0
Q1<= share of "managerial staff" <Q2	20.1	22.6	21.6	21.9
Q2<= share of "managerial staff" <Q3	21.2	22.7	21.3	19.9
>= Q3	21.1	22.6	20.5	21.2
Share of part-time workers in employment				
No part-time work	25.6	43.1	18.0	29.1
<Q1	18.8	14.6	21.0	18.2
Q1<= share of part-time workers <Q2	18.9	14.2	19.8	17.5
Q2<= share of part-time workers < Q3	18.8	14.2	20.6	18.4
>= Q3	17.9	13.9	20.6	16.8
Degree of competition				
Local	52.1	47.1	51.8	60.8
National	35.4	27.3	49.1	52.7
International	29.7	31.8	27.9	25.1
Relevance of the questions on competition	87.2	83.5	84.4	88.4
Collective agreement on working time and/or operating time	71.6	67.6	79.0	53.2
Fluctuations in demand				
Daily fluctuations (foreseeable)	8.4	9.3	9.5	12.2
Daily fluctuations (unforeseeable)	11.7	14.6	8.9	16.0
Weekly fluctuations (foreseeable)	10.8	14.6	12.7	17.5
Weekly fluctuations (unforeseeable)	16.0	17.0	10.8	19.8
Annual fluctuations (foreseeable)	21.4	24.8	16.0	23.7
Annual fluctuations (unforeseeable)	22.8	18.3	13.4	25.3
Number of observations	2,862	2,225	1,866	1,355

Appendix 2.3 Sectoral distribution

Table A2.3.A Country models (% of establishments)

Sector of economic activity	NACE codes (two-digits)	Germany	France	Netherlands	UK
Primary sector	1 to 14	2.6	8.8	8.3	4.8
Manufacture of food products, beverages and tobacco	15 and 16	2.0	3.1	1.8	0.2
Manufacture of textile and textile products leather and leather products wood and wood products pulp, paper and paper products	17 to 21	2.0	2.3	1.6	1.4
Publishing, printing and reproduction of recorded media	22	0.9	1.9	1.8	2.0
Manufacture of coke, refined petroleum products and nuclear fuel chemicals, chemical products and man-made fibres rubber and plastic products other non-metallic mineral products	23 to 26	3.8	4.8	3.0	2.3
Manufacture of basic metals and fabricated metal products	27 and 28	3.8	3.9	2.7	2.9
Manufacture of machinery and equipment n.e.c electrical and optical equipment transport equipment Manufacturing n.e.c	29 to 37	10.2	8.1	7.9	12.6
Electricity, gas and water supply	40 and 41	1.0	1.0	0.3	0.6
Construction	45	6.2	7.4	9.2	7.5
Sale, maintenance and repair of motor vehicles and motorcycles; retail trade of automotive fuel	50	2.7	1.6	1.2	0.2
Wholesale trade and commission trade, except of motor vehicles and motorcycles	51	4.9	4.1	5.0	3.9
Retail trade, except of motor vehicles and motorcycles; repair of personal and household goods	52	4.9	7.0	5.3	0.8
Hotels and restaurants	55	2.5	4.6	3.0	0.4
Transport and storage	60 to 63	4.6	2.6	3.8	15.6
Post and telecommunications	64	0.8	2.0	0.8	1.6
Financial intermediation	65 to 67	4.3	2.3	2.9	6.1
Real estate, renting and business activities	70 to 74	10.9	10.2	11.6	17.5
Public administration and defence; compulsory social security	75	9.3	8.8	4.5	0.1
Education	80	4.4	0.9	6.1	0.1
Health and social work	85	12.9	9.8	13.4	11.5
Other community, social and personal service activities; activities of households	90 to 95	5.5	5.0	5.9	8.2
Number of observations		2,862	2,225	1,866	1,355

Table. A2.3.B Overall sample (% of establishments)

Sector of economic activity	**NACE codes (two-digits)**	
Primary sector	1 to 14	5.9
Manufacture of food products, beverages and tobacco	15 and 16	2.0
Manufacture of textile and textile products, leather and leather products, wood and wood products, pulp, paper and paper products	17 to 21	1.9
Publishing, printing and reproduction of recorded media	22	1.5
Manufacture of coke, refined petroleum products and nuclear fuel, chemicals, chemical products and man-made fibres, other non-metallic mineral products	23 and 24	1.6
Manufacture of rubber and plastic products	25	1.1
Manufacture of other non metallic mineral product	26	1.0
Manufacture of basic metals	27	0.9
Manufacture of fabricated metal products, except machinery and equipment	28	2.6
Manufacture of machine and equipment, n.e.c	29	2.6
Manufacture of office machinery and computers, electrical machinery and apparatus n.e.c	30 and 31	1.2
Manufacture of radio, television and communication equipment and apparatus	32	0.9
Manufacture of medical, precision and optical instruments, watches and clocks	33	1.0
Manufacture of motor vehicles, trailers and semi-trailers	34	1.0
manufacture of other transport equipment	35	1.1
Manufacturing n.e.c	36 and 37	1.8
Electricity, gas and water supply	40 and 41	0.8
Construction	45	7.4
Sale, maintenance and repair of motor vehicles and motorcycles; retail trade of automotive fuel	50	1.7
Wholesale trade and commission trade, except of motor vehicles and motorcycles	51	4.5
Retail trade, except of motor vehicles and motorcycles; repair of personal and household goods	52	4.9
Hotels and restaurants	55	2.8
Transport and storage	60 to 63	5.7
Post and telecommunications	64	1.3
Financial intermediation, except insurance and pension funding	65	2.2
Insurance and pension funding, except compulsory social security	66	0.9
Activities auxiliary to financial intermediation	67	0.6
Real estate activities	70	1.2
Computer and related activities	72	1.5
Research and development	73	0.6
Renting of machinery and equipment without operator and of persona land household goods; Other business activities	71 and 74	8.6
Public administration and defence; compulsory social security	75	6.6
Education	80	3.1
Health and social work	85	11.9
Sewage and refuse disposal, sanitation and similar activities	90	0.4
Activities of membership organisations n.e.c	91	2.0
Recreational, cultural and sporting activities	92	1.8
Other personal activities	93	1.7
Number of observations		8,308

Appendix 2.4 The regression results

A – national samples

Table A2.4.1 Shift work (yes/no)

	France	Germany	Netherlands	UK
Legal form of organisation				
Enterprise	Ref.	Ref.	Ref.	Ref.
Public institution		-0.456		
		(0.296)		
Non-profit organisation	-0.839	-0.551	0.522	
	(0.354)**	(0.245)**	(0.323)	
Other				
Company size (number of employees)				
1-9	Ref.	Ref.	Ref.	Ref.
10-19	0.847	1.138	0.704	1.159
	(0.416)**	(0.348)***	(0.512)	(0.341)**
20-49	1.314	1.905	1.428	1.925
	(0.346)***	(0.271)***	(0.442)***	(0.299)***
50-249	2.401	2.927	2.615	3.083
	(0.354)***	(0.280)***	(0.445)***	(0.317)***
>= 250	3.333	4.075	3.766	4.582
	(0.360)***	(0.283)***	(0.449)***	(0.360)***
Share of women in employment				
<Q1[a]	Ref.	Ref.	Ref.	Ref.
Q1<= share of women <Q2[a]	-0.645			-0.331
	(0.199)***			(0.232)
Q2<= share of women <Q3[a]	-0.988		-1.082	-0.361
	(0.219)***		(0.310)***	(0.261)
>= Q3[a]	-1.238		-0.505	0.712
	(0.244)***		(0.377)	(0.280)**
Share of "managerial staff" in employment				
<Q1[a]	Ref.	Ref.	Ref.	Ref.
Q1<= share of "managerial staff" <Q2[a]	0.667	0.210		-0.277
	(0.192)***	(0.148)		(0.203)
Q2<= share of "managerial staff" <Q3[a]				-0.860
				(0.238)***
>= Q3[a]	-0.831	-0.515		-1.951
	(0.231)***	(0.167)***		(0.291)***
Share of part-time workers in employment				
No part-time work	Ref.	Ref.	Ref.	Ref.
<Q1[a]	0.293			
	(0.188)			
Q1<= share of part-time workers <Q2[a]				0.391
				(0.261)
Q2<= share of part-time workers < Q3[a]		-0.340		0.984
		(0.187)*		(0.286)***
>= Q3[a]		-0.291		0.766
		(0.193)		(0.302)**

	France	Germany	Netherlands	UK
Degree of competition				
Absence of local competition	Ref.	Ref.	Ref.	Ref.
Local competition	-0.518 (0.194)***	-0.345 (0.146)**		-0.465 (0.193)**
Absence of national competition	Ref.	Ref.	Ref.	Ref.
National competition	-0.228 (0.163)		-0.275 (0.201)	
Absence of international competition	Ref.	Ref.	Ref.	Ref.
International competition	0.786 (0.189)***	0.508 (0.156)***	0.769 (0.220)***	
Irrelevant questions	Ref.	Ref.	Ref.	Ref.
Relevant questions				-0.730 (0.350)**
Collective agreement on working time and/or operating time				
No	Ref.	Ref.	Ref.	Ref.
Yes	0.593 (0.173)***			0.450 (0.163)***
Fluctuations in demand				
Absence of daily fluctuations	Ref.	Ref.	Ref.	Ref.
Daily fluctuations (foreseeable)				
Daily fluctuations (unforeseeable)				
Absence of weekly fluctuations	Ref.	Ref.	Ref.	Ref.
Weekly fluctuations (foreseeable)			0.562 (0.325)*	
Weekly fluctuations (unforeseeable)				0.582 (0.300)*
Absence of annual fluctuations	Ref.	Ref.	Ref.	Ref.
Annual fluctuations (foreseeable)	0.306 (0.175)*	0.216 (0.151)		
Annual fluctuations (unforeseeable)	0.289 (0.197)			
Sector of economic activity				
Primary sector	Ref.	Ref.	Ref.	Ref.
Manufacture of food products, beverages and tobacco	1.403 (0.428)***		2.784 (0.710)***	
Manufacture of textile and textile products, leather and leather products, wood and wood products, pulp, paper and paper products			1.465 (0.789)*	-1.725 (0.801)**
Publishing, printing and reproduction of recorded media	1.358 (0.493)***		3.099 (0.759)***	
Manufacture of coke, refined petroleum products and nuclear fuel, chemicals, chemical products and man-made fibres, rubber and plastic products, other non-metallic mineral products.	1.591 (0.374)***		2.995 (0.644)***	-1.573 (0.619)**
Manufacture of basic metals and fabricated metal products	0.658 (0.371)*		1.770 (0.659)***	-0.924 (0.581)
Manufacture of machinery and equipment n.e.c, electrical and optical equipment, transport equipment, Manufacturing n.e.c.			1.010 (0.588)*	-0.868 (0.387)**

	France	Germany	Netherlands	UK
Electricity, gas and water supply			2.785	
			(1.243)**	
Construction	-2.173	-2.147	-1.098	-1.275
	(0.453)***	(0.525)***	(0.825)	(0.445)***
Sale, maintenance and repair of motor vehicles and motorcycles; retail trade of automotive fuel	-1.448			
	(0.842)*			
Wholesale trade and commission trade, except of motor vehicles and motorcycles	-0.624	-1.634		-0.724
	(0.451)	(0.439)***		(0.508)
Retail trade, except of motor vehicles and motorcycles; repair of personal and household goods		-1.628	1.895	-2.791
		(0.475)***	(0.701)***	(1.401)**
Hotels and restaurants	2.312	1.335	3.360	-2.488
	(0.367)***	(0.474)***	(0.688)***	(1.357)*
Transport and storage			2.754	-1.068
			(0.619)***	(0.381)***
Post and telecommunications				
Financial intermediation		-2.975		
		(0.491)***		
Real estate, renting and business activities		-1.565	1.185	-1.072
		(0.401)***	(0.602)**	(0.372)***
Public administration and defence; compulsory social security		-1.452	1.513	
		(0.482)***	(0.710)**	
Education		-1.300		
		(0.470)***		
Health and social work	3.151	1.789	2.613	-0.589
	(0.409)***	(0.422)***	(0.662)***	(0.390)
Other community, social and personal service activities; activities of households	0.668		2.132	-1.011
	(0.436)		(0.665)***	(0.426)**
Intercept	-3.467	-2.555	-5.530	-2.188
	(0.417)***	(0.435)***	(0.710)***	(0.523)***
Number of observations	2,211	2,799	1,820	1,313
P-value LR	<.0001	<.0001	<.0001	<.0001
P-value Score	<.0001	<.0001	<.0001	<.0001
P-value Wald	<.0001	<.0001	<.0001	<.0001
Concordance	90.2	89.1	90.7	86.7

a Samples on which medians and quartiles are computed differ from samples used in estimation since independent variables may be missing; "Ref.", reference situation; *** 1% significance level; ** 5% significance level; * 10% significance level; coefficients not reported if significance level >20%.

Table A2.4.2 Staggered working times (yes/no)

	France	Germany	Netherlands	UK
Legal form of organisation				
Enterprise	Ref.	Ref.	Ref.	Ref.
Public institution			-1.042 (0.388)***	
Non-profit organisation				
Other				-0.420 (0.243)*
Company size (number of employees)				
1-9	Ref.	Ref.	Ref.	Ref.
10-19	0.352 (0.223)	0.346 (0.206)*	1.176 (0.261)***	0.590 (0.223)***
20-49	0.585 (0.191)***	0.533 (0.164)***	0.720 (0.254)***	0.521 (0.202)***
50-249		0.712 (0.177)***	1.136 (0.279)***	0.731 (0.219)***
>= 250	0.395 (0.216)*	0.786 (0.175)***	1.455 (0.279)***	0.808 (0.256)***
Share of women in employment				
<Q1[a]	Ref.	Ref.	Ref.	Ref.
Q1<= share of women <Q2[a]			0.651 (0.206)***	0.427 (0.197)**
Q2<= share of women < Q3[a]	0.396 (0.186)**		0.341 (0.238)	
>= Q3[a]		0.546 (0.157)***		
Share of "managerial staff " in employment				
<Q1[a]	Ref.	Ref.	Ref.	Ref.
Q1<= share of "managerial staff" <Q2[a]	0.351 (0.168)**		0.436 (0.209)**	
Q2<= share of "managerial staff" <Q3[a]	0.271 (0.163)*			
>= Q3[a]		0.180 (0.123)		
Share of part-time workers in employment				
No part-time work	Ref.	Ref.	Ref.	Ref.
<Q1[a]				0.409 (0.213)*
Q1<= share of part-time workers <Q2[a]				0.694 (0.206)***
Q2<= share of part-time workers <Q3[a]				0.696 (0.232)***
>= Q3[a]				0.721 (0.247)***
Degree of competition				
Absence of local competition	Ref.	Ref.	Ref.	Ref.
Local competition	0.315 (0.170)*	0.294 (0.123)**		
Absence of national competition	Ref.	Ref.	Ref.	Ref.
National competition		0.273 (0.101)***		

	France	Germany	Netherlands	UK
Absence of international competition	Ref.	Ref.	Ref.	Ref.
International competition				
Irrelevant questions	Ref.	Ref.	Ref.	Ref.
Relevant questions				
Collective agreement on working time and/or operating time				
No	Ref.	Ref.	Ref.	Ref.
Yes	0.203		0.444	
	(0.130)		(0.205)**	
Fluctuations in demand				
Absence of daily fluctuations	Ref.	Ref.	Ref.	Ref.
Daily fluctuations (foreseeable)	0.451	0.344	1.141	
	(0.232)*	(0.216)	(0.285)***	
Daily fluctuations (unforeseeable)	0.327	0.279	0.600	0.893
	(0.205)	(0.191)	(0.301)**	(0.261)***
Absence of weekly fluctuations	Ref.	Ref.	Ref.	Ref.
Weekly fluctuations (foreseeable)	0.267	0.393		
	(0.206)	(0.204)*		
Weekly fluctuations (unforeseeable)	0.563	0.370		
	(0.199)***	(0.174)**		
Absence of annual fluctuations	Ref.	Ref.	Ref.	Ref.
Annual fluctuations (foreseeable)	0.335	0.474		
	(0.146)**	(0.119)***		
Annual fluctuations (unforeseeable)				
Sector of economic activity				
Primary sector	Ref.	Ref.	Ref.	Ref.
Manufacture of food products, beverages and tobacco	0.925 (0.327)***	0.825 (0.412)**	0.672 (0.523)	1.972 (1.313)
Manufacture of textile and textile products, leather and leather products, wood and wood products, pulp, paper and paper products	-0.816 (0.467)*			
Publishing, printing and reproduction of recorded media				
Manufacture of coke, refined petroleum products and nuclear fuel, chemicals, chemical products and man-made fibres, rubber and plastic products, other non-metallic mineral products.				
Manufacture of basic metals and fabricated metal products	-0.762 (0.397)*			
Manufacture of machinery and equipment n.e.c, electrical and optical equipment, transport equipment, Manufacturing n.e.c.	-0.505 (0.301)*			0.559 (0.343)
Electricity, gas and water supply	1.117			
	(0.502)**			
Construction	-1.154	-0.685		
	(0.339)***	(0.360)*		
Sale, maintenance and repair of motor vehicles and motorcycles; retail trade of automotive fuel	0.899 (0.406)**	1.744 (0.386)***		
Wholesale trade and commission trade, except of motor vehicles and motorcycles		0.529 (0.341)	0.981 (0.401)**	

	France	Germany	Netherlands	UK
Retail trade, except of motor vehicles and motorcycles; repair of personal and household goods	0.440 (0.285)	0.742 (0.347)**	2.140 (0.394)***	1.364 (0.766)*
Hotels and restaurants	1.204 (0.308)***	0.901 (0.402)**	2.170 (0.448)***	
Transport and storage	0.575 (0.358)		0.945 (0.417)**	
Post and telecommunications	1.911 (0.439)***		1.047 (0.707)	
Financial intermediation				
Real estate, renting and business activities			0.803 (0.359)**	
Public administration and defence; compulsory social security	0.573 (0.383)		1.701 (0.549)***	
Education	1.515 (0.568)***			
Health and social work	0.724 (0.334)**	0.560 (0.340)*	1.988 (0.413)***	
Other community, social and personal service activities; activities of households	0.914 (0.319)***	0.692 (0.349)**	1.979 (0.410)***	
Intercept	- 2.522 (0.298)***	- 2.035 (0.334)***	- 4.004 (0.425)***	- 2.168 (0.433)***
Number of observations	2,099	2,589	1,714	1,230
P-value LR	<.0001	<.0001	<.0001	<.0001
P-value Score	<.0001	<.0001	<.0001	<.0001
P-value Wald	<.0001	<.0001	<.0001	.0002
Concordance	73.3	69.2	78.0	67.8

a Samples on which medians and quartiles are computed differ from samples used in estimation since independent variables may be missing; "Ref.", reference situation; *** 1% significance level; ** 5% significance level; * 10% significance level; coefficients not reported if significance level >20%.

Table A2.4.3 Decoupling (yes/no)

	France	Germany	Netherlands	UK
Legal form of organisation				
Enterprise	Ref.	Ref.	Ref.	Ref.
Public institution			-0.887 (0.346)**	
Non-profit organisation	-0.372 (0.283)	-0.464 (0.224)**		
Other			-0.713 (0.384)*	-0.379 (0.226)*
Company size (number of employees)				
1-9	Ref.	Ref.	Ref.	Ref.
10-19		0.581 (0.213)***	1.067 (0.259)***	0.791 (0.218)***
20-49	0.404 (0.191)**	0.926 (0.173)***	0.884 (0.247)***	0.974 (0.196)***
50-249	0.755 (0.207)***	1.538 (0.191)***	1.678 (0.272)***	1.704 (0.217)***
>= 250	1.566 (0.215)***	2.259 (0.195)***	2.610 (0.278)***	2.868 (0.286)***
Share of women in employment				
<Q1[a]	Ref.	Ref.	Ref.	Ref.
Q1<= share of women <Q2[a]			0.404 (0.197)**	0.272 (0.194)
Q2<= share of women < Q3[a]				
>= Q3[a]	-0.312 (0.198)	0.512 (0.173)***		0.642 (0.241)***
Share of "managerial staff" in employment				
<Q1[a]	Ref.	Ref.	Ref.	Ref.
Q1<= share of "managerial staff" <Q2[a]	0.872 (0.170)***	0.334 (0.143)**	0.334 (0.205)	
Q2<= share of "managerial staff" < Q3[a]	0.429 (0.160)***			-0.323 (0.195)*
>= Q3[a]	-0.355 (0.168)**			-0.679 (0.197)***
Share of part-time workers in employment				
No part-time work	Ref.	Ref.	Ref.	Ref.
<Q1[a]			0.366 (0.253)	0.459 (0.206)**
Q1<= share of part-time workers <Q2[a]	0.372 (0.166)**			0.534 (0.203)***
Q2<= share of part-time workers < Q3[a]				0.797 (0.229)***
>= Q3[a]				0.833 (0.240)***
Degree of competition				
Absence of local competition	Ref.	Ref.	Ref.	Ref.
Local competition				-0.349 (0.164)**
Absence of national competition	Ref.	Ref.	Ref.	Ref.
National competition		0.228 (0.114)**		

	France	Germany	Netherlands	UK
Absence of international competition	Ref.	Ref.	Ref.	Ref.
International competition	0.573 (0.159)***	0.263 (0.147)*	0.313 (0.176)*	
Irrelevant questions	Ref.	Ref.	Ref.	Ref.
Relevant questions				-0.564 (0.280)**
Collective agreement on working time and/or operating time				
No	Ref.	Ref.	Ref.	Ref.
Yes	0.521 (0.128)***		0.551 (0.200)***	0.272 (0.136)**
Fluctuations in demand				
Absence of daily fluctuations	Ref.	Ref.	Ref.	Ref.
Daily fluctuations (foreseeable)			1.181 (0.297)***	0.396 (0.298)
Daily fluctuations (unforeseeable)				0.480 (0.265)*
Absence of weekly fluctuations	Ref.	Ref.	Ref.	Ref.
Weekly fluctuations (foreseeable)	0.283 (0.215)	0.363 (0.259)		
Weekly fluctuations (unforeseeable)	0.517 (0.209)**	0.689 (0.218)***		
Absence of annual fluctuations	Ref.	Ref.	Ref.	Ref.
Annual fluctuations (foreseeable)	0.397 (0.146)***	0.590 (0.139)***	0.403 (0.207)*	
Annual fluctuations (unforeseeable)	0.218 (0.169)			
Sector of economic activity				
Primary sector	Ref.	Ref.	Ref.	Ref.
Manufacture of food products, beverages and tobacco	1.975 (0.371)***		1.578 (0.508)***	
Manufacture of textile and textile products, leather and leather products, wood and wood products, pulp, paper and paper products				-0.954 (0.643)
Publishing, printing and reproduction of recorded media	1.315 (0.407)***		1.427 (0.533)***	
Manufacture of coke, refined petroleum products and nuclear fuel, chemicals, chemical products and man-made fibers, rubber and plastic products, other non-metallic mineral products.	1.814 (0.348)***		1.856 (0.449)***	-1.267 (0.541)**
Manufacture of basic metals and fabricated metal products	0.607 (0.315)*		1.328 (0.438)***	
Manufacture of machinery and equipment n.e.c, electrical and optical equipment, transport equipment, Manufacturing n.e.c.	0.474 (0.263)*			
Electricity, gas and water supply			2.023 (1.150)*	-1.707 (1.196)
Construction	-1.566 (0.312)***	-1.669 (0.353)***	-0.956 (0.447)**	-0.600 (0.382)

	France	Germany	Netherlands	UK
Sale, maintenance and repair of motor vehicles and motorcycles; retail trade of automotive fuel	0.882 (0.419)**	0.957 (0.398)**		
Wholesale trade and commission trade, except of motor vehicles and motorcycles		-0.634 (0.338)*	0.935 (0.400)**	-0.755 (0.455)*
Retail trade, except of motor vehicles and motorcycles; repair of personal and household goods	0.441 (0.289)		2.474 (0.389)***	
Hotels and restaurants	2.123 (0.326)***		2.722 (0.454)***	
Transport and storage			1.575 (0.408)***	
Post and telecommunications	1.391 (0.479)***		1.803 (0.758)**	-0.809 (0.622)
Financial intermediation		-1.475 (0.363)***		
Real estate, renting and business activities		-0.671 (0.308)**	0.924 (0.345)***	-0.582 (0.334)*
Public administration and defence; compulsory social security		-0.990 (0.392)**	1.414 (0.509)***	
Education	1.951 (0.600)***	-0.542 (0.367)	0.468	
Health and social work	1.893 (0.340)***	0.924 (0.343)***	2.285 (0.400)***	
Other community, social and personal service activities; activities of households	1.218 (0.323)***		2.271 (0.404)***	-0.641 (0.375)*
Intercept	-2.239 (0.285)***	-1.089 (0.327)***	-3.889 (0.407)***	-1.305 (0.420)***
Number of observations	2,093	2,555	1,699	1,218
P-value LR	<.0001	<.0001	<.0001	<.0001
P-value Score	<.0001	<.0001	<.0001	<.0001
P-value Wald	<.0001	<.0001	<.0001	<.0001
Concordance	82.4	80.5	84.3	76.9

a Samples on which medians and quartiles are computed differ from samples used in estimation since independent variables may be missing; "Ref.", reference situation; *** 1% significance level; ** 5% significance level; * 10% significance level; coefficients not reported if significance level > 20%.

Table A2.4.4 Daily operating time (greater than national median, yes/no)

	France	Germany	Netherlands	UK
Legal form of organisation				
Enterprise	Ref.	Ref.	Ref.	Ref.
Public institution	-0.907			
	(0.285)***			
Non-profit organisation	-0.389	-0.611		-0.432
	(0.278)	(0.211)***		(0.191)**
Other	-0.547			
	(0.369)			
Company size (number of employees)				
1-9	Ref.	Ref.	Ref.	Ref.
10-19	0.665	0.833	0.297	0.625
	(0.208)***	(0.207)***	(0.190)	(0.203)**
20-49	0.781	0.753	0.298	1.215
	(0.178)***	(0.168)***	(0.179)*	(0.181)***
50-249	1.325	1.457	0.330	1.634
	(0.196)***	(0.182)***	(0.207)	(0.203)***
>= 250	2.160	2.378	0.786	2.131
	(0.210)***	(0.186)***	(0.210)***	(0.249)***
Share of women in employment				
<Q1[a]	Ref.	Ref.	Ref.	Ref.
Q1<= share of women <Q2[a]		-0.215		
		(0.134)		
Q2<= share of women < Q3[a]	-0.339			-0.350
	(0.176)*			(0.197)*
>= Q3[a]	-0.247			
	(0.189)			
Share of "managerial staff" in employment				
<Q1[a]	Ref.	Ref.	Ref.	Ref.
Q1<= share of "managerial staff" <Q2[a]	0.467	0.194	0.277	
	(0.161)***	(0.131)	(0.168)*	
Q2<= share of "managerial staff" < Q3[a]	0.383			-0.550
	(0.155)**			(0.183)***
>= Q3[a]	0.326		-0.358	-0.821
	(0.154)**		(0.151)**	(0.182)***
Share of part-time workers in employment				
No part-time work	Ref.	Ref.	Ref.	Ref.
<Q1[a]			-0.345	
			(0.188)*	
Q1<= share of part-time workers <Q2[a]				
Q2<= share of part-time workers < Q3[a]	0.331			
	(0.174)*			
>= Q3[a]				0.412
				(0.222)*
Degree of competition				
Absence of local competition	Ref.	Ref.	Ref.	Ref.
Local competition		-0.169		
		(0.128)		
Absence of national competition	Ref.	Ref.	Ref.	Ref.
National competition		0.200		
		(0.106)*		

	France	Germany	Netherlands	UK
Absence of international competition	Ref.	Ref.	Ref.	Ref.
International competition	0.486 (0.152)***	0.379 (0.139)***	0.347 (0.143)**	0.220 (0.164)
Irrelevant questions	Ref.	Ref.	Ref.	Ref.
Relevant questions				
Collective agreement on working time and/or operating time				
No	Ref.	Ref.	Ref.	Ref.
Yes			0.244 (0.143)*	
Fluctuations in demand				
Absence of daily fluctuations	Ref.	Ref.	Ref.	Ref.
Daily fluctuations (foreseeable)	0.553 (0.248)**			
Daily fluctuations (unforeseeable)	0.403 (0.213)*			0.407 (0.251)
Absence of weekly fluctuations	Ref.	Ref.	Ref.	Ref.
Weekly fluctuations (foreseeable)			0.387 (0.230)*	
Weekly fluctuations (unforeseeable)		0.312 (0.192)	0.375 (0.242)	
Absence of annual fluctuations	Ref.	Ref.	Ref.	Ref.
Annual fluctuations (foreseeable)		0.482 (0.130)***		
Annual fluctuations (unforeseeable)	0.390 (0.162)**	0.318 (0.130)**	0.301 (0.185)	0.261 (0.187)
Sector of economic activity				
Primary sector	Ref.	Ref.	Ref.	Ref.
Manufacture of food products, beverages and tobacco	2.318 (0.397)***	1.336 (0.447)***	1.662 (0.455)***	
Manufacture of textile and textile products, leather and leather products, wood and wood products, pulp, paper and paper products				
Publishing, printing and reproduction of recorded media	1.433 (0.424)***	-0.772 (0.523)		
Manufacture of coke, refined petroleum products and nuclear fuel, chemicals, chemical products and man-made fibres, rubber and plastic products, other non-metallic mineral products.	1.385 (0.338)***		0.759 (0.339)**	
Manufacture of basic metals and fabricated metal products				
Manufacture of machinery and equipment n.e.c, electrical and optical equipment, transport equipment, Manufacturing n.e.c.		-0.684 (0.312)**	-0.372 (0.263)	
Electricity, gas and water supply				
Construction	-0.452 (0.252)*	-1.038 (0.330)***	-0.353 (0.261)	
Sale, maintenance and repair of motor vehicles and motorcycles; retail trade of automotive fuel		0.905 (0.376)**		

	France	Germany	Netherlands	UK
Wholesale trade and commission trade, except of motor vehicles and motorcycles		-0.836 (0.330)**	0.427 (0.289)	
Retail trade, except of motor vehicles and motorcycles; repair of personal and household goods	0.487 (0.271)*	-0.548 (0.341)	1.447 (0.302)***	
Hotels and restaurants	3.177 (0.396)***	1.928 (0.432)***	1.397 (0.361)***	
Transport and storage	0.986 (0.354)***	1.303 (0.372)***	0.873 (0.312)***	
Post and telecommunications	1.648 (0.513)***		1.534 (0.689)**	0.757 (0.560)
Financial intermediation		-1.368 (0.355)***		
Real estate, renting and business activities	0.584 (0.240)**	-0.643 (0.301)**	0.637 (0.243)***	
Public administration and defence; compulsory social security		-1.430 (0.387)***	1.003 (0.393)**	
Education	2.537 (0.641)***	-1.327 (0.373)***	1.371 (0.325)***	
Health and social work	2.562 (0.335)***	1.141 (0.330)***	1.379 (0.289)***	
Other community, social and personal service activities; activities of households	1.248 (0.312)***	-0.444 (0.338)	1.024 (0.294)***	
Intercept	-1.829 (0.269)***	-1.054 (0.318)***	-1.326 (0.267)***	-0.850 (0.394)**
Number of observations	2,221	2,847	1,850	1,335
P-value LR	<.0001	<.0001	<.0001	<.0001
P-value Score	<.0001	<.0001	<.0001	<.0001
P-value Wald	<.0001	<.0001	<.0001	<.0001
Concordance	81.1	80.8	71.0	75.2

a Samples on which medians and quartiles are computed differ from samples used in estimation since independent variables may be missing; "Ref.", reference situation; *** 1% significance level; ** 5% significance level; * 10% significance level; coefficients not reported if significance level > 20%.

Table A2.4.5 Weekly operating time (greater than national median, yes/no)

	France	Germany	Netherlands	UK
Legal form of organisation				
Enterprise	Ref.	Ref.	Ref.	Ref.
Public institution	- 0.422		-0.938	-0.523
	(0.294)		(0.290)***	(0.271)*
Non-profit organisation	- 0.786	-0.422		-0.410
	(0.281)***	(0.207)**		(0.191)**
Other	- 0.753	-0.296		
	(0.392)*	(0.194)		
Company size (number of employees)				
1-9	Ref.	Ref.	Ref.	Ref.
10-19	0.295	0.559		0.462
	(0.222)	(0.201)***		(0.203)**
20-49	0.406	0.664	0.290	0.995
	(0.187)**	(0.164)***	(0.188)	(0.181)***
50-249	1.215	1.386	0.835	1.179
	(0.203)***	(0.181)***	(0.219)***	(0.202)***
>= 250	2.045	2.402	1.781	1.985
	(0.215)***	(0.186)***	(0.228)***	(0.254)***
Share of women in employment				
<Q1[a]	Ref.	Ref.	Ref.	Ref.
Q1<= share of women <Q2[a]	-0.325			
	(0.160)**			
Q2<= share of women <Q3[a]	-0.484			-0.719
	(0.178)***			(0.199)***
>= Q3[a]	-0.639		-0.416	
	(0.192)***		(0.217)*	
Share of "managerial staff " in employment				
<Q1[a]	Ref.	Ref.	Ref.	Ref.
Q1<= share of "managerial staff" <Q2[a]	0.544	0.210	0.246	
	(0.165)***	(0.134)	(0.179)	
Q2<= share of "managerial staff" <Q3[a]				-0.365
				(0.181)**
>= Q3[a]		0.251		-1.076
		(0.127)**		(0.185)***
Share of part-time workers in employment				
No part-time work	Ref.	Ref.	Ref.	Ref.
<Q1[a]				
Q1<= share of part-time workers <Q2[a]				
Q2<= share of part-time workers <Q3[a]	0.368			0.363
	(0.176)**			(0.210)*
>= Q3[a]				0.361
				(0.222)
Degree of competition				
Absence of local competition	Ref.	Ref.	Ref.	Ref.
Local competition		-0.220	0.205	
		(0.130)*	(0.138)	
Absence of national competition	Ref.	Ref.	Ref.	Ref.
National competition		0.226		-0.186
		(0.108)**		(0.142)
Absence of international competition	Ref.	Ref.	Ref.	Ref.

	France	Germany	Netherlands	UK
International competition	0.532 (0.156)***	0.197 (0.142)		
Irrelevant questions	Ref.	Ref.	Ref.	Ref.
Relevant questions		-0.317 (0.206)		-0.424 (0.262)
Collective agreement on working time and/or operating time				
No	Ref.	Ref.	Ref.	Ref.
Yes	0.194 (0.126)			
Fluctuations in demand				
Absence of daily fluctuations	Ref.	Ref.	Ref.	Ref.
Daily fluctuations (foreseeable)	0.385 (0.246)	0.378 (0.253)		
Daily fluctuations (unforeseeable)				0.500 (0.257)*
Absence of weekly fluctuations	Ref.	Ref.	Ref.	Ref.
Weekly fluctuations (foreseeable)	0.270 (0.210)		0.434 (0.250)*	
Weekly fluctuations (unforeseeable)	0.453 (0.200)**	0.343 (0.195)*	0.468 (0.265)*	
Absence of annual fluctuations	Ref.	Ref.	Ref.	Ref.
Annual fluctuations (foreseeable)	0.220 (0.143)	0.428 (0.131)***		0.326 (0.178)*
Annual fluctuations (unforeseeable)	0.337 (0.162)**		0.291 (0.198)	
Sector of economic activity				
Primary sector	Ref.	Ref.	Ref.	Ref.
Manufacture of food products, beverages and tobacco	2.145 (0.377)***	0.677 (0.465)		
Manufacture of textile and textile products, leather and leather products, wood and wood products, pulp, paper and paper products	-0.537 (0.363)	-1.247 (0.416)***	-0.722 (0.437)*	
Publishing, printing and reproduction of recorded media	1.170 (0.408)***	-1.880 (0.527)***	-0.987 (0.437)**	
Manufacture of coke, refined petroleum products and nuclear fuel, chemicals, chemical products and man-made fibres, rubber and plastic products, other non-metallic mineral products.	1.089 (0.319)***	-0.802 (0.381)**		
Manufacture of basic metals and fabricated metal products		-1.202 (0.360)***	-0.709 (0.364)*	
Manufacture of machinery and equipment n.e.c, electrical and optical equipment, transport equipment, Manufacturing n.e.c.		-1.473 (0.319)***	-1.425 (0.268)***	
Electricity, gas and water supply		-1.761 (0.509)***		
Construction	-1.251 (0.283)***	-1.568 (0.326)***	-1.064 (0.254)***	
Sale, maintenance and repair of motor vehicles and motorcycles; retail trade of automotive fuel	0.842 (0.411)**	1.011 (0.433)**		

	France	Germany	Netherlands	UK
Wholesale trade and commission trade, except of motor vehicles and motorcycles		-1.293 (0.334)***	-0.417 (0.293)	
Retail trade, except of motor vehicles and motorcycles; repair of personal and household goods	1.021 (0.276)***		1.378 (0.334)***	
Hotels and restaurants	3.166 (0.370)***	0.862 (0.427)**	1.472 (0.441)***	
Transport and storage	1.034 (0.358)***	0.774 (0.396)*		
Post and telecommunications	1.720 (0.485)***			
Financial intermediation		-2.412 (0.362)***	-1.072 (0.372)***	
Real estate, renting and business activities	0.396 (0.248)	-1.377 (0.305)***	-0.758 (0.247)***	
Public administration and defence; compulsory social security		-2.052 (0.388)***		
Education	1.953 (0.562)***	-1.926 (0.371)***	-0.522 (0.334)	
Health and social work	2.732 (0.338)***		0.385 (0.295)	
Other community, social and personal service activities; activities of households	1.213 (0.318)***	-0.679 (0.341)**	0.534 (0.305)*	
Intercept	- 1.772 (0.275)***		-0.411 (0.270)	
Number of observations	2,221	2,847	1,850	1,335
P-value LR	<.0001	<.0001	<.0001	<.0001
P-value Score	<.0001	<.0001	<.0001	<.0001
P-value Wald	<.0001	<.0001	<.0001	<.0001
Concordance	83.0	80.7	76.4	76.5

a Samples on which medians and quartiles are computed differ from samples used in estimation since independent variables may be missing; "Ref.." reference situation; *** 1% significance level; ** 5% significance level; * 10% significance level; coefficients not reported if significance level > 20%.

Table A2.4.6 Annual operating time (greater than national median, yes/no)

	France	Germany	Netherlands	UK
Legal form of organisation				
Enterprise	Ref.	Ref.	Ref.	Ref.
Public institution			-0.618	-0.478
			(0.272)**	(0.291)
Non-profit organisation	-0.679			-0.448
	(0.285)**			(0.206)**
Other				
Company size (number of employees)				
1-9	Ref.	Ref.	Ref.	Ref.
10-19		0.693		0.652
		(0.215)***		(0.225)***
20-49	0.565	1.057		1.041
	(0.197)***	(0.169)***		(0.198)***
50-249	1.237	1.683	0.425	1.361
	(0.213)***	(0.182)***	(0.203)**	(0.218)***
>= 250	2.019	2.337	0.902	2.270
	(0.222)***	(0.184***	(0.208)***	(0.257)***
Share of women in employment				
<Q1[a]	Ref.	Ref.	Ref.	Ref.
Q1<= share of women <Q2[a]	-0.412	-0.170		
	(0.163)**	(0.130)		
Q2<= share of women < Q3[a]	-0.542			-0.361
	(0.180)***			(0.210)*
>= Q3[a]	-0.714			
	(0.196)***			
Share of "managerial staff" in employment				
<Q1[a]	Ref.	Ref.	Ref.	Ref.
Q1<= share of "managerial staff" <Q2[a]	0.548			-0.361
	(0.165)***			(0.173)**
Q2<= share of "managerial staff" < Q3[a]	0.259			-0.431
	(0.161)			(0.187)**
>= Q3[a]	-0.237		-0.233	-1.465
	(0.169)		(0.148)	(0.214)***
Share of part-time workers in employment				
No part-time work	Ref.	Ref.	Ref.	Ref.
<Q1[a]				
Q1<= share of part-time workers <Q2[a]	0.236			0.267
	(0.169)			(0.204)
Q2<= share of part-time workers <Q3[a]	0.417			0.552
	(0.180)**			(0.226)**
>= Q3[a]				0.868
				(0.237)***
Degree of competition				
Absence of local competition	Ref.	Ref.	Ref.	Ref.
Local competition				
Absence of national competition	Ref.	Ref.	Ref.	Ref.
National competition		0.286		
		(0.102)***		
Absence of international competition	Ref.	Ref.	Ref.	Ref.
International competition	0.499	0.306		-0.232
	(0.160)***	(0.134)**		(0.172)
Irrelevant questions	Ref.	Ref.	Ref.	Ref.

	France	Germany	Netherlands	UK
Relevant questions				-0.815 (0.289)***
Collective agreement on working time and/or operating time				
No	Ref.	Ref.		
Yes		-0.202 (0.110)*		
Fluctuations in demand				
Absence of daily fluctuations	Ref.	Ref.		
Daily fluctuations (foreseeable)				
Daily fluctuations (unforeseeable)				
Absence of weekly fluctuations	Ref.	Ref.		
Weekly fluctuations (foreseeable)	0.421 (0.208)**			
Weekly fluctuations (unforeseeable)	0.309 (0.200)	0.255 (0.181)		
Absence of annual fluctuations	Ref.	Ref.		
Annual fluctuations (foreseeable)	0.512 (0.145)***			
Annual fluctuations (unforeseeable)	0.641 (0.163)***	-0.293 (0.127)**		
Sector of economic activity				
Primary sector	Ref.	Ref.		
Manufacture of food products, beverages and tobacco	1.890 (0.359)***	1.228 (0.434)***		
Manufacture of textile and textile products, leather and leather products, wood and wood products, pulp, paper and paper products				
Publishing, printing and reproduction of recorded media	0.916 (0.404)**			
Manufacture of coke, refined petroleum products and nuclear fuel, chemicals, chemical products and man-made fibres, rubber and plastic products, other non-metallic mineral products.	1.029 (0.312)***			
Manufacture of basic metals and fabricated metal products				
Manufacture of machinery and equipment n.e.c, electrical and optical equipment, transport equipment, Manufacturing n.e.c.		-0.702 (0.307)**		
Electricity, gas and water supply		-1.051 (0.492)**		
Construction	-1.371 (0.300)***	-1.436 (0.345)***		
Sale, maintenance and repair of motor vehicles and motorcycles; retail trade of automotive fuel		0.565 (0.366)		
Wholesale trade and commission trade, except of motor vehicles and motorcycles	-0.489 (0.337)	-0.848 (0.328)***		
Retail trade, except of motor vehicles and motorcycles; repair of personal and household goods	0.849 (0.285)***	-0.526 (0.336)		

	France	Germany	Netherlands	UK
Hotels and restaurants	2.897 (0.341)***	1.410 (0.401)***		
Transport and storage	1.034 (0.351)***	0.897 (0.350)**		
Post and telecommunications	1.416 (0.456)***			
Financial intermediation		-1.443 (0.350)***		
Real estate, renting and business activities		-1.007 (0.300)***		
Public administration and defence; compulsory social security	-0.636 (0.406)	-1.607 (0.381)***	0.559 (0.391)	
Education	0.925 (0.589)	-1.330 (0.364)***		
Health and social work	2.610 (0.337)***	0.653 (0.324)**	0.903 (0.284)***	
Other community, social and personal service activities; activities of households	1.180 (0.325)***	-0.582 (0.333)*		
Intercept	-2.131 (0.285)***	-0.902 (0.313)***	-0.430 (0.256)*	-1.329 (0.415)***
Number of observations	2,221	2,847	1,850	1,335
P-value LR	<.0001	<.0001	<.0001	<.0001
P-value Score	<.0001	<.0001	<.0001	<.0001
P-value Wald	<.0001	<.0001	<.0001	<.0001
Concordance	83.9	79.3	66.7	78.0

a Samples on which medians and quartiles are computed differ from samples used in estimation since independent variables may be missing; "Ref. " reference situation; *** 1% significance level; ** 5% significance level; * 10% significance level; coefficients not reported if significance level > 20%.

B – Overall sample

	Shift work	Staggered working times	De-coupling	Daily operating time	Weekly operating time	Annual operat-ing time
Legal form of organisation						
Enterprise	Ref.	Ref.	Ref.	Ref.	Ref.	Ref.
Public institution				-0.553	-0.175	-0.214
				(0.129)***	(0.131)	(0.129)*
Non-profit organisation	0.201			-0.304	-0.151	-0.141
	(0.127)			(0.103)***	(0.103)	(0.103)
Other						
Company size (number of employees)						
1-9	Ref.	Ref.	Ref.	Ref.	Ref.	Ref.
10-19	0.941	0.601	0.651	0.553	0.291	0.299
	(0.186)***	(0.108)***	(0.108)***	(0.098)***	(0.102)***	(0.104)***
20-49	1.672	0.609	0.846	0.850	0.607	0.652
	(0.152)***	(0.091)***	(0.091)***	(0.083)***	(0.084)***	(0.085)***
50-249	2.650	0.744	1.444	1.320	1.187	1.041
	(0.154)***	(0.099)***	(0.099)***	(0.092)***	(0.092)***	(0.093)***
>= 250	3.713	0.843	2.227	2.018	2.127	1.720
	(0.157)***	(0.102)***	(0.105)***	(0.097)***	(0.098)***	(0.096)***
Share of women in employment						
<Q1[a]	Ref.	Ref.	Ref.	Ref.	Ref.	Ref.
Q1<= share of women <Q2[a]	-0.140	0.372	0.150		-0.127	-0.156
	(0.094)	(0.081)***	(0.082)*		(0.077)*	(0.076)**
Q2<= share of women < Q3[a]	-0.594	0.359		-0.112	-0.282	-0.283
	(0.107)***	(0.090)***		(0.084)	(0.085)***	(0.084)***
>= Q3[a]		0.502	0.280		-0.219	-0.126
		(0.096)***	(0.098)***		(0.092)**	(0.090)
Share of "managerial staff" in employment						
<Q1[a]	Ref.	Ref.	Ref.	Ref.	Ref.	Ref.
Q1<= share of "managerial staff" <Q2[a]	0.224	0.121	0.275	0.136	0.145	0.157
	(0.086)***	(0.078)	(0.081)***	(0.076)*	(0.076)*	(0.074)**
Q2<= share of "managerial staff" < Q3[a]			0.104			
			(0.080)			
>= Q3[a]	-0.953		-0.261	-0.100	-0.280	-0.383
	(0.111)***		(0.083)***	(0.076)	(0.078)***	(0.078)***
Share of part-time workers in employment						
No part-time work	Ref.	Ref.	Ref.	Ref.	Ref.	Ref.
<Q1[a]	0.135		0.191		-0.111	
	(0.096)		(0.087)**		(0.083)	
Q1<= share of part-time workers <Q2[a]		0.219	0.145	0.124		
		(0.084)***	(0.085)*	(0.080)		
Q2<= share of part-time workers < Q3[a]	0.142	0.137	0.252	0.112	0.126	0.240
	(0.109)**	(0.089)	(0.091)***	(0.085)	(0.086)	(0.085)***
>= Q3[a]			0.164	0.130	0.119	0.230
			(0.097)*	(0.089)	(0.089)	(0.089)***

	Shift work	Staggered working times	De-coupling	Daily operating time	Weekly operating time	Annual operating time
Degree of competition						
Absence of local competition	Ref.	Ref.	Ref.	Ref.	Ref.	Ref.
Local competition	-0.343 (0.084)***	0.217 (0.074)***				
Absence of national competition	Ref.	Ref.	Ref.	Ref.	Ref.	Ref.
National competition	-0.181 (0.074)**	0.178 (0.064)***				
Absence of international competition	Ref.	Ref.	Ref.	Ref.	Ref.	Ref.
International competition	0.464 (0.088)***		0.250 (0.078)***	0.242 (0.074)***	0.290 (0.074)***	0.230 (0.073)***
Irrelevant questions	Ref.	Ref.	Ref.	Ref.	Ref.	Ref.
Relevant questions	-0.183 (0.138)		-0.167 (0.121)			
Collective agreement on working time and/or operating time						
No	Ref.	Ref.	Ref.	Ref.	Ref.	Ref.
Yes	0.229 (0.080)***		0.208 (0.064)***			
Fluctuations in demand						
Absence of daily fluctuations	Ref.	Ref.	Ref.	Ref.	Ref.	Ref.
Daily fluctuations (foreseeable)		0.490 (0.119)***	0.384 (0.132)***		0.273 (0.124)**	0.194 (0.119)
Daily fluctuations (unforeseeable)		0.477 (0.109)***	0.238 (0.119)**	0.221 (0.113)*	0.271 (0.112)**	0.161 (0.109)
Absence of weekly fluctuations	Ref.	Ref.	Ref.	Ref.	Ref.	Ref.
Weekly fluctuations (foreseeable)		0.189 (0.111)*		0.158 (0.112)	0.164 (0.112)	0.190 (0.108)*
Weekly fluctuations (unforeseeable)	0.196 (0.123)	0.280 (0.105)***	0.439 (0.113)***	0.185 (0.106)*	0.313 (0.106)***	0.269 (0.103)***
Absence of annual fluctuations	Ref.	Ref.	Ref.	Ref.	Ref.	Ref.
Annual fluctuations (foreseeable)	0.168 (0.089)*	0.281 (0.075)***	0.385 (0.078)***	0.148 (0.074)**	0.243 (0.074)***	0.105 (0.073)
Annual fluctuations (unforeseeable)				0.270 (0.079)***	0.136 (0.079)*	
Country						
France	Ref.	Ref.	Ref.	Ref.	Ref.	Ref.
Germany	0.407 (0.086)***	0.588 (0.071)***	0.517 (0.074)***	0.557 (0.069)***	0.376 (0.069)***	0.878 (0.068)***
UK	0.954 (0.115)***		0.326 (0.096)***		0.143 (0.091)	0.129 (0.091)
Netherlands	-0.539 (0.106)***	-0.189 (0.088)**	-0.530 (0.087)***	-0.909 (0.079)***	-0.611 (0.081)***	-0.353 (0.080)***

	Shift work	Staggered working times	De-coupling	Daily operating time	Weekly operating time	Annual operating time
Sector of economic activity						
Primary sector	Ref.	Ref.	Ref.	Ref.	Ref.	Ref.
Manufacture of food products, beverages and tobacco	1.049 (0.254)***	0.830 (0.213)***	1.309 (0.230)***	1.411 (0.232)***	1.173 (0.224)***	1.205 (0.213)***
Manufacture of textile and textile products, leather and leather products, wood and wood products, pulp, paper and paper products	0.347 (0.250)		0.320 (0.218)		-0.538 (0.208)***	
Publishing, printing and reproduction of recorded media	0.938 (0.273)***		0.553 (0.236)**	0.410 (0.227)*		
Manufacture of coke, refined petroleum products and nuclear fuel, chemicals, chemical products and man-made fibres, other non-metallic mineral products	1.041 (0.277)***	0.394 (0.241)	1.189 (0.282)***	0.703 (0.263)***		0.540 (0.235)**
Manufacture of rubber and plastic products	2.235 (0.356)***		1.635 (0.335)***	0.737 (0.292)**	0.808 (0.300)***	0.901 (0.278)***
Manufacture of other non metallic mineral product	0.517 (0.324)			0.358 (0.277)		
Manufacture of basic metals	1.630 (0.402)***		1.770 (0.442)***	0.440 (0.335)	0.611 (0.361)*	0.787 (0.329)**
Manufacture of fabricated metal products, except machinery and equipment	0.333 (0.230)		0.345 (0.195)*	-0.246 (0.185)	-0.726 (0.187)***	
Manufacture of machine and equipment, n.e.c	0.479 (0.229)**		0.550 (0.204)***		-0.616 (0.190)***	
Manufacture of office machinery and computers, electrical machinery and apparatus n.e.c	0.426 (0.287)			0.426 (0.274)		0.458 (0.257)*
Manufacture of radio, television and communication equipment and apparatus			0.402 (0.311)		-0.391 (0.284)	
Manufacture of medical, precision and optical instruments, watches and clocks					-0.681 (0.279)**	-0.432 (0.278)
Manufacture of motor vehicles, trailers and semi-trailers						
manufacture of other transport equipment		0.622 (0.270)**	0.617 (0.288)**			
Manufacturing n.e.c	-0.427 (0.259)*	-0.347 (0.257)	-0.426 (0.225)*	-0.882 (0.218)***	-1.473 (0.226)***	-0.840 (0.223)***

	Shift work	Staggered working times	De-coupling	Daily operating time	Weekly operating time	Annual operat-ing time
Electricity, gas and water supply						
Construction	-1.487 (0.229)***	-0.547 (0.176)***	-1.072 (0.164)***	-0.348 (0.139)**	-0.972 (0.142)***	-0.740 (0.147)***
Sale, maintenance and repair of motor vehicles and motorcycles; retail trade of automotive fuel	-0.476 (0.319)	1.211 (0.221)***	0.876 (0.227)***	0.797 (0.225)***	0.892 (0.222)***	0.668 (0.217)***
Wholesale trade and commission trade, except of motor vehicles and motorcycles	-0.816 (0.223)***	0.382 (0.170)**			-0.619 (0.157)***	-0.222 (0.159)
Retail trade, except of motor vehicles and motorcycles; repair of personal and household goods	-0.909 (0.241)***	0.830 (0.170)***	0.574 (0.170)***	0.371 (0.158)**	0.542 (0.157)***	0.510 (0.158)***
Hotels and restaurants	1.500 (0.224)***	1.259 (0.195)***	1.480 (0.201)***	2.040 (0.214)***	1.948 (0.211)***	1.811 (0.194)***
Transport and storage	0.325 (0.187)*	0.429 (0.165)***	0.457 (0.159)***	0.655 (0.150)***	0.336 (0.148)**	0.562 (0.148)***
Post and telecommunications		0.890 (0.261)***	0.738 (0.283)***	1.067 (0.281)***	0.596 (0.269)**	1.053 (0.261)***
Financial intermediation, except insurance and pension funding	-1.456 (0.283)***		-0.890 (0.220)***	-0.530 (0.205)***	-1.390 (0.212)***	-0.810 (0.211)***
Insurance and pension funding, except compulsory social security	-1.882 (0.414)***		-0.617 (0.306)**		-0.397 (0.296)	-0.498 (0.295)*
Activities auxiliary to financial intermediation			0.483 (0.351)			
Real estate activities	-1.140 (0.440)***				-0.963 (0.279)***	
Computer and related activities	-0.780 (0.326)**		-0.340 (0.248)		-0.388 (0.230)*	
Research and development	-1.385 (0.457)***		-0.922 (0.360)**		-0.548 (0.343)	-0.619 (0.352)*
Renting of machinery and equipment without operator and of persona land household goods;	-0.433 (0.188)**				-0.305 (0.135)**	
Other business activities						
Public administration and defence; compulsory social security	-1.296 (0.237)***		-0.688 (0.201)***	-0.277 (0.186)	-1.064 (0.189)***	-0.813 (0.191)***
Education	-1.088 (0.273)***		-0.372 (0.204)*		-0.894 (0.197)***	-0.333 (0.193)*
Health and social work	1.200 (0.182)***	0.542 (0.157)***	0.946 (0.152)***	1.125 (0.142)***	0.806 (0.139)***	1.029 (0.141)***
Sewage and refuse disposal, sanitation and similar activities	0.727 (0.469)					

	Shift work	Staggered working times	De-coupling	Daily operating time	Weekly operating time	Annual operat-ing time
Activities of membership organisations n.e.c	-1.008 (0.317)***	0.312 (0.228)			-0.466 (0.214)**	-0.520 (0.224)**
Recreational, cultural and sporting activities	0.468 (0.281)*	0.980 (0.222)***	0.995 (0.227)***	1.288 (0.220)***	1.081 (0.217)***	1.023 (0.213)***
Other personal activities		0.473 (0.240)**	0.368 (0.240)	0.371 (0.215)*		
Intercept	-3.441 (0.221)***	-2.740 (0.167)***	-2.180 (0.159)***	-1.160 (0.144)***	-0.949 (0.143)***	-1.466 (0.146)***
Number of observations	8,143	7,632	7,565	8,253	8,253	8,253
P-value LR	<.0001	<.0001	<.0001	<.0001	<.0001	<.0001
P-value Score	<.0001	<.0001	<.0001	<.0001	<.0001	<.0001
P-value Wald	<.0001	<.0001	<.0001	<.0001	<.0001	<.0001
Concordance	88.1	71.0	80.4	78.4	79.3	78.0

"Ref.", reference situation; *** 1% significance level; ** 5% significance level; * 10% significance level; coefficients not reported if significance level > 20%.

3 Operating Hours in the EU: the Role of Strategy, Structure and Context

Lei Delsen and Jeroen Smits

3.1 Introduction

Long and flexible operating hours, and opening and service hours are key indicators of economic performance. Extending operating times and a more flexible organisation of work are important policy instruments to improve competitiveness of a single enterprise, a sector or an economy (European Commission, 1995; Betancourt and Clague, 1981; Anxo *et al.*, 1995; Delsen *et al.*, 2007). A prolongation of operating times and opening hours may increase average capital productivity and ultimately increase profitability, reduce unit costs, and generate more jobs and/or higher wages. For these reasons, both governments and companies consider operating hours a strategic goal of macroeconomic policy (European Commission, 1995).

At the macro level, operating hours depend on the openness of the economy, its industrial and sectoral structure, and the size of plants in the country. Also the business cycle situation is of importance. Figure 3.1 shows that among the six EU countries covered by the EUCOWE survey there are considerable differences in the weekly operating hours – defined as the weekly business hours, including preparation times and times for maintenance – ranging from 60.4 hours in Germany to 47.3 hours in Spain. These figures concern the *direct* measurement of operating hours of establishments. The direct measure is calculated from the answers given by the respondents to the question "How many hours did your establishment operate in a typical week in March or April 2003?".[1]

1 For more details see the EUCOWE questionnaire in the Appendix of this volume. The indirect measure of weekly operating hours is constructed on the ba-

L. Delsen et al., *Comparative Analyses of Operating Hours and Working Times in the European Union*,
DOI: 10.1007/978-3-7908-2185-7_3,

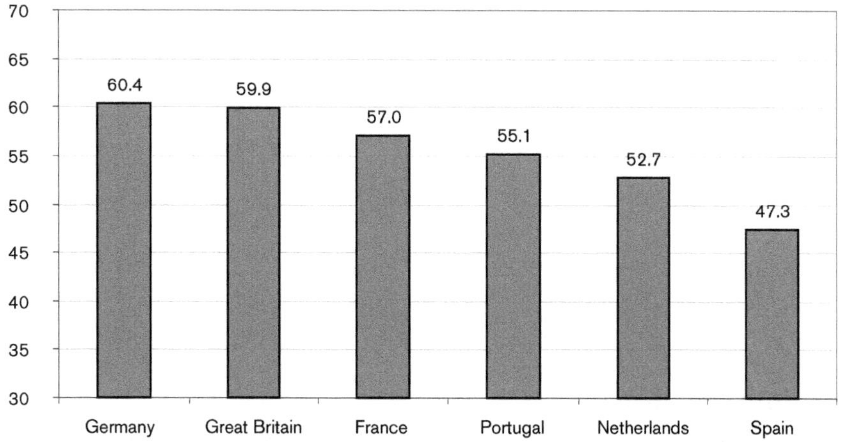

Figure 3.1 Directly measured weekly operating hours in the six EUCOWE countries

According to the *endogenous capital utilisation* theory, in the short run the capital stock is fixed and capital utilisation is variable (Anxo *et al.*, 1995). In this theory, capital utilisation not only concerns the firms' organisational choices that vary with market conditions, but also labour supply behaviour. The starting point of this chapter is that weekly operating hours and the working-time arrangements used to realise these operating hours are the result of both demand and supply factors. There may be a trade-off between economic and social objectives, as the decoupling of operating hours and individual working times may require employees to work at less social hours, which interfere with social life and affect the so called work-life balance. The extent to which a trade-off takes place depends on the way in which these long and flexible operating hours are achieved. At the establishment level, it depends on the organisation of work. To match preferences of firms concerning weekly operating times, opening hours and service hours, and preferences of workers concerning hours and times of work some compromise has to be reached. This compromise reflects the relative bargaining power positions of the employer and the employee and

sis of the number of employees and the duration of the various working time patterns (see Chapter 1 this volume). Hence it measures the number of employees that experience the various operating hour regimes (see also Delsen et al., 2007).

is influenced by economic conditions as well as by the institutional environment of the establishment.

In this chapter, we want to find out to what extent weekly operating hours are determined by working time strategies, by internal characteristics of the establishment, and by the economic and institutional context in which the establishment operates. The working time options concern the use of shift work, staggered working times, Saturday and Sunday work, overtime (including the premia paid for it), part-time work and on-call labour. Also the use of temporary workers (agency workers plus fixed-term employees) is included in our analysis. Characteristics of establishments used to explain the variation in weekly operating time include sector of activity, establishment's age, ownership (multinational), sector and size class, capital intensity, and skill and gender composition of the workforce. The economic and institutional environment variables concern fluctuations in product demand, the business cycle situation, the degree to which the establishment experiences competition and the coverage by collective labour agreements.

The chapter is organised as follows. In Section 3.2 the hypotheses concerning the determinants of operating hours are derived. These hypotheses are grouped according to internal and external dimensions. The internal dimension concerns the working-time strategies and the establishment characteristics. The external dimension concerns the economic and institutional environment. In the results section, first bivariate relationships are established between weekly operating hours and the working-time patterns (Section 3.3.1), between weekly operating hours and establishment characteristics (Section 3.3.2), and between weekly operating hours and the economic and institutional environment (Section 3.3.3). After that the results of a multivariate regression analysis are presented (Section 3.4), explaining the weekly operating hours in the six countries *ceteris paribus* from establishments' characteristics, the use of the various working-time options and the economic and institutional context. In Section 3.5 conclusions are drawn.

3.2 Hypotheses concerning determinants of operating hours

3.2.1 Working time strategies

An increase in the weekly operating hours means that equipment will operate longer: earlier in the morning, later in the evening, at night, and/or at weekends. In the economic literature it is assumed that longer operating hours require longer working hours (Anxo *et al.*, 1995; Dupaigne, 2000; 2001; Betancourt and Clague, 1981). However, throughout Europe, in collective labour agreements longer operating hours have been exchanged for shorter but more flexible working hours. The UK, where industry-wide collective bargaining is absent, is the exception. Decoupling of operating time and working time allows reconciling workers' demands for shorter hours with industry needs for increased production (see *e.g.* Delsen, 1995; European Commission, 1995; Contensou and Vranceanu, 2000; Golden and Figart, 2000). Moreover, in the EU the share of part-time jobs has increased strongly over the past two decades (Delsen, 1995; Garibaldi and Mauro, 2002; Buddelmeyer, Mourre and Ward, 2008). Hence, the relationship between weekly operating hours and average *contractual* weekly working time has become more ambiguous.

The organisation of work is a very important determinant of the capability of a firm to adjust production to fluctuations in demand. Evidence for Europe shows that the use of shift work is not only predetermined by technological requirements (continuous operation), but that economic conditions play an important role, too. Once shift work has been introduced in an establishment, it is used for a relative long period of time. Changes in shift work are related to a medium or long term adjustment of production or demand (see Anxo *et al.*, 1995; Jirjahn, 2008). Shift work is one of the most important factors determining the length of the operating times (European Commission, 1995; Anxo *et al.*, 1995; Dupaigne, 2000; 2001; Betancourt and Clague, 1981). Establishments that use shift work, therefore tend to have longer weekly operating hours relative to establishments that use no shifts.

Apart from shift work, also staggered (i.e. overlapping), working times, overtime work, and working on Saturdays and on Sundays are important alternative and interrelated work schedules to extend the period of daily and weekly productivity and service hours (see Delsen *et al.*, 2007). Staggered working hours may also be used to vary staffing levels within given opening and operating hours (Kümmerling and Lehndorff, 2007). Furthermore supply factors play a role. Staggered working hours offer some flexibility in working hours to the employees and may contribute to improving work-life balance.

Like staggered working hours, also overtime hours may be used for other purposes than to extend operating hours. Overtime enables firms to effectively manage variable workloads without increasing staffing levels. Overtime allows matching the preference of firms to extend operating hours to evenings or weekends and preferences of workers concerning the *actual* weekly hours of work. Overtime may be used on a permanent basis or temporarily to cope with unpredicted short-term fluctuations or to replace absent workers. The association between overtime work and establishment size is ambiguous. For example, workers in larger German manufacturing establishments are more likely to work overtime: both the incidence and the hours of overtime per worker increase with establishment size. This is related to the higher absence rates. German manufacturing establishments using shifts are less likely to use overtime (see Jirjahn, 2008). A higher proportion of temporary workers who are unfamiliar with the organisation and have to be settled in or have to be trained by senior employees may lead to more overtime work by core employees (Delsen, 1995; Jirjahn, 2008). Böckerman (2002) found that in small Finnish establishments the share of overtime hours is relatively high, because such establishments are confronted with more volatility in demand and production. In West European countries the incidence of overtime increases with establishment size, while the number of overtime hours per employee decreases with establishment size (see Delsen *et al.*, 2007). We expect weekly operating hours to be longer in establishments that use staggered working times, overtime hours, working on Saturday and working on Sunday relative to establishments that do not use these working-time options.

Research shows that there is a trade-off between lower capital costs and higher labour costs related to the extension of capital utilisation. For the employer, extending weekly operating hours implies increasing labour costs as wage premia must be paid if longer or unusual hours (overtime, weekend and shift work) are worked (Betancourt and Clague, 1981; Anxo *et al.*, 1995; Kostiuk, 1990). Management must balance extra costs of premia against the flexibility gain and the avoidance of costs of hiring additional labour. The extension of operating hours may also be accompanied by attempts to reduce unsocial hours premia. These premia mirror employee preferences for leisure time. A reduction in leisure raises the wage rate for less social durations or schedules of work. In this respect the overtime allowance, like extra time off in lieu, can be considered a bonus used to remunerate an employee for his/her willingness to work long hours or at less social times. It also serves as an incentive for an employee to work long hours. Empirical results indicate that the higher the overtime and shift-work premia, the lower the level of capital utilisation (see Bautista *et al.*, 1981; Dupaigne, 2000; 2001). Premia paid and extra time off in lieu for various working time patterns have a negative impact on the number of weekly operating hours.

Part-timers may be brought in at (predictable) peak times and to cover regular and anticipated variations in demand. They prevent underemployment of full-time staff during off-peak periods and overtime payments in busy periods. Part-timers may also enable establishments to remain open longer, *e.g.* on evenings or weekends. Apart from these demand factors supply factors also play a role. Employees may prefer and choose to work part time for personal reasons, to improve their work-life balances (Delsen, 1995; Buddelmeyer, Mourre and Ward, 2008). We expect weekly operating hours to be longer in establishments with a higher part-time rate.

Fixed-term employment contracts may be used when fluctuations are predictable and overtime and agency work when fluctuations are unpredictable. In the case of irregular variations in demand, also on-call labour (hours not agreed) contracts are a solution. The incidence of these forms of work shows a procyclical movement. Flexible work arrangements have long been standard practice in order to match working time with variations in customer volume. These contracts are mainly associated with an extension of operating hours, which are mostly determined by social factors (consumers' demands) rather than economic ones (Delsen, 1995; Böckerman, 2002; Mitlacher, 2007). Agency workers may also be used to introduce additional but reversible shifts (Delsen and Smits, 2007). Again supply factors play a role. Relative to core workers, temporary workers may be more willing to work less social hours. We expect weekly operating hours to be longer in establishments with a higher proportion of agency workers, fixed-term employees, and employees without an agreed number of working hours.

3.2.2 Structural characteristics of establishments

Increasing returns to scale and indivisibilities in the production process influence the minimum efficient size of establishments. Savings in administrative and supervision costs due to indivisibilities in production imply that smaller firms will generally have a lower level of capital utilisation. Empirics confirm this: capital utilisation is greater in large-scale plants than in small-scale plants (Bautista *et al.*, 1981; Eriksson and Fellman, 1995). Moreover, shift work is positively associated with establishment size (Cette, 1989). We therefore expect weekly operating hours to be longer the larger the size of the establishment.

In the producing sector, technical reasons (high costs of starting up or stopping production) may explain continuous operation in certain branches of industry (see Anxo *et al.*, 1995; Delsen *et al.*, 2007). Apart from economic and technical grounds, long opening and operating hours may also be determined on social grounds. For instance, certain social services, like accident and emergency, police and fire brigade, and certain personal services, like hotels, must be available 24 hours-a-day. In construction and producer services, including financial intermediation, the proportion of employees working on non-standard times is small and weekly operating hours are relatively short (see Parent-Thirion *et al.*, 2007; Delsen *et al.*, 2007). Production and service processes increasingly look alike. On the one hand, the development of technology and the consequent changes in production processes produce greater service functions at all phases of transformation processes. The pure production costs have continued to decrease. On the other hand, services have become more standardised and mechanised. Modern technology has forced the service sector to make radical changes to some of its functioning modes through the introduction of processes which are very close to the capital intensive processes in manufacturing (see Giarini and Stahel, 1993; Bauer and Groß, Chapter 4, this volume). Evening, night and/or weekend work may be used for enlarging operating and opening times or service hours, but also to perform sector-specific tasks which cannot or need not to be done during normal day time, like cleaning, repairing machinery or introducing new soft- or hardware. From these empirical results we expect weekly operating hours to be relatively long in social services and personal services and relatively short in construction and producer services.

Capital intensity is another important establishment characteristic that influences operating hours and working-time management. For highly capital-intensive establishments, the extension of operating hours may lead to a more efficient use of capital and reduced unit capital costs. Capital intensive processes tend to have higher levels of utilisation (Winston, 1974; Anxo *et al.*, 1995; Eriksson and Fellman, 1995). Weekly operating hours are longer in capital intensive establishments relative to labour intensive establishments.

Also gender is of importance for weekly operating hours. There may be legal constraints governing the times at which women can work. Also working-time preferences (regarding both duration and schedules) may play a role. Empirics show that women are less likely to work evenings, and are less involved in shift work and in overtime hours (Anxo *et al.*, 1995; Böckerman, 2002). Here reverse causality may also play a role. Establishments with a high proportion of women face difficulty in using these work schedules, while establishments making use of overtime or shift work may be reluctant to hire women (Jirjahn, 2008). These results concern manufacturing. Also in certain sectors of the female-dominated service sector, *e.g.* health care, round the clock service is provided (see Bauer and Gross, Chapter 4, this volume). We expect operating hours and the proportion of females in the workforce to be ambiguous.

Also the proportion of skilled personnel may influence operating hours. In part the same reasoning as with capital intensity applies: in establishments where highly trained employees are the most important capital, extension of operating hours and working times might lead to a more efficient use of that human capital. However, in contrast with capital goods, the maximum working time of employees is often legally restricted and hence the possibility to let them work longer maybe restricted. The extension of operating hours will, therefore, generally make it necessary to hire additional personnel, which in establishments with many skilled employees is relatively expensive. Investments in human capital of their employees, representing fixed costs per employee, may induce employers to demand overtime. This leads to the expectation that the proportion of skilled workers and overtime incidence are positively associated (Jirjahn, 2008). In the EU the higher skilled and better qualified workers tend to work longer hours than the average employee; managers, professionals and technicians also have more work autonomy (Parent-Thirion *et al.*, 2007; Fernández Macías and Muñoz de Bustillo Llorente, Chapter 7, this volume). However, the opposite relationship between weekly operating hours and human capital may also apply. This is related to working-time preferences. For manual employees, financial motives to work overtime prevail. For low-wage earners overtime pay may be essential to earn a living by supplementing their earnings. Also the level of skill is important. Higher educated (non-manual) workers have been found to be less willing to work unsocial hours, overtime and shifts (see Anxo *et al.*, 1995: 30). Hence, it requires higher compensating differentials in order to encourage overtime and shift work. This would imply that the costs of extending operating hours are higher for establishments with more skilled workers and thus that the proportion of skilled workers and overtime are negatively associated

(Anxo *et al.*, 1995; Böckerman, 2002). The relationship between weekly operating hours and the proportion of skilled workers is thus ambiguous.

One may expect that newly established companies and young establishments, in order to compete for and gain a share in the market, are more likely to have longer weekly operating hours than those establishments that are already settled in the market. Research in Finland indicates that young service sector firms have longer operating hours, while for manufacturing firms this relationship is not significant (Eriksson and Fellman, 1995). We expect establishment age and weekly operating hours to be inversely related.

Also ownership may influence weekly operating hours. One may expect that establishments that are part of multinational companies (MNCs) have longer operating hours than national organisations. This may be related to the size effect. Foreign-owned establishment tend to be larger than domestically owned establishments. Also the sector effect plays a role. Globalising pressure varies between sectors; it may be expected to be stronger in the producing sector. MNCs have greater propensity to use working-time patterns likely to increase operating times, including shift work (see also Schief, Chapter 6, this volume).

3.2.3 The economic and institutional environment

In the short run, capital and labour are complementary production factors; increases in labour input and capital services coincide (Baxter and Farr, 2001). Hence, weekly operating hours might be positively associated with the business cycle situation.

Building flexibility into a plant means sacrificing the lowest achievable unit costs. Uncertainty reduces optimal utilisation of capacity. Short-term fluctuations may be driving the move toward extended operating hours. Firms which experience cyclical increases in demand are more likely to increase the utilisation of their capital stock, by introducing new shifts, extending the working week (Eriksson and Fellman, 1995). We thus expect establishments that experience considerable fluctuations in business activity to have longer weekly operating hours than establishments that do not.

Competition between employers at national and international levels creates pressure to drive down unit labour costs and unit costs associated with utilisation of plant and equipment. Pressure to reduce labour costs and costs associated with the utilisation of plant and equipment may also create pressures to extend operating hours. Competition may force firms to improve technical and productive efficiency, *i.e.* a more optimal use of available capital and labour in the production process. Technical efficiency refers to the physical relation between resources (capital and labour) and economic output. Productive efficiency refers to the maximisation of outcomes for a given cost, or the minimisation of costs for a given outcome. Longer operating times may be considered important in this respect to increasing capital utilisation and hence economic performance.

Collective bargaining coverage implies that standards for weekly working time, premia, bonuses, extra time-off for overtime or unsocial working hours, and differences in working time patterns become institutionalised. Firms may compensate workers involved in these types of arrangements by providing them with a more stable and regulated job. As far as collective agreements increase premia for overtime hours, shift work and less social hours, this may have a negative impact on operating hours. Contractual working times may be shorter in sectors covered by collective bargaining than elsewhere. If so, this may induce covered establishments to use overtime and shift work to prevent operating time from falling (Jirjahn, 2008). Throughout Europe, longer operating hours have in collective labour agreements been exchanged for shorter but more flexible working hours to avoid these premia (see Chapter 1 this volume). Flexible working patterns are more frequent when there is a collective labour agreement (Delsen, 1995; European Commission, 1995; Contensou and Vranceanu, 2000; Golden and Figart, 2000; Cette, Kocoglu and Sylvain, Chapter 2, this volume). Weekly operating hours therefore are expected to be longer in establishments that are covered by collective agreements.

3.3 Bivariate results

3.3.1 Operating hours and working time patterns

To gain insight into the factors that influence the operating hours of establishments in the six EUCOWE countries, Table 3.1 presents bivariate regression coefficients between the directly measured weekly operating hours and characteristics of the establishments, their working-time patterns and of the environment in which they are operating.

Table 3.1 Bivariate regression coefficients of selected establishment characteristics on weekly operating hours

	DE	ES	FR	UK	NL	PT
Working time patterns						
Shift work	44.518	46.791	67.894	67.275	36.070	65.904
Staggered working times	12.361	x	19.331	15.014	18.978	33.641
Saturday work	23.376	23.809	22.758	35.023	18.758	38.758
Sunday work	36.843	40.065	38.893	54.886	31.144	56.252
Percentage part-time (< 35 hours)	-0.059	0.264	0.259	0.545	0.290	0.904
Percentage part-time square	Ns	-0.003	-0.003	-0.005	-0.003	-0.009
Average overtime hours	1.127	8.360	*-0.174*	4.197	2.363	8.194
Average overtime hours square	ns	ns	ns	-0.125	-0.104	-0.660
Overtime premium	7.650	x	4.449	14.263	5.632	20.911
Percentage agency & fixed-term employees	0.372	0.257	*0.049*	-0.092	0.288	0.354
Percentage agency & ft square	-0.004	-0.003	ns	ns	-0.003	-0.004
Percentage contract hours not agreed	*0.049*	x	0.067	0.540	0.464	0.592
Percentage hours not agreed square	ns	x	ns	-0.005	-0.005	-0.007
Average contractual working time	0.219	1.461	-0.941	1.868	0.963	-0.471
Average contractual working time square	ns	-0.022	0.023	-0.031	-0.022	ns
Establishment characteristics						
1-19 employees	-45.175	-51.933	-48.017	-51.741	-41.364	-47.286
20-249 employees	-26.840	-33.912	-26.359	-25.505	-31.229	-33.351
250+ employees	ref.	ref.	ref.	ref.	ref.	ref.
Primary sector	5.044	*6.073*	*-1.156*	*0.281*	3.355	*-8.138*
Secondary sector	*0.052*	*-0.324*	*2.403*	*-1.875*	*-1.554*	-4.580
Construction	-9.217	-7.523	-13.491	*2.532*	-6.454	-15.244
Distributive services	2.381	*-0.968*	*-1.002*	*3.161*	*1.049*	*-1.867*
Producer services	-6.409	-5.727	-4.074	-6.040	-8.077	-12.704
Social services	*-1.023*	-3.839	*-0.956*	8.332	*1.296*	19.951
Personal services	9.172	12.308	18.278	-6.391	10.385	22.582
Establishment age < 10 years	4.562	*-0.782*	*1.940*	-11.255	5.013	*-1.106*
Percentage skilled employees	-0.070	x	*-0.030*	-0.996	-0.108	x
Percentage skilled employees square	ns	x	ns	0.006	ns	x
Percentage labour costs	-0.089	2.063	0.527	*-0.048*	-0.090	0.302
Percentage labour costs square	ns	-0.042	-0.005	ns	ns	-0.003
Labour costs increased since 1998	*1.411*	15.195	6.668	12.830	2.663	7.363
Percentage female employees	0.240	0.379	0.413	-0.437	0.317	0.481

	DE	ES	FR	UK	NL	PT
Percentage female employees square	-0.002	-0.004	-0.004	0.004	-0.003	-0.003
Multinational	*4.297*	3.706	7.390	*1.410*	*3.616*	*-0.198*
Economic and institutional environment						
International competition	4.674	3.287	4.122	*0.245*	5.125	-3.677
Employment increased since 1998	8.717	6.022	*0.721*	*3.296*	5.862	*1.087*
Experiencing fluctuations	3.922	x	7.256	*2.466*	9.695	8.632
Collective labour agreement	*-1.260*	8.859	4.931	*2.203*	8.607	6.174

x = variable not available in country; ns – Quadratic term not significant
Non-significant coefficients are printed in grey and italic

The data largely confirm our expectations concerning the relationship between weekly operating hours and the various working-time patterns. The rather high significant positive regression coefficients in all countries between weekly operating hours and the use of shifts, staggered working times and Saturday and Sunday working can be rather straightforwardly interpreted as resulting from the fact that these all are major working time options used to extend weekly operating hours. The data produce similar pictures for all six countries: shift work shows the highest coefficients, followed by working on Sunday and working on Saturday. The weakest effects are for staggered working times.

The average overtime hours per employee have the expected positive relationship with weekly operating hours in all countries, except France. The added quadratic term is negatively associated with weekly operating hours, indicating a parabolic relation for the UK, the Netherlands and Portugal. In these countries, longer overtime hours per employee are associated with longer weekly operating hours, but the impact of overtime diminishes with its volume. Within the range covered by our data, the effect of overtime remains positive. Contrary to our hypothesis, the overtime premium is strongly positively associated with weekly operating hours in all six countries. The use of overtime premium and/or extra time off in lieu of overtime seems to serve mainly to induce employees to work long hours or at unsocial times.

We expected longer contractual working times of employees to increase operating time. This is confirmed for Germany and the UK, the countries with the longest weekly operating hours, as well as for the Netherlands and Spain, the countries with the shortest weekly operating hours (see Figure 3.1). However, the significant negative coefficients of the quadratic terms for Spain, UK and Netherlands indicate that in these countries the positive impact of contractual weekly working hours on weekly operating hours becomes weaker if the contractual working hours are longer, suggesting an inverted U-shaped relationship. In Germany the relationship is linearly positive. For France and Portugal, countries with intermediate weekly operating hours, the relationship is negative. In these last two countries longer weekly operating hours are accompanied by shorter average weekly working time, suggesting a trade-off between operating time and contractual working time. In France the relationship is nonlinear; the negative impact decreases with the length of the average contractual weekly working hours, pointing towards a U-shape relationship. In Portugal the negative relationship is linear. The trade-off between operating time and contractual working time may be explained from legislation and collective labour agreements that require special working time reductions for shift workers, for employees working at nights or during the weekend. Also specific strategic use of part-time contracts may play a role here. For instance, in Portugal part-time employment is not used to extend operating hours, but to guarantee the operation of some type of business, and is associated with shorter operating hours (see Castro and Varejão, 2007: 164-165). These businesses are predominantly in the retail trade and leisure services and closely linked to weekend operations (a small number of establishments operate from Fridays to Sundays only). These inter-country differences may also be partly related to employee preferences. From this mixed picture, it may be concluded that longer weekly contractual working hours are not a condition *sine qua non* for extending weekly operating hours, as suggested in the economic literature.

Weekly operating hours increase with the part-time rate in all countries, except Germany where weekly operating hours decrease with the part-time rate.[2] Germany also is the only country where the (negative) relationship is linear. In the other five countries the positive relationship is nonlinear: the added quadratic term is negative in these countries, indicating an inverted U-shaped relation between the part-time rate and weekly operating hours. The expected strategic use of part-time employment as an instrument for permanently extending weekly operating and opening hours is confirmed. However, its impact on weekly operating hours diminishes the higher the part-time rate. Employee preferences and coverage of regular fluctuations in demand may play a role here. The latter may also partly explain the negative relation in Germany.

2 Part-time employment refers to less than 35 contractual weekly working hours, and may therefore in certain economic sectors also include full-time contracts.

The percentage of agency workers and fixed-term employees has a significant positive effect on weekly operating hours in Germany, Spain, the Netherlands and Portugal. The significant negative coefficients of the quadratic term indicate that this positive impact on weekly operating hours is weaker in establishments with a high percentage of agency and fixed-term employees. The expected strategic use of agency workers and fixed-term employees as an instrument for extending weekly operating and opening hours is confirmed. In the UK this relationship is negative and linear and contradicts our hypothesis, suggesting that agency workers and fixed-term employees are mainly used to cope with unpredicted short-term fluctuations or to replace absent workers.

The percentage of employees without an agreed number of hours (on-call contracts) has a positive impact on weekly operating hours in France, the UK, the Netherlands and Portugal. Like in the case of agency workers and fixed-term employees, the significant negative coefficients of the added quadratic term indicate that this positive impact on weekly operating hours is hump-shaped. For France the positive relationship is linear. The expected strategic use of on-call labour as an instrument for extending weekly operating and opening hours is confirmed, except for Germany where the relation is not significant.

3.3.2 Operating hours and establishment characteristics

Table 3.1 also presents the bivariate regression coefficients of characteristics of establishments on the directly measured weekly operating hours for the EUCOWE countries. In all six countries, weekly operating hours increase considerably with establishment size, *i.e.* the number of employees of establishments. Small establishments have the shortest and large establishments have the longest weekly operating hours. Our hypothesis is confirmed.

Concerning the weekly operating hours in the different sectors of the economy the bivariate analysis shows a mixed picture that partly conflicts with our expectation. In most countries weekly operating hours in the primary sector, the secondary sector and in construction do not differ significantly from the average and hence do not contribute to explaining weekly operating hours at the national level. Producer services have the expected significant negative impact on average weekly operating hours in all six countries, and personal services have the expected significant positive impact on average weekly operating hours in all countries; the UK being the exception. The impact of social services on weekly operating hours varies between countries: an expected positive impact in the UK and Portugal while in Spain it has a negative impact on weekly operating time.

Young establishments (aged less than 10 years) only have the expected significant longer operating hours in Germany and the Netherlands. In the UK the relation is reversed. The latter may be related to the fact that a considerable part of the new establishments concern are in the producer services where operating times are often shorter (see Section 3.4.2).

In our model we use the percentage of labour costs in total costs of the establishment as a proxy for capital intensity. Table 3.1 shows a mixed picture. The expected linear negative relationship with operating hours is confirmed for Germany and the Netherlands. In the Southern European countries – Spain, France and Portugal – this relationship is positive. Here labour intensive establishments have significantly longer operating hours and the impact is nonlinear. These inter-country differences may relate to differences in the way the management of the establishments weigh up the increasing labour costs resulting from extra wage premia and the costs of hiring additional labour and the gains from extending operating hours. Our bivariate analysis supports the trade-off between lower capital costs and higher labour costs of more intensive utilisation of capital. The growth in the share of labour costs in total costs between 1998 and 2003 is positively associated with weekly operating hours in all countries, except Germany. Hence, in establishments with long weekly operating hours in 2003 this rise in operating hours was accompanied by an increasing proportion of labour costs in the preceding five year period.

The regression coefficients of the proportion of skilled employees – in the EUCOWE survey measured by the percentage of managerial, professional and higher technical staff – on weekly operating hours is negative in Germany, the Netherlands and the UK. The significant quadratic term implies that in the UK this relationship is nonlinear: the negative impact of skilled employees on weekly operating hours decreases the higher the proportion of skilled employees in the workforce. These results seem to indicate the importance of working-time preferences of skilled employees, *i.e.* their lower willingness to work unsocial hours, to work overtime and to work shifts.

Unlike our expectation, the regression coefficients for the proportion of female employees on the operating hours are nonlinear and positive in all countries, except in the UK, where it is nonlinear and negative. Hence, in most countries a high proportion of women in the workforce is favourable for the extension of operating hours. In part this may be related to differences between male and female employees in the sectoral distribution.

Women are overrepresented in personnel services with above average weekly operating hours and underrepresented in producer services, with below average weekly operating hours. As already pointed out, the negative relationship in the UK is the exception.

The regression coefficient of MNCs on weekly operating hours has the expected positive sign in Spain and France. In these countries foreign owned establishments have longer weekly operating hours, suggesting that foreign capital ownership is a more important determinant of weekly operating hours than the “local environment”. For the other countries no significant influence was found.

3.3.3 Operating hours and the economic and institutional environment

The coefficients for the economic and institutional context variables presented in Table 3.1 are lower than those for working time options, indicating a relatively low significance of this group of variables. We see that in line with our expectations, in Germany, Spain, France and the Netherlands the establishments that mainly compete on international markets have significantly longer weekly operating hours. These results suggest that longer operating hours are used as a measure to improve productive and technical efficiency to address international competition. For Portugal the relationship is negative. This finding disappears in the multivariate analysis and hence is the result of other organisational characteristics that are related to the operating hours and experiencing international competition.

Weekly operating hours may also be influenced by the business cycle. We used employment growth as a proxy for the business cycle situation. Past employment growth (1998-2003), *i.e.* a boom, has the expected significant positive association with the length of weekly operating time in Germany, Spain and the Netherlands. In the other countries the business cycle has no impact on the usual weekly operating hours.

In Germany, the Netherlands, France and Portugal, establishments that experienced considerable fluctuations in business activity in 2002 recorded significantly longer weekly operating hours in 2003 than establishments that did not experience those fluctuations. This is in line with our expectations. These longer operating hours to cope with fluctuations may be inefficient, *i.e.* increase unit costs, and reduce competitiveness. In the UK no significant impact of fluctuations was found.

Establishments covered by a collective labour agreement on working time or operating hours were found to operate significantly more hours per week in Spain, France, the Netherlands and Portugal. In these countries our expectation is confirmed. Collective agreements could be accompanied by cost increases or conditions that might hamper the extension or reduce the length of operating and opening hours. Our results indicate that, on balance, coverage by collective agreements facilitate and promote the extension of operating and opening hours by employers. In Germany and the UK the impact of collective labour agreements is not statistically significant. For Germany, Bauer *et al.* (2002) found similar operating hours for establishments covered and not covered by sectoral collective agreements.

3.4 Multivariate results

In Table 3.2 the results of a multivariate regression analysis are presented to establish, *ceteris paribus*, the impact of establishment's characteristics, working-time patterns and the institutional and economic environment on the number of weekly operating hours in a typical week in March or April 2003. The proportion of explained variance in the models is high, ranging from 43% in the Netherlands to 69% in Portugal. However, these percentages are high due to the presence of the working time patterns in the model. Shift work, staggered working times, Saturday and Sunday work are, among others, used as strategies to extend operating hours. Hence the fact that they have strong positive effects on operating hours and explain a substantial part of the variance comes as no surprise. Still it is important to have them in the multivariate models, because we know that the use of these working-time patterns varies among sectors and among establishments with different characteristics. Hence if we leave them out, we do not know whether the effects of the other variables in the model are real, or compositional effects due to the fact that establishment with different characteristics make different use of these working-time patterns.

To get an idea of the proportion of the variance in weekly operating hours explained by the other variables in the model, at the bottom of Table 3.2 the percentages of explained variance are also presented for models without the shift, staggered, Saturday and Sunday work variables. These percentages range from 17% in Germany to 27% in the UK. In this section, where relevant, the multivariate results are compared with the bivariate results in Table 3.1 to highlight similarities and differences.

Table 3.2 Multivariate regression coefficients of selected establishment characteristics on weekly operating hours

	DE	ES	FR	UK	NL	PT
Intercept	55.289	60.630	46.726	23.264	48.171	73.099
Working time patterns						
Shift work	31.613	33.125	46.299	40.477	20.831	37.724
Staggered working times	5.180	x	7.694	6.745	8.492	13.078
Saturday work	10.117	2.905	9.180	8.565	7.477	12.168
Sunday work	22.356	21.736	25.046	29.278	21.991	28.970
Percentage part-time (< 35 hours)	0.246	-0.068	0.102	0.438	*0.008*	-0.069
Percentage part-time square	-0.002	ns	-0.002	-0.003	ns	ns
Average overtime hours	*0.261*	3.510	*-0.266*	0.892	2.318	-1.866
Average overtime hours square	ns	ns	ns	ns	-0.135	ns
Overtime premium	3.399	x	2.503	3.265	*-0.776*	8.657
Percentage agency & fixed-term employees	*-0.018*	*-0.002*	*-0.027*	-0.096	*-0.045*	*0.000*
Percentage agency & ft square	ns	ns	ns	ns	ns	ns
Percentage contract hours not agreed	-0.185	x	*0.001*	*0.025*	0.376	*-0.044*
Percentage hours not agreed square	0.002	x	ns	ns	-0.005	ns
Average contractual working time	0.248	*0.044*	0.184	0.747	0.713	-1.004
Average contractual working time square	ns	ns	ns	ns	-0.013	0.015
Establishment characteristics						
1-19 employees	-19.204	-23.628	-16.374	*-6.012*	-18.670	-15.992
20-249 employees	-12.947	-16.612	*-8.297*	*-0.038*	-15.039	*-11.950*
250+ employees	ref.	ref.	ref.	ref.	ref.	ref.
Primary sector	*-0.527*	*1.109*	*-0.659*	*0.615*	*1.190*	*-0.432*
Secondary sector	*-0.938*	*-0.032*	*-0.165*	*-0.662*	*-1.931*	*-0.528*
Construction	*-0.555*	*-2.243*	*-0.123*	2.827	*-1.869*	*-1.884*
Distributive services	*1.367*	*0.419*	-3.910	*-0.213*	*0.665*	-2.639
Producer services	*0.302*	*-0.912*	*0.636*	-5.531	-3.515	-4.104
Social services	*-1.350*	*-1.642*	*1.916*	*0.386*	3.486	10.350
Personal services	*1.702*	3.300	2.306	*2.578*	*1.976*	*-0.762*
Establishment age < 10 years	3.416	*-0.373*	*1.512*	-3.904	3.309	-1.457
Percentage skilled employees	0.184	x	*-0.025*	-0.323	-0.082	x
Percentage skilled employees square	-0.003	x	ns	0.002	ns	x
Percentage labour costs	*-0.028*	0.351	0.088	*0.046*	*0.007*	0.038
Percentage labour costs square	ns	-0.008	ns	ns	ns	ns
Labour costs increased since 1998	-1.539	2.810	2.505	6.422	*1.180*	*1.155*
Percentage female employees	-0.031	0.034	*-0.009*	*-0.012*	*-0.025*	*0.020*

	DE	ES	FR	UK	NL	PT
Percentage female employees square	ns	ns	ns	ns	ns	ns
Multinational	-6.270	*-2.324*	*4.479*	*1.209*	*-0.664*	*1.695*
Economic and institutional environment						
International competition	*0.654*	*0.725*	2.946	*2.399*	3.238	*-0.330*
Employment increased since 1998	4.051	*0.656*	*-0.449*	*2.014*	*1.969*	*0.449*
Experiencing fluctuations	*0.825*	x	*1.538*	-2.043	3.020	-2.885
Collective labour agreement	*-0.203*	*1.627*	*-0.332*	-2.838	2.899	*0.218*
Number of cases	2,946	5,934	2,227	1,412	1,826	2,810
R^2 adjusted	0.489	0.486	0.621	0.642	0.434	0.687
R^2 adjested without working time options*	0.171	0.207	0.225	0.269	0.203	0.252

x = variable not available in country; ns – Quadratic term not significant
Non-significant coefficients are printed in grey and italic

3.4.1 Working time strategies

The multivariate analysis to a large extent confirms the results from our bivariate analysis concerning working-time strategies. In all six countries, controlled for all the other characteristics, shift work is the most important determinant and Sunday working the second most important determinant of weekly operating hours. Also staggered working times and Saturday working are statistically significant working-time schedules to lengthen operating hours. The effect of the latter two varies between countries. In Germany, France and the UK Saturday work is a stronger determinant of weekly operating hours than staggered working times, while in Portugal and the Netherlands staggered working times is stronger than working on Saturdays (see also Fernández Macías and Muñoz de Bustillo Llorente, Chapter 7, this volume).

In Germany, the UK and the Netherlands again a positive relationship between weekly operating hours and average contractual weekly working time is found. Now also France shows the expected positive relationship. For Portugal, again, the relationship is negative, suggesting a trade-off between operating hours and contractual working hours. This may be related to specific strategic use of part-time contracts. In Portugal part-time employment is not used to extend operating hours, but allows establishments to operate only during weekends, *e.g.* in leisure and retail trade. Also from the multivariate results it can be concluded that longer weekly contractual working hours are not a necessary condition for long weekly operating hours, as suggested in the economic literature. Decoupling of weekly operating hours and individual working time does not necessarily mean shorter operating hours.

The impact of the proportion of part-time employees on weekly operating hours shows again a mixed picture. In three of the countries, Germany, France and the UK, the effect is nonlinear, with an initial increase followed by a decrease of operating hours. These results point towards the expected strategic use of part-time employment as an instrument for extending weekly operating and opening hours in these countries. However, its impact on weekly operating hours decreases the higher the part-time rate, pointing towards an inverted U-shape relationship. Unlike the bivariate results, in Spain and Portugal the impact is significantly negative and linear. Hence, higher proportions of part-time employment in these countries are accompanied by shorter weekly operating hours. These results can be explained from the fact that in these countries the majority of establishments do not use part-time work. In Spain this is the case with 62% of the establishments. Moreover, the establishments using part-time work are small and mainly located in retail trade and social services (see Fernández Macías and Muñoz de Bustillo Llorente, 2007). This also applies to Portugal where 86% of establishments do not use part-time work (Castro and Varejão, 2007). It is important to note that in the Netherlands, where 70% of the establishments use part-time employment contracts[3], no significant impact was found. This finding is in line with the fact that the high proportion of part-time work in the Netherlands is mainly the results of the preferences of employees and much less the result of strategic use for extending weekly operating hours (see Delsen and Smits, 2007).

Average overtime hours per employee again have the expected positive relationship with weekly operating hours in the Netherlands, Spain and the UK. As the EUCOWE data on operating hours concern a usual week, this points towards strategic use of structural (permanent) overtime to extend operating times, opening hours or service hours. In Spain only 3% of the establishments use overtime (Fernández Macías and Muñoz de Bustillo Llorente, 2007: 189). Table 3.2 shows that in these establishments overtime hours have a strong positive impact on weekly operating hours. The case of the Netherlands is also interesting in this respect, the only country were the relation is not linear. Hence, in the Netherlands longer overtime

3 To compare: in the UK 71% of the establishments use part-time work, in Germany 60% of the establishments and in France 52% of the establishments (see Smith, Bosworth and Carroll, 2007; Bauer et al., 2007; Cette, Kocoglu and Sylvain, 2007).

hours per employee are associated with longer weekly operating hours, but the impact of overtime diminishes with its volume. In contrast with the bivariate results, in Germany overtime hours are no longer statistically significant and in Portugal the negative effect points towards a trade-off between operating hours and overtime. In Portugal only 5.5% of the establishments use overtime hours (Castro and Varejão, 2007: 156, 166). The results suggest that here overtime hours, like part-time employment, are not used to extend operating hours, but to guarantee the operation of some types of business with shorter operating hours.

As in the bivariate analysis and contrary to our hypothesis, the overtime premium again is positively associated with weekly operating hours in Germany, France, the UK and Portugal. In these countries overtime premium and/or extra time off in lieu of overtime seems to serve to induce employees to work longer hours or to work at unsocial times. Unlike the bivariate results, in the Netherlands the relationship is no longer statistically significant.

The positive relationship between weekly operating hours and the percentage of agency workers and fixed-term employees found in the bivariate analysis is completely absent in the multivariate analysis. Contrary to our expectation, the percentage of agency workers and fixed-term employees again has a significant linear negative effect on operating hours in the UK but in the other countries not significant. This seems to indicate that these contracts and employees are mainly used as strategies for coping with fluctuations and not for extending operating hours permanently.

The multivariate results concerning on-call contracts (hours not agreed) differ considerably from the bivariate results too. The percentage of on-call contracts now has a nonlinear negative effect on weekly operating hours in Germany and a nonlinear positive effect in the Netherlands. In France, Portugal and the UK the positive relationship found in the bivariate analysis is absent; suggesting that, like agency workers and fixed-term employees, employees with on-call employment contracts are mainly used as strategies for coping with fluctuations and not for permanently extending operating hours. Hence, the Netherlands seems to be the only country where on-call labour is used to extend weekly operating hours.

3.4.2 Establishment characteristics

The multivariate regression results in Table 3.2 confirm the statistic and economic significance of establishment size in explaining operating hours. In all countries, except the UK, weekly operating hours increase with establishment size. As in the bivariate analysis, in Germany, Spain, and the Netherlands weekly operating hours are significantly lower in small (1-19 employees) establishments than in medium sized (20-249 employees) establishments, and in these medium sized establishments weekly operating hours are again significantly lower than in large (250+ employees) establishments. In France and Portugal the differences between the medium-sized establishments and the largest establishments are smaller than in the other countries (except the UK) and not significant.

In relation to weekly operating hours in the different sectors of the economy, the multivariate analysis shows that in most sectors of industry operating hours do not differ significantly from the national average. This holds for the primary and secondary sectors in all six countries. In the UK, weekly operating hours in construction are higher than average. Operating hours in the different service sectors show a mixed picture that moreover varies between countries. In producer services, operating hours are signifycantly lower than average in the UK, the Netherlands and Portugal and in the social services, operating hours are significantly higher than average in the Netherlands and Portugal. In the personal services, operating hours are higher than average in Spain and France and in distributive services they are lower than average in France and Portugal. The higher than average operating hours in personal and social services and the lower than average operating hours in the producer and distributive services are in line with our expectations.

Young establishments (aged less than 10 years) have the expected longer operating hours in Germany and the Netherlands. In the UK and Portugal the relation is the reverse of what was expected: young establishments there have shorter weekly operating hours. The latter may be related to the fact that a considerable share of new establishments are in the producer services where operating hours are shorter.

Unlike the bivariate analysis, the multivariate analysis confirms the ambiguous relationship between weekly operating hours and the proportion of skilled workers (managerial, professional and higher technical staff). In the UK and the Netherlands establishments with higher percentages of skilled staff have significantly shorter weekly operating hours. In these two countries the negative impact of employee preferences and the costs of extending operating hours seem to be more important than the benefits of the extension of operating hours and the demand for overtime by the employer induced by the investments in human capital of their employees. Unlike the bivariate results, in Germany the percentage of skilled employees has a significant positive impact on weekly operating hours. Here managerial, professional and higher technical staff seems to be considered as fixed costs. It may also relate to high-value manufacturing using shifts where a high share of employees are classified as technical. Extending operating hours allows reducing unit fixed costs. In Germany and the UK the relationships are nonlinear. In the Netherlands the relationship is linear.

The multivariate results on the impact of capital intensity on weekly operating hours differ from the mixed bivariate results. The proportion of labour costs in total costs of the establishment is used as a proxy for capital intensity.[4] The negative linear relationship in Germany and the Netherlands turns statistically insignificant. For the UK, the relationship remains insignificant. Contrary to our expectation, in Spain, France and Portugal the proportion of labour costs is again positively associated with weekly operating hours. Here labour intensive establishments have longer weekly operating hours than capital intensive establishments. Like the bivariate results, only for Spain was this relationship nonlinear. The coefficients indicate that the economic significance is low. The trade-off between lower capital costs and higher labour costs of more intensive utilisation of capital is confirmed again in Spain, France and the UK. In these countries, establishments that experienced a growth in the share of labour costs between 1998 and 2003 had longer than average operating hours. In Germany, however, the effect is negative, indicating that in this country long weekly operating hours in 2003 were preceded by capital-deepening investments in the preceding five year period.

The proportion of females in total employment of the establishment has an (unexpected) positive relationship with weekly operating hours in Spain and an (expected) negative relationship with weekly operating hours in Germany. In the other four countries no significant impact was found.

Foreign ownership (multinational) has a significant negative impact on weekly operating hours in Germany. This effect was not expected. In the other countries no impact was found. This suggests that the "local environment" is a more important determinant of weekly operating hours than foreign ownership.

---

4 There has been an indication that capital intensity may be highly correlated with shift work (Cette, 1989), causing multicollinearity problems. However, in our data the relationship between the proportion of labour costs in total costs and shift work is not statistically significant.

3.4.3 Economic and institutional environment

In the multivariate analysis, few significant effects of the economic and institutional environment on weekly operating hours were found. Regarding the effect of international competition, only for France and the Netherlands were significant relationships identified; establishments that experience international competition in these countries have longer operating hours. Hence, for the other countries, unlike our expectations and contrary to the bivariate findings, international competitive pressure does not force establishments to increase operating hours.

With regard to the effect of the business cycle, in the bivariate analyses positive effects of employment growth in the period 1998-2003 were found for Germany, Spain and the Netherlands. However, in the multivariate analysis, this effect is only significantly Germany. Hence in the other five countries no clear effects of the business cycle situation on the average number of weekly operating hours seems to exist.

The bivariate analysis showed that most countries that experienced considerable fluctuations in business activity in 2002 had significantly longer weekly operating hours in 2003. In the multivariate analysis, this is only the case in the Netherlands. Here longer operating hours to cope with fluctuations may be inefficient since building flexibility into a plant may imply the sacrifice of the lowest achievable unit costs. Moreover, contrary to the bivariate results, for Portugal the relationship is negative.

In the Netherlands, establishments covered by a collective labour agreement on working time or operating hours also tend to operate more hours per week. In this country, collective labour agreements facilitate and promote the extension of operating and opening hours by employers. Most Dutch firms and employees are covered by legally extended sectoral labour agreements that limit the power of the insiders, *i.e.* incumbent personnel within establishments. In the UK the opposite applies. Here establishments covered by collective agreements have lower weekly operating hours, possibly because of accompanying cost increases or conditions that hamper the extension of or reduce operating and opening hours. This constraint may be related to insider power of employees resulting from decentralised collective bargaining.

3.5 Conclusions

Our results indicate that in West European countries shift work and Sunday working are the most important working-time options used to extend weekly operating and opening hours, followed by staggered working times and Saturday working. Another economic and statistically significant determinant of weekly operating hours in West Europe is establishment size; operating hours are generally longer in larger establishments. Structural overtime hours also contribute significantly to the length of weekly operating hours in most countries, France and Portugal being the exception. Inter-country differences may partly relate to differences in employee preferences for working overtime or the reliance of overtime pay to boost basic wages. Contrary to earlier research we found that overtime premia are positively related to weekly operating hours.

The contribution of part-time employment to operating hours shows a mixed picture: in Spain and Portugal it is linear and negative, while in Germany, France and the UK it is non-linear and positive. In the Netherlands it is insignificant. Employee preferences most likely play a role here too. Concerning the use of temporary workers, the bivariate results differ from the multivariate results. Bivariate results show positive and nonlinear effect on weekly operating hours. Multivariate results show insignificant or negative effects, the Netherlands being the exception. Hence, agency workers, fixed-term employees and employees with on-call (hours not agreed) contracts seem to be mainly used for coping with unpredicted short-term fluctuations or to replace absent workers, and not for extending operating hours permanently. Our results also show that, unlike the assumption posited by economic literature, longer weekly contractual working hours are not a condition *sine qua non* for extending weekly operating hours.

Other establishment characteristics help determine weekly operating hours. Operating hours in the service sector vary between branches: producer services and distributive services have lower than average operating hours, while social services and personal services have higher than average operating hours. In no country do operating hours in the primary and secondary sectors differ significantly from the national average. The effect of the proportion of skilled workers (managerial, professional and higher technical staff) on operating hours was for two of the four countries for which this information is available (UK and Netherlands) negative and for Germany nonlinearly positive. Hence the expected mixed relationship between weekly operating hours and the proportion of skilled workers was confirmed in our data. The multivariate results concerning the impact of capital intensity on weekly operating hours confirm the trade-off between lower capital costs and higher labour costs of more intensive utilisation of capital. Only for Spain, France and Portugal, was a positive effect on operating hours found.

The impact of the age of the establishments on weekly operating hours shows a mixed picture; in some countries (Germany, Netherlands) operating hours are significantly longer in younger establishments, while in other countries (UK and Portugal) they are significant shorter in younger establishments. In most countries the proportion of female employees and being part of a multinational does not have an impact on weekly operating hours. The latter suggests that the "local environment" is a more important determinant of weekly operating hours than foreign ownership.

The economic and institutional context also explains part of the weekly operating hours. Bivariate results differ from multivariate results here. In the multivariate analyses, the positive impact of the business cycle on weekly operating hours was found in fewer countries. In most countries, international competitive pressure does not force establishments to increase operating hours. The impact of fluctuations in business activity on weekly operating hours is ambiguous. Bivariate analysis shows that in most EU countries, except Germany and the UK, establishment covered by collective labour agreements have longer operating hours. The multivariate analysis reveals a different picture: only in the Netherlands is the relationship is positive, while in the UK it is negative.

Concerning the central question of this chapter, our research results indicate that weekly operating hours in Europe are largely determined by working time strategies. Internal characteristics of the establishment play a lesser role, and the economic and institutional context in which the establishment operates is least important.

References

Anxo, D., G. Bosch, D. Bosworth, G. Cette, T. Sterner and D. Taddei (1995) *Work patterns and capital utilisation – an international comparative study*, Dordrecht: Kluwer Academic Publishers.

Bauer, F., H. Groß, E. Munz and S. Sayin (2002) *Arbeits- und Betriebszeiten 2001. Neue Formen des betrieblichen Arbeits- und Betriebszeitmanagements. Ergebnisse einer repräsentativen Betriebsbefragung*, Berichte des ISO 67, Köln: Institut zur Erforschung sozialer Chancen.

Bauer, F., H. Groß, S. Lehndorff, S. Schief and G. Sieglen (2007) Operating hours, working times and employment in Germany, in: L. Delsen, D. Bosworth, H. Groß, R. Muñoz de Bustillo y Llorente (eds.) *Operating Hours and Working Times. A Survey of Capacity Utilisation and Employment in the European Union,* Heidelberg: Physica-Verlag, 95-120.

Bauer, F., H. Groß, R. Muñoz de Bustillo y Llorente, E. Fernández Macias and G. Sieglen (2007) Cross-country Comparison of Operating Hours, Capacity Utilisation, Working Times and Employment, in: L. Delsen, D. Bosworth, H. Groß, R. Munoz de Bustillo y Llorente (eds.) *Operating Hours and Working Times. A Survey of Capacity Utilisation and Employment in the European Union,* Heidelberg: Physica-Verlag, 41-72.

Bautista, R. M., H. Hughes, D. Lim, D. Morawetz and F. Thoumi (1981) *Capital Utilization in Manufacturing: Colombia, Israel, Malaysia and the Philippines,* New York: Oxford University Press.

Baxter, M. and D. D. Farr (2001) The Effects of Variable Capital Utilization on the Measurement and Properties of Sectoral Productivity: Some International Evidence, *NBER Working Papers 8475*, Cambridge: National Bureau of Economic Research.

Betancourt, R. R. and C. K. Clague (1981) *Capital Utilization: A Theoretical and Empirical Analysis*, Cambridge: Cambridge University Press.

Böckerman, P. (2002) Overtime in Finland, *Finnish Economic Papers*, 15 (1): 36-54.

Buddelmeyer, H., G. Mourre and M. Ward (2008) Why do Europeans work part-time? A cross-country panel analysis, *ECB Working Papers Series 872*, Frankfurt am Main: European Central Bank.

Burns, R. N. and M. W. Carter (1985) Work force size and single shift schedules with variable demands, *Management Science*, 31, May: 599-607.

Castro, A. and J. Varejão (2007) Operating hours, working times and employment in Portugal, in: L. Delsen, D. Bosworth, H. Groß and R. Muñoz de Bustillo y Llorente (eds.), *Operating Hours and Working Times. A survey of Capacity Utilisation and Employment in the European Union,* Heidelberg: Physica-Verlag, 147-167.

Cette, G. (1989) Recours au travail posté et caractéristiques des entreprises, *Economie et Prévision*, 87: 43-48.

Contensou, F. and R. Vranceanu (2000) *Working time. Theory and policy implications,* Cheltenham: Edward Elgar.

Delsen, L. (1995) *Atypical Employment: An International Perspective. Causes, Consequences and Policy*, Groningen: Wolters Noordhoff.

Delsen, L., D. Bosworth, H. Groß and R. Muñoz de Bustillo y Llorente (eds.) (2007) *Operating Hours and Working Times. A Survey of Capacity Utilisation and Employment in the European Union,* Heidelberg: Physica-Verlag.

Delsen. L. and J. Smits (2007) Operating hours, working times and employment in the Netherlands, in: L. Delsen, D. Bosworth, H. Groß and R. Muñoz de Bustillo y Llorente (eds.), *Operating Hours and Working Times. A survey of Capacity Utilisation and Employment in the European Union,* Heidelberg: Physica-Verlag, 121-146.

Dupaigne, M. (2000) *Capital utilization and the willingness to rest: A general equilibrium analysis*, Econometric Society World Congress 2000 Contributed Papers 0391, Econometric Society, August 11-16, Seattle.

Dupaigne, M. (2001) Capital utilization and work schedules: the welfare costs of shiftworking, *Economics Letters*, 73: 195-200.

Eriksson, T. and S. Fellman (1995) Determinants of firms' operating times – Some evidence from firm level data, *Discussion Paper 542*, Helsinki: ETLA, the Research Institute of the Finnish Economy.

EC (1995) Performance of the European Union labour market. Results of an ad hoc labour market survey covering employers and employees. *European Economy*, Reports and Studies No. 3, Brussels/Luxembourg: European Commission, Directorate-General for Economic and Financial Affairs.

Garibaldi, P. and P. Mauro (2002) Anatomy of employment growth, *Economic policy*, 17 (34): 67-114.

Giarini, O. and W. M. Stahel (1993) *The Limits to certainty. Facing risks in the new service economy*, Dordrecht: Kluwer Academic Publishers.

Golden, L. and D. M. Figart (eds.) (2000) *Working time. International trends, theory and policy perspectives*, London: Routledge.

Jirjahn, U. (2008) On the determinants of shift work and overtime work: evidence from German establishment data, *British Journal of Industrial Relations*, 46 (3): 133-168.

Kostiuk, P. (1990) Compensating differentials for shift work, *Journal of Political Economy*, 98 (5): 1054-1075.

Kümmerling, A. and S. Lehndorff (2007) *Extended and unusual working hours in European companies*, Dublin: European Foundation for Improvement of the Living and Working Conditions.

Mitlacher, L. W. (2007) The role of temporary agency work in different industrial Relations Systems – A comparison between Germany and the USA, *British Journal of Industrial Relations*, 45 (3): 581-606.

Muñoz de Bustillo y Llorente, R. and E. Fernández Macias (2007) Operating hours, working times and employment in Spain, in: L. Delsen, D. Bosworth, H. Groß and R. Muñoz de Bustillo y Llorente (eds.) (2007) *Operating Hours and Working Times. A Survey of Capacity Utilisation and Employment in the European Union,* Heidelberg: Physica-Verlag, 169-195.

Parent-Thirion, A., E. Fernández Macías, J. Hurley and G. Vermeylen (2007) *Fourth European Working Conditions Survey*, Dublin: European Foundation for the Improvement of Living and Working Conditions.

Smith, M., D. Bosworth and M. Carroll, (2007) Operating hours, working times and employment in the UK, in: L. Delsen, D. Bosworth, H. Groß and R. Muñoz de Bustillo y Llorente (eds.) (2007) *Operating Hours and Working Times. A Survey of Capacity Utilisation and Employment in the European Union,* Heidelberg: Physica-Verlag, 197-223.

Winston G. C. (1974) The theory of capital utilization and idleness, *Journal of Economic Literature*, 12 (4): 1301-1320.

4 Exploring Terra Incognita – Operating Hours in the Service Sector

Frank Bauer and Hermann Groß

4.1 Introduction

The (developed) European economies are characterised by an increasing tertiarisation and, today, a clear majority of jobs and establishments are allocated in the service sector. In 2005, the overall sectoral employment structure of the EU-25 shows that 4.9% of total employment took place in agriculture, 27.5% in industry and 67.7% in services (EC, 2006: 57). Moreover, the development of the service sector is often presented as one of the most promising solutions for the employment crisis of the members of the European Union; Member States with a high share of service jobs also tend to do well with regard to employment. Empirical evidence shows indeed that between 2000 and 2005 the service sector was mainly responsible for the rise of employment:

> "Since 2000 total employment in the EU has increased by over 8.5 million, mainly driven by strong net employment creation of almost 11.5 million in the service sector. The latter has more than made up for the employment contraction in industry (down 1.6 million) and agriculture (down 1.2 million) since 2000." (EC, 2006: 62)

A more detailed analysis for Germany shows that all but one of the producing sectors lost employment over the same period, while amongst the service industries, on the other hand, there were a lot of employment winners in the same period, for example producer services and transport (Amend and Bauer, 2005; 2006; Bauer and Otto, 2006). But it is not only this development which makes the service sector of interest; recently in a lot of European countries there have been legal interventions, which

L. Delsen et al., *Comparative Analyses of Operating Hours and Working Times in the European Union*,
DOI: 10.1007/978-3-7908-2185-7_4,

strongly influence operating hours in the service sector. Shop opening hours have been extended in the Netherlands, Spain, Portugal and Germany. In France collective working time reduction has not only influenced operating hours in manufacturing. Additionally, the perennial political discussion about inevitable cost reduction in the public services suggests another special feature of the service industries: a lot of social services are publicly financed and operating time management is set by societal necessity and political discretion rather than by the market.

Against this background, it is astonishing that operating hours in the service sector have not been analysed in depth up to now.[1] Research on the topic has focussed on the producing industries, both conceptually and empirically (see Delsen *et al.*, Chapter 1, this volume). At the international level there are no data available on operating hours in the service sector at all. This means that we are entering more or less unknown territory here and that is why we first sketch central differences between operating hours' management in producing and service industries, hinting at some of their consequences for the measurement and the assessment of operating hours. We do so in Section 4.2 by exploring some of the most prominent definitions of the service sector and by contrasting two stylised models of production and service work.[2] In Section 4.3 we show that the calculation of operating hours still has a "production bias", because it is historically founded on the need to calculate the capital operating time of expensive machinery in the secondary sector. The empirical Section 4.4 contains firstly descriptive statistics and secondly multivariate analyses on the most important determinants for the duration of operating hours. In Section 4.5 conclusions are drawn.

The main aim of the chapter is to show some specifics of the service sector in duration and constitution of operating hours and to explain these differences considering information on establishment size classes, sub sectors of the service industries, country variables, *etc.*

---

1 The exceptions are Delsen et al., 2007; Groß, Stille and Thoben, 1991; Bauer et al., 1999a; 1999b; Bauer et al., 2001, that covered the service sector.

2 We have already highlighted the difference in Delsen et al. (2007: 6-17) referring to some characteristic examples from an economic point of view. Here we will try to examine the difference more systematically from a sociological perspective.

4.2 A heuristic definition of the service sector

There is no generally accepted definition of the service sector or the special character of service work. This makes it difficult to systematically explore the special challenges of operating hours' management in this sector. Haukness (1999) claims that in the face of the heterogeneity of the sector, and its rapid change owing to developments in information and communication technology, a strict definition is neither possible nor desirable. Giarini and Stahel (1993: 45) even declare "the end of the theory of the three sectors of economy". We think it is still helpful to discuss essential differences between different types of work highlighting ideal-typical problems, especially when we are discussing the measurement of operating hours.

The classical definitions, which identify one or more positive features of the quality of services and generalise them, can be contested. Fourastié's (1954) fundamental theory of tertiarisation identifies two driving forces: "prices based on productivity and demand based on hierarchical needs" (Schmid, 2001: 183). This theory is still influential, even though only with respect to one feature at one time; services as "laggards of productivity" (Haukness, 1999: 6), since resistant to methods of rationalisation since wages in the service sector are linked to those in the more productive secondary sector, is at the heart of Baumol's cost disease (Baumol, 1967). Esping-Andersen (1999) follows Baumol when he discusses the problem of the job potential in the service sector as a "service trilemma". However, Bosch (2000) does not and argues that these authors are debating over different types of service work: while resistance to rationalisation is conceded for some personal or social services it is rejected for some business and distributive services owing to the ground-breaking progress in IC-technologies, overcoming the *uno actu* principle to a large extent.

Similarly Fourastié's considerations on the development of needs and their impact on the employment potential are controversial. Criticism focuses on the time budget problem: one needs time to consume especially personal services, but a look at modern time budget studies shows that this time is not always available. Schmid mentions two further strands of criticism besides the Baumol argument:

> "First, services can also, to some extent, be transformed through innovation into (secondary) manufactured goods plus self-servicing if one thinks of typewriters (now PCs), cars or washing machines (Gershuny, 1983). Second, since self-servicing and consumption of services require time, and since individual time budgets are chronically restricted, expectations of job miracles in services should be rejected (Scharpf, 1998)." (Schmid, 2001:183 *ff.*)

Bell's (1975) sociological emphasis on the pre-eminence of the professional and technical class as a result of tertarisation is clearly an overgeneralisation, because it cannot explain the proportion of bad- or "Mc-jobs" mushrooming in the service industry.[3] The debate on low-wage services as a motor for employment shows this plainly. Gartner and Riessman (1977; 1978) overemphasise the interactive character of services and draw far reaching conclusions of the inherent "charity" of this face-to-face character of services. This might prove to be correct for some personal or social services, but fails to be an acceptable definition for business or distributive services.

The "mainstream-definitions" of service work attempt to start from a definition of the service output. This is very clearly formulated by Singelmann:

> "The central feature of services that distinguishes them from other industries is the absence of a tangible product. This characteristic has several important ramifications for work and its organisation. Associated with the nonmaterial product of services it is difficult to stockpile them. As a result, the production of services is closely linked to their consumption: in many cases, production and consumption of services occur at the same time. This situation creates special problems for the scheduling of production hours and for the organisation of work, even in those cases where the demand can somewhat be channelled through office hours and appointments." (Singelmann, 1978: 126)

One of the consequences of these features is the *uno actu* principle: user and producer of services have to be present at the same time and the same place. In a critical adaptation of this element, Haukness stresses two features, which can be seen as a short conclusion of the "positive" features of service work: "the ephemerality, *i.e.*, the fleeting existence, of service products, and the intense user/producer interaction, with a strong element of customisation" (Haukness, 1999: 5).

To complement this quality of the outcome starting point for the definition of services, we propose to tie in a macro sociological functional definition. Here we start from a sociological assumption that total societal production is conceived as consisting of two partial functions: firstly, "the social achievement of the physical conditions of survival through respective extractive and transformative work" (Offe, 1984: 232); and secondly, the "activities aiming at preserving and transforming the forms of the first

3 This is just one criticism beside those points which refer to the technocratic approach Bell has.

partial function" (*ibid.*). The relationship of the two functions can be described as the framework of institutional and cultural forms in which the process of material production of social systems takes place. This is determined by forms, which are variable but claim validity at any one time. The second partial function in the general societal process of reproduction safeguards and maintains the respective identity of a society, characterised by the abovementioned framework of institutional and cultural norms. Differences in this respect are, for example, incorporated in the different welfare regimes (see Esping-Andersen, 1993; 1999; 2000). They do not only influence the extent to which opening and operating hours are determined by economic or social reasons but also the number of enterprises belonging to the public sector or non-profit-organisations (see Delsen *et al.*, 2007: 7 and 13).

The service sector[4] embraces the totality of these functions within the process of social reproduction which are directed towards the reproduction of formal structures – the formal social manners and dealings and the cultural framework of material social reproduction. It is necessary to avoid an overly narrow understanding of the concept of social reproduction:

> "... it encloses the maintenance of the physical conditions of social life as well as the preserving of cultural and legal norm systems, the conveyance and development of the social knowledge. It also embraces the social systems of information, communication and traffic." (Offe, 1984b: 233)

Furthermore, "reproduction" should not be conceived as a static concept, but contains proactive processes of innovative adaptation of the cultural, normative, administrative and political framework of rules, routines and expectations, which are safeguarded by service activities. Services are often activities to guarantee social normality. This guarantee means the protection and maintenance of the differentiated elements of the social structure and the mediation between them.

A lot of service activities deal with the absorption of risks, cope with crises and emergencies, and monitor and control. These activities include peculiar problems for the estimation of operating hours: what is the status

4 It is very important to note the conceptualisation of the service sector in this section is not to be understood as a mere classification of NACE departments. It is a theoretical definition referring to a concept of service sector and service work independent whether it is taking place in a public-sector hospital or in a logistics department of a steel producing enterprise. Thus it of course also covers the problems of the internal tertiarisation of the producing industries.

of stand-by services in hospitals, emergency services for the police, the firefighters and medics, or an alert-situation in the army? These employees are on duty, but they are not working; they may even be sleeping or playing tennis until an emergency ensues. Similar problems can be seen in all social or personal services, which include the task of maintaining security: employees have to be there to avoid something happening. Furthermore, in distributive and producer services similar problems occur.

Ultimately service work has to deal with zones of uncertainty. One can distinguish between "input- and output-uncertainty" (Berger and Offe, 1984: 275). Input uncertainties appear whenever the type and amount of work necessary to achieve a certain result is not totally determined and known. Thus any sort of work dealing with persons who do not belong to the organisation and who have to cooperate and interact with the worker is characterised by input uncertainties. The success of the working process depends to a good deal on a successful interaction with the client, customer or patient. This can make it difficult to define or even technically determine what exactly has to be done at each step of the process as is the case in a standardised production process. Input uncertainty is a feature of all services with a strong need for understanding and interpreting case specificity. However, this is only one type of input uncertainty, they generally appear when there are no unequivocal, tried and tested technical rules that establish the type and quantity of actions necessary to achieve the desired aim. Input uncertainties thus apply to processes of education, care, consultation, but also to all working processes which contain moments of interaction, innovation and cooperation.

On the other hand, output uncertainties[5] derive from uncertainties relating to the ends and functions of working, appearing if it can not unequivocally be determined what amount of labour is required to be able to react to future incidents which would have critical consequences if not enough personnel were available. The classical case for output uncertainties are police, firefighters, and emergency personnel in hospitals or the army. To guarantee public order, public health or public security, personnel have to be on stand-by even if nothing actually happens. The same is true for technical personnel to guarantee the functioning of technical plants. Output

5 A typical reaction to these uncertainties is to estimate the labour demand on the basis of experience. Managers often do know about peaks in demand (*e.g.* Friday night in accident and emergency, lunch times in banks, *etc.*). Another typical reaction is to try to influence demand, for example, by the organisation of happy hours, *etc.*

uncertainty is found especially when there is a changeable customer demand, therefore they are very obvious in retail trade, when it is uncertain when customers appear and in what quantity and with what demands. Obviously input and output uncertainties can also occur in combination.

In contrast to this theoretical model of service work the stylised production model can be understood as the result of a process of resolving the production process from input and output uncertainties. This process reached its historical peak in the Fordistic-Tayloristic production paradigm: mass production of homogenous standardised products with extensive stock holding freed organisations from volatile customer wishes and peaks and troughs in demand. Work was organised rationally, with expected results determined, and minimal variations in operating capital and working time. The organisation of work permitted the monitoring of working-activities and reduced the autonomy of individual employees. The working process had to be standardised and uniform and thus became mechanised and faster.

It is obvious that this stylised contrast is a black-and-white-portrayal, but it has become clear, that "uncertainty" is a central category of differentiation as well as the degree to which industries are determined by economic and/or social grounds. The internal difference within the service sector between social and personal services on the one hand, where just because of input- and output-uncertainties rationalisation is difficult and, on the other hand, producer and distributive services, where it is regularly observed, is another feature of the theoretic debate, which is relevant for the empiric part. The topic "uncertainty" is strongly discussed in the debate on the actual production model. Here we find a wide range of contributions which state paradigmatic changes, marking the "end of mass production", a post-Tayloristic, a post-Fordist production and regulation model and the end of the theory of three economic sectors (see Piore and Sable, 1984; Kern and Schumann,1984; Giarini and Stahel, 1993), because the service and production process have become alike. By contrast, empirical evidence shows (Bosch, 2000; Nordhause-Janz and Pekruhl, 2000) that there is a persistent stock of Tayloristically-organised jobs and an increase in services becoming standardised and mechanised.

As a heuristic perspective we prefer starting with the contrast between two ideal types, instead of a picture of blurring perspectives. In producing industries, slack times and unproductive leeway can be regarded as an inefficiency to be eliminated but this may be harder in the service sector. Here it may be part of the reality, which cannot be eliminated; operating hours' management and working time organisation have to address that problem. Organising alternative jobs, for example in stock management, for employees in retail or wholesale trade while there are no customers is one strategy; gaining influence over customer flows or adjusting labour to them are others, for example by organising "happy hours", *etc*. Nevertheless as much as operating hours and working time management attempts to deal with variation, it will not be able to eliminate the problem as effectively as in the classical productive industries.

Finally, there is a further tension to be dealt with. Managing operating hours in the service sector in a comprehensive way requires the inclusion of the public services. However, here the "guaranteeing" feature of the service sector is more strongly accentuated than in private services. If a state has to guarantee public order, security, or health the difference between effectiveness and efficiency has to be taken into account. According to Kaufmann (1977) the concept of effectiveness sees an organisation's performance from the point of view of its capacity to achieve its ascribed aims. On the other hand, efficiency can rely on the alternative use of means to meet given aims. In contrast to private enterprises, public work does not only have to be organised efficiently; it also has to be organised effectively. The latter aspect applies very obviously to public services like hospitals, traffic or the police and the army. Such services have to guarantee a population's health, security or justice services. "That is why a proportion of these establishments in all countries will be determined wholly on social grounds" (Delsen *et al.*, 2007:14). Although, it is also important that those services are efficiently organised, as the public sector faces cost pressures, the main strategic point of reference remains effectiveness: the supply of services may have to be guaranteed, even if its utility cannot be calculated in terms of profit. The extent to which supply is necessary is not only a question of economic revenues, but predominantly of political decision making. The topic is of big importance for the empirical part of this chapter, where we distinguish between social services – with a high amount of public enterprises in all countries under study – and other services.

4.3 Theoretical discussions on the measurement of operating hours in the service sector

The measurement of operating hours has historically been motivated by interest in measuring the time that expensive machinery is busy. Within the concept of the indirect measurement of operating hours, based on both the "employee concept" and the "workstation concept"[6], the assumption of a continuous production process of each worker in the shift system is hidden. Shift systems make variable use of available workstations: a one-shift system of eight hours occupies each workstation just once while in a two-shift system of two eight-hour shifts each work station is occupied twice, and so one. An establishment can only simultaneously deploy as many employees as there are workstations available, in a continuous production process a maximum is reached.

When we use the "employee concept" of weighting operating hours (as a proxy for capital usage), we are making the abovementioned assumptions on the design of workstations and their occupation by the workforce. Such a concept is highly plausible for a continuous production process in the secondary sector, but it does not necessarily fit services, as implied above. The basic assumption of a continuous production (of services) process is not met, because of the *uno actu* principle and the fundamental uncertainty zones in services. Another condition not met by services in the traditional approach to operating hours' measurement is the existence of physical workstations. In a shop there are no workstations, just the necessity to balance out customer flows and available personnel, the same is true for an emergency service. Of course, it is always possible that the medical personnel, buildings and costly equipment remain idle, in the absence of an emergency, but it can also be the case that too many emergencies occur and only the most serious are dealt with, while less urgent cases have to wait. There is an uncertainty one can not eliminate in services and which can lead to unavoidable idleness of personnel, machinery and buildings.

Thus operating hours in the service sector can mean something quite different to operating hours in the production of goods. Whenever we analyse operating hours in the service sector, times will be included when equipment, buildings and personnel are idle. Maintaining a ready status is an important and integrative part of operating hours in parts of the service sector which is not the case in manufacturing industries. The density of operating hours is thus probably less in the service industries even when the same measured hours appear. However, since in detail it seems to be impossible to measure this "lower density" effect we argue here for the use of the "employee model" of measurement of operating hours in the service industry, but keep in mind the difference. Apart from systematic measurement problems we should expect relatively long operating hours in social

6 For the direct and indirect measurement and calculation of operating hours see Bauer, Groß and Sieglen (2007) and Delsen et al., Chapter 1, this volume.

services, since a huge share of them have to be delivered 24 hours a day, seven days a week, utilising shift systems to cover the necessary 168 hours operating hours. Additionally, we can expect that a lot of the establishments in social services are not private establishments but public sector bodies or non-profit organisations. Those should have longer operating hours than, for example, small private health services. Also in personal services long operating hours can be expected, but with a smaller share of shift work. Staggered working times may be found here, because personal services are not subject to a duty of care for 24 hours a day. Staggered working times can be implemented more flexibly and with less bureaucratic effort than shift work systems. Thus it is possible to decouple individual working times and collective operating hours to achieve highly flexible operating hours which are not as long as those utilising shift systems, but longer than the effective working time of full-time employees.

4.4 Empirical results

The empirical section starts with descriptive statistics on selected establishment characteristics in the service industries (4.4.1), on the duration of operating hours in the overall sample according to sub sectors and size classes and on the constitution of operating hours by the different forms of working time organisation (4.4.2). The global perspective is complemented by the most important national variations (4.4.3). The descriptive statistics are followed by a multivariate analysis, establishing the most important determinants of the duration of operating hours in the service sector (4.4.4).

4.4.1 Establishment characteristics

The variation coefficients (standard deviation/mean) of operating hours, which show the relative dispersion around the mean, (Table 4.1) show that the operating hours heterogeneity in the service sector is clearly larger than in producing industries. Within the service sector, operating hours in social services and personal services are less homogeneously distributed than in the other sectors.[7] In social services we find a lot of establishments with very short and very long operating hours, while the distribution within

7 We use the Singelmann-classification to differentiate between four sub sectors of the service sector (Singelmann, 1978).

distributive services is even more homogenous than in the producing sector as a whole. This is true for all countries under study.

Table 4.1 Relative variance of operating hours by country and economic sector

	Germany	Spain	France	Portugal	Netherlands	UK	Total
Primary sector	0.49	0.35	0.26	0.41	0.41	0.71	0.52
Secondary sector	0.51	0.34	0.49	0.45	0.42	0.62	0.49
Construction	0.40	0.13	0.17	0.09	0.19	0.70	0.42
All producing sectors	0.49	0.26	0.43	0.37	0.36	0.66	0.48
Distributive services	0.48	0.34	0.36	0.54	0.57	0.59	0.47
Producer services	0.49	0.32	0.28	0.31	0.39	0.72	0.51
Social services	0.64	0.69	0.79	0.64	0.70	0.64	0.67
Personal services	0.69	0.55	0.62	0.50	0.86	0.71	0.65
All service sectors	0.59	0.45	0.53	0.55	0.59	0.66	0.57
Total	0.56	0.41	0.51	0.52	0.55	0.66	0.55

As we have seen another central feature of the service sector is that part of it produces public goods. In most parts of Europe, these services are only partly organised by the market, alongside public institutions or in non-profit organisations, this is especially true for social services, here only 45% of the establishments are private enterprises. This becomes clearer when we look at the distribution of employees over the organisational forms in the three sectors of economy. Employees in producing industries and other services work, almost without exception, are in private enterprises in all countries under study – with the United Kingdom the main exception (see Table 4.2). Social services clearly differ from the other sectors with the vast majority of employees employed in public bodies or non profit organisations. The respective figures are: for Germany 72.5%, for France 86.7%, for the Netherlands 85.6% and for Portugal 50.4%. Even in Spain and the United Kingdom where the respective figures are much lower (37.2% respectively 26.9%) the share of employees working in public bodies or in non-profit organisations is larger in social services than in the producing industries and in other parts of the service sector.[8]

Another key characteristic of the service sector is the high share of female employees and part-timers. A quarter of all jobs in the service sector are part-time; this compares to only 12% of the jobs in the producing

8 Spain is a good example of the relevance of the employee-oriented view in this context. While in Spain only 3.5% of the establishments in social services belong to public bodies or non-profit organisations, 37.2% of the employees working in social services are employed in these establishments (Table 4.2).

industries. Furthermore, almost half (49%) of the employees in the service sector are female compared to only 26% in the producing sector. Social services have especially high shares of female employees (56%) and part-time jobs (29%), the respective figures for personal services are 52% and 31%.

Table 4.2 Distribution of establishments and employees over the three sectors of economy

	Producing industries		Social services		Other services		Total	
	Est.	**Empl.**	**Est.**	**Empl.**	**Est.**	**Empl.**	**Est.**	**Empl.**
Germany								
Enterprise	94.8	97.3	26.5	15.4	87.7	89.7	74.0	70.2
Public	0.5	0.8	42.2	72.5	2.8	5.3	12.2	23.7
Other	4.7	1.9	31.3	12.1	9.5	5.0	13.8	7.1
Spain								
Enterprise	99.3	97.7	96.5	62.8	99.5	96.6	99.2	92.6
Public	0.7	1.1	3.5	37.2	0.5	3.4	0.8	7.4
Other*	-	-	-	-	-	-	-	-
France								
Enterprise	99.2	98.2	20.0	9.3	88.9	90.9	82.0	74.6
Public	0.5	1.1	78.9	86.7	8.8	6.5	16.3	23.0
Other	0.4	0.7	1.1	4.0	2.3	2.6	1.7	2.4
UK								
Enterprise	60.1	72.3	56.8	65.3	50.3	62.7	54.1	65.9
Public	28.8	19.3	31.4	26.9	35.0	25.0	33.2	24.3
Other	11.0	8.4	11.8	7.8	14.8	12.3	12.7	9.8
Netherlands								
Enterprise	95.3	91.9	37.9	7.5	89.2	90.9	84.3	67.7
Public	1.2	5.9	49.3	85.6	5.6	7.0	10.0	28.8
Other	3.5	2.2	12.8	6.9	5.2	2.1	5.7	3.5
Portugal								
Enterprise	93.3	93.9	48.4	33.6	94.6	91.6	91.5	88.7
Public	2.0	3.2	37.6	50.4	2.5	4.5	4.3	6.7
Other	4.8	2.9	14.0	16.0	3.0	3.9	4.1	4.3

* Due to the special survey design in Spain there is no data available for the operating times in public administration, see Muñoz de Bustillo y Llorente and Fernández Macías (2007).

Finally we consider some figures on the qualification structure across sectors. The establishments in the EUCOWE survey were asked what percentage of their employees were administrative, technical or managerial, to provide an idea of the human capital deployed. While in the service sector the respective percentage is 19%, in the producing sector it is 14% (Table 4.3). The two sectors with the lowest share of highly skilled employees are construction for the producing industries and personal services for the service industries. Thus, we find a low-skill sector dominated by male full-timers in the producing sector and one characterised by female part-timers in services.

Table 4.3 Share of female employees, part-time jobs and administrative, technical or managerial employees (%)

Economic sector	Share of female employees	Share of part-time jobs	Share of admin, tech or management
Primary sector	28.2	20.4	15.7
Secondary sector	29.5	12.4	14.6
Construction	14.6	4.0	12.2
All producing sectors	26.0	12.2	14.1
Distributive services	41.6	22.0	17.5
Producer services	44.8	20.4	22.5
Social services	55.6	29.0	18.5
Personal services	51.6	30.8	13.5
All service sectors	48.5	25.1	18.6
Total	41.7	21.2	17.3

4.4.2 Duration and constitution of operating hours in the service sector - global perspective

A look at the overall mean operating hours across the countries for which we have data reveals that operating hours in the service sector (55.9 hours) are clearly below the level of the producing industries (59.3 hours). This is partly due to the huge difference in the number of large establishments, where the average operating hours amount to 76.4 hours in the producing sector, but to only 68.1 hours in services. In the smaller categories of firm size, the service sectors actually show slightly higher operating hours; in small enterprises 43.3 hours compared to 41.6 hours and in the medium enterprises 58.5 hours compared to 57.9 hours (Table 4.4).

The overall totals disguise even more dramatic differences within the service sector. The average operating hours in establishments in social services (61.6 hours) and in personal services (61.1 hours) are slightly above the values for the producing industries; especially in the larger establishments in social services (75.8 hours) and in personal services (68.3 hours). Distributive and producer services present a different pattern. In both sub sectors the operating hours are clearly below average (52.2 hours and 49.6 hours). In the smallest size classes they are comparable to the working times of a full-time employee; there is almost no decoupling of working times and operating hours in these sectors (For a comparison of decoupling indicators over all sectors and countries see Bauer *et al.*, 2007: 47 *ff.*). In producer services we find the lowest operating hours in the whole service sector, even in the larger size classes. We thus see a divide between producing industries and service sector, which is mainly caused by the divide within the service sector: social and personal services with relatively long operating hours and a marked large enterprises effect on the one hand and, on the other, distributive and producer services with short operating hours, including the big enterprises in producer services (Table 4.4).

Table 4.4 Indirectly measured operating hours in all countries under study (hours per week)

Economic sector	1-19 employees	20-249 employees	250+ employees	Total
Primary sector	45.9	57.7	103.1	58.7
Secondary sector	42.0	62.5	77.0	64.8
Construction	40.3	43.6	54.2	42.6
All producing sectors	41.6	57.9	76.4	59.3
Distributive services	41.1	56.9	65.1	52.2
Producer services	43.4	50.1	56.2	49.6
Social services	41.4	61.3	75.8	61.6
Personal services	52.4	72.0	68.3	61.1
All service sectors	43.3	58.5	68.1	55.9
Total	42.9	58.3	70.9	57.0

The divide within the service sector between social and personal services reflects the composition of operating hours by shift work, staggered working times and individual effective working times. The largest influence[9] of shift work within the service sector (47.7%) on the operating hours is found in social services, and here especially in the large enterprises, where it contributes to 61.4% of operating hours. There is no comparable sector among the service sub sectors; the figures are rather similar to large enterprises in production. Personal services are markedly different; operating times are not really shorter but the contribution of shift work (35.9%) is just below the service sector average (36.9%). On the other hand, it is interesting and typical for the service sector that in personal services the contribution of staggered working times (32%) is substantially higher than

9 The calculation of the constitution of operating hours is explained in Bauer *et al.* (2007: 21-39).

in social services (17.6%) (Table 4.5). Operating hours which are similar in duration are achieved by different means, either by an above average utilisation of shift work and a below average usage of staggered working times or the other way around.

Table 4.5 Working time elements contributing to operating hours (in percent)

a The contribution of shift work to operating hours ...

	1-19	20-249	250+	Total
Primary sector	16.8	30.1	87.0	40.3
Secondary sector	10.2	49.8	67.9	54.0
Construction	9.1	13.6	28.8	12.8
All producing sectors	10.4	42.7	67.0	46.6
Distributive services	9.7	32.7	41.3	27.6
Producer services	13.8	28.4	42.5	28.8
Social services	18.0	44.9	61.4	47.7
Personal services	24.6	43.3	53.6	35.9
All service sectors	15.3	38.1	52.7	36.9
Total	14.1	39.5	57.9	39.9

b The contribution of staggered working times to operating hours ...

	1-19	20-249	250+	Total
Primary sector	14.5	24.0	1.2	14.6
Secondary sector	17.4	12.5	9.3	11.5
Construction	4.5	7.7	19.8	7.2
All producing sectors	11.8	12.1	9.5	10.9
Distributive services	21.9	24.7	26.0	24.2
Producer services	21.7	17.0	11.5	16.5
Social services	27.0	17.7	14.0	17.6
Personal services	33.9	32.1	24.5	32.0
All service sectors	25.2	21.2	16.6	20.8
Total	21.9	18.3	14.0	17.7

c The contribution of effective working times to operating hours ...

	1-19	20-249	250+	Total
Primary sector	68.7	45.9	11.8	45.1
Secondary sector	72.4	37.7	22.8	34.5
Construction	86.4	78.7	51.4	80.0
All producing sectors	77.8	45.2	23.5	42.5
Distributive services	68.4	42.6	32.7	48.2
Producer services	64.5	54.6	46.0	54.7
Social services	55.0	37.4	24.6	34.7
Personal services	41.5	24.6	21.9	32.1
All service sectors	59.5	40.7	30.7	42.3
Total	64.0	42.2	28.1	42.4

The respective figures add to 100% on the respective cells are summed up.

Establishments in social services also utilise a larger volume of work than the establishments of the other services[10]: a finding that can be put down to the fact that establishments in social services use shift work to a greater extent than those of the other services. First, the overall share of employees working shifts is 20.3% in social services, while the respective share is only 13.0% in the other services. Secondly, the overall average duration of shift work amounts to 140 hours per week in social services, whereas the figure for other services is just 118 hours per week. Thirdly, 44.2% of all part-timers in social services are involved in shift work compared to only 25.2% for the other services (see Table 4.6).

Table 4.6 Operating hours+ and volume of work by country, hours per week (index of volume of work in parentheses*)

	France	Germany	Netherlands	Portugal	Spain	UK
All producing sectors	61.50	63.44	51.06	51.47	51.57	59.40
	(1.30)	(1.20)	(1.40)	(1.40)	(1.30)	(1.20)
All service sectors	57.23	55.16	51.52	50.06	51.58	58.57
	(0.90)	(0.90)	(0.90)	(0.80)	(0.90)	(0.90)
Total	58.47	58.10	51.18	54.77	51.58	58.77
Distributive services	51.53	55.70	47.40	56.64	49.98	52.46
	(1.00)	(0.70)	(0.60)	(0.80)	(0.80)	(1.00)
Producer services	43.49	47.89	45.01	44.88	44.26	61.92
	(1.00)	(0.80)	(0.90)	(1.10)	(1.30)	(0.90)
Social services	71.86	56.60	58.23	64.70	61.70	61.91
	(1.50)	(1.20)	(2.00)	(1.00)	(1.50	(1.00)
Personal services	64.72	63.21	60.29	73.47	58.57	53.30
	(0.50)	(0.60)	(0.80)	(0.50)	(0.50)	(0.60)

Note: + indirect measurement; * Overall average volume of work = 1.

4.4.3 Duration and constitution of operating hours in the service sector – the most important national variations

With the exception of the UK (see Table 4.6) operating hours in social and personal services are clearly longer than those in distributive and producer services in the countries under study. If one compares these operating hours to the averages of the producing industries, they are on the same level or even considerably above average (as in France, the Netherlands, Portugal and Spain). In the UK the operating hours in social services

10 The overall average of the volume of work by establishments corresponds to a value of 1. Therefore a value of 1.2, for example, in German social services establishments means that these establishments use a volume of work, which is 20% larger than the overall average.

(61.9) and especially in personal services (53.3) are relatively short and those in producer services with an average of 61.9 are extremely long, almost 13 hours longer than in Germany. The UK is the only country in the study where operating hours in personal services are clearly below the aggregate averages of producing and service industries and the other way around: where producer services have operating hours above the average, even of the producing industries.

In France and Spain operating hours are longer in social services than in personal services. This is very clear in France where the operating hours in the former amount to 71.9 hours and the latter to 64.7 hours. The figure for social services is far and away above the rest of the countries. Portugal represents the other extreme; here establishments in personal services operate for extremely long hours (for 73.5 hours). In Spain and the Netherlands the differences between social services and personal services are quite small. Both countries have rather short operating hours in both sectors and rank in the last two places on the duration of operating hours in the service sector (Table 4.6).

With regard to the constitution of operating hours the share of shift work in social services is about twice as large as in the other services in France, the Netherlands, Germany and Spain. In the Netherlands, the volume of work utilised by establishments in other services is 65% lower than the volume of work in social services (2.0 compared to 0.7). The respective figures for Spain and France are 46.7%, for Germany are 41.7%, for Portugal are 20% and for the United Kingdom are 10% (Table 4.6). In all countries under study, the establishments in social services employ nearly the same volume of work as those of the producing industries (Table 4.6).

It is interesting that social services differ from the other services more in the volume of work than in the duration of operating hours in Germany, Spain, France and the Netherlands. This finding points to the fact that the density of operating hours is less in other service areas than in social services. This suggests that against the background of nearly identical operating hours establishments in social services (and also establishments in producing industries) employ a larger volume of work than establishments in other parts of the service sector.

The general characteristic of the way Spanish establishments constitute operating hours, without the utilisation of staggered working times, is a feature which is also reflected in the Spanish service sector. While in the producing industries staggered working times do not play any role at all, in the service sector there is a small contribution of 3.6% to operating hours, based mainly in distributive services, where the contribution of staggered working times amounts to 7.4% (see Table 4.7). This has two interesting results. The first one is that in Spanish services the contribution of individual effective working times to the constitution of operating hours is bigger than in all the other countries studied, amounting to 50.4%. The second result is that the contribution of shift work is noticeably higher than in the other countries and amounts to 46%. This might be expected since to achieve operating hours of more than 50 hours a week (the Spanish average for the service industries) it is necessary to decouple operating hours and individual working times; and if staggered working time is not used, shift work has to compensate for this. Thus shift work and staggered working times can be seen as functional equivalents, which in the case of Spain shows a big shift work contribution combined with small one from staggered working time.

Something similar takes place in the UK, where the contribution of staggered working time is considerably bigger than in Spain (15.7%), but still a lot smaller than in the other countries studied. And again, shift work has a distinctive higher influence on the operating hours. Conversely, in Portugal the share of shift work is well below the mean of all the countries in the sample and even when shift work it utilised, it shows a weaker influence on the duration of the operating hours in return. France, Germany and the Netherlands show a different pattern. In these countries shifts contribute one third of operating hours, around a quarter by staggered working times and about two fifth by individual effective working times (Table 4.7).

Here we see one of the fundamental components of the comparison of the constitution of operating hours′ within the service sector. In Spain we find a clear divide: there are above-average contributions from shift work in social services (67.6%), personal services (64.4%), and in distributive services (35.1%) while in producer services the respective values are below average. In producer services about two thirds (68.8%) of operating hours are based on individual effective working times, so here shift work and staggered working times are the exception, operating hours are mainly the sum of contractual working hours plus overtime. Portugal is in sharp contrast to Spain, particularly in social services where operating hours are long: here the share of shift work is 40 points below the Spanish figure, and for staggered working times about the same amount above; one way or the other long operating hours can only be achieved by decoupling (Table 4.7).

If we have a look at the countries of the "continental-group" the similarities vanish as soon as the sub division of the service sector is taken into consideration. In distributive services in Germany there is a higher influence from shift work (30.1%) than in France (17.8%) and the Netherlands (19.1%). In producer services in the Netherlands there is a higher contribution of shift work, while this is true for France for social services, where 57% of the operating hours are achieved by shift work. In personal services in Germany shift work has quite a lot of influence on operating hours, but it is in the Netherlands that 55.4% of the operating hours are constituted by staggered working times. This shows that the heterogeneity of the service sector is even greater if we compare the operating hours and their constitution between countries. Not only do operating hours of the same sub sectors differ, as for example in social services where operating

Table 4.7 Constitutive elements of operating hours by country and sector (in percent; the three columns per cell sum up to 100% vertically)

	France	Germany	Netherlands	Portugal	Spain	UK
All producing sectors						
Shift	52.7	51.1	35.2	31.5	40.4	40.6
Staggered working times	6.7	13.3	7.1	8.9	0.4	19.4
Effective working times	41.6	35.6	57.7	59.6	59.6	39.9
All service sectors						
Shift	33.6	33.1	31.6	21.3	46.0	42.2
Staggered working times	23.6	27.9	25.7	33.8	3.6	15.7
Effective working time	42.8	38.9	42.7	44.9	50.4	42.1
Total						
Shift	39.4	40.1	32.4	25.6	44.0	41.8
Staggered working times	18.1	22.3	21.6	23.3	2.5	16.7
Effective working times	42.5	37.6	46.0	51.1	53.5	41.5
Distributive services						
Shift	17.8	30.1	19.1	21.3	35.1	33.8
Staggered working times	30.7	32.6	32.1	30.1	7.4	16.3
Effective working times	51.5	37.3	48.8	48.6	57.6	49.9
Producer services						
Shift	14.1	18.1	24.8	10.6	28.9	49.1
Staggered working times	15.7	29.2	18.6	19.7	2.0	11.8
Effective working times	70.2	52.8	56.6	69.7	68.8	39.3
Social services						
Shift	57.1	40.3	46.1	27.4	67.6	46.1
Staggered working times	15.6	22.9	19.7	42.5	0.4	15.9
Effective working times	27.3	36.8	34.2	30.1	32.0	38.0
Personal services						
Shift	29.6	34.8	25.6	64.4	64.4	24.6
Staggered working times	42.0	37.4	23.3	1.3	1.3	26.8
Effective working times	28.5	27.8	51.0	34.3	34.3	48.6
Distributive, producer and personal services						
Shift	19.0	26.9	21.5	20.3	39.5	39.0
Staggered working times	28.5	32.4	29.9	32.5	4.6	15.6
Effective working times	52.5	40.7	48.6	47.2	55.9	45.4

hours vary from 71.86 hours a week (France) to 56.6 hours (Germany), but also the way these hours are achieved. The example of Portugal and Spain shows that national features can be far stronger than structural similarities between sectors (Table 4.7).

4.4.4 Multivariate analyses

The descriptive statistics show that the average duration and the constitution of operating hours in the service sector are strongly correlated with the size of the establishment and different sub sectors within the service sector. Moreover, they show that also the country, where establishments are located has an influence on duration and constitution of operating hours. In the following, we present results of multivariate regression-models to see how far variances in (indirect) weekly operating hours of establishments can be explained by the sector the establishment belongs to, controlling for the size of the establishment, the country where it is located and other explanatory variables.

The estimations include a set of six country dummy variables, with the Netherlands chosen as reference category, since it shows the lowest operating hours on average; then a set of six industry dummies is integrated, with social services as reference category. To control for establishment size effects we use four banded size-class dummies (small establishments: 10-49 employees; medium establishments: 50-249 employees and large enterprises with 250 and more employees) with micro-establishments (1-9 employees) as the reference category. Furthermore we use dummy variables to estimate the effect of being a private establishment, a single establishment instead of an establishment being part of bigger enterprise, and of being at least partly under foreign control instead of being solely under national control. Additionally, we include a dummy that indicates whether the company is covered by a collective agreement on working time and/or operating hours. To account for different effects we the multivariate analysis separately for the four service sub sectors.

In a second step, we present multivariate analyses with the contribution of shift work, of staggered working times and of effective working times of full-time employees to operating hours[11] to explain variances by sector

11 As a result of problems of endogeneity the first group of regression models do not include explanatory variables for shift work, staggered working times and weekly working times. This is due to the fact that the dependent variable (indirect weekly operating hours) is calculated referring to the number of employees in the respective working time forms and their volume of work.

controlling for the identical explanatory variables as in the first group of models. The descriptive analyses have also shown that there are considerable differences in the average use of these constitutive elements between the countries under study. The analyses additionally serve the aim of showing how far country differences can be understood as a result of specific patterns of working times organisation.

Operating hours

As expected, the establishment size has the biggest positive influence on the duration of the operating hours, large establishments have significantly longer operating hours than micro establishments, but also medium establishments have clearly longer hours of operation (Table 4.8) Only belonging to personal services is associated with longer operating hours compared to social services, all other industry dummies show significant negative coefficients, especially construction and producer services. Compared to being located in the Netherlands there are significant positive effects of being located in any other country in the sample. The location factors are strongest in Germany followed by the UK and Spain. Less important, but still positive are the effects on the duration of operating hours exerted by being an establishment under foreign control and being covered by a collective agreement. Being a single, a private establishment both have small relative negative effects on the duration of the operating hours. This is a result of the fact that these establishments use shift work and also staggered working times to a smaller extent than others (see also Table 4.9).

Against the background of the descriptive results it is of interest to look at the effects in sub sectors of the service sector separately. Both size and country effects differ more strongly in social services and personal services than in distributive and producer services. The operating hours' extension effect of large establishments is almost twice as big as in producer and distributive services, it amounts to 41.5, respectively 39.3 hours a week in the former, whereas the estimations for the latter yield 14.0 and 22.8 hours of weekly operating hour. In social and personal services even the medium establishments exert a positive effect relative to micro establishments, which is bigger than the large establishment effect in production and distributive services. This very clearly confirms the descriptive findings concerning the heterogeneity of the service sector and shows how strongly this is associated with size and country effects. Looking at the significant effects of establishment location shows, that the most important country differences can be found in personal services, where for Portuguese establishments weekly operating hours are estimated to be more than 23 hours longer than in the Netherlands and also clearly longer than in all other countries. British establishments have exceptionally long operating hours in producer services, which are according to the estimation about 12.9 hours longer, because they are located there and not in the Netherlands. For social services strong positive location effects are estimated for Portugal (12.3 hours), Germany (14.3 hours) and France (11.6 hours). There is no service sub sector, which shows a significant negative location effect, relative to being located in the Netherlands.

Table 4.8 Regression results for indirectly measured weekly operating hours

	All	Distributive services	Producer services	Social services	Personal services
Private establishment yes=1)	-1.79*	0.68	2.89	3.07	9.12***
Foreign control (yes=1)	6.22***	0.96	3.20*	-1.28	5.51
Single-establishment organisation (yes=1)	-3.26***	-3.97***	-0.05	-5.57***	-8.19***
Collective agreement (yes=1)	3.44***	2.44***	2.34**	6.03***	2.83
Company size					
Micro	Ref.	Ref.	Ref.	Ref.	Ref.
Small	5.53***	4.27***	5.44***	10.71***	18.51***
Medium	12.47***	9.72***	8.31***	22.24***	26.94***
Large	26.32***	22.83***	14.01***	41.48***	39.31***
Country					
Netherlands	Ref.	Ref.	Ref.	Ref.	Ref.
Germany	10.14***	9.60***	5.32***	14.32***	16.82***
Spain	8.29***	5.79***	3.79**	2.98	10.83***
France	7.33***	5.56***	2.25	11.62***	12.56***
UK	8.99***	6.38***	12.94***	7.53***	-0.06
Portugal	7.54***	9.75***	3.63**	12.34***	23.25***
Sector					
Social services	Ref.	Ref.	Ref.	Ref.	Ref.
Primary	-7.43***				
Secondary	-3.54***				
Construction	-13.82***				
Distributive services	-7.87***				
Producer services	-13.74***				
Personal services	7.49***				
Constant	40.78***	35.12***	29.35***	30.07***	30.04***
Number of observations	15,191	3,209	2,245	1,920	1,222
F	178.43***	34.30***	15.10***	39.68***	24.23***
R^2	0.1736	0.1347	0.0628	0.1609	0.1787

*** Significant on the 1%-level; ** Significant on the 5%-level ; * Significant on the 10%-level.

The coverage by a collective agreement on working times and operating hours has positive effects on operating hours in all service sub sectors, but there are differences in the strength of the effect. It is strongest in social services and on the same level in all the other sub sectors. Being a private enterprise only shows a significant effect in personal services, where it is strongly positive in contrast to the estimation for the complete sample. This is probably due to the fact that public enterprises, which are generally covered by collective agreements, in social and distributive services utilise shift work far more than private establishments, since they have to deliver 24 hours services for emergencies, public transport, *etc.* The dummy on single establishments yields negative significant effects everywhere except for producer services where it is not significant. The strongest negative effect on the duration of operating hours is found in personal services.

Contribution of shift work to operating hours

As far as the contribution of shift work to the duration of operating hours is concerned, again we find strong associations with establishment size and the sub sectors of service industries (Table 4.9). The bigger the establishments' size class, the greater the contribution of shift work to the given operating hours. In the large establishments the contribution of shift work to the constitution of operating hours is estimated 32.58 percentage points higher than in micro establishments, for medium establishments the estimated effect still amounts to 13.84%. Only in personal services and the secondary sector is the contribution of shift work to the operating hours bigger than in social services; in producer services and construction these effects are significantly negative.

Looking at the location effects the first result is, that being not located in the Netherlands exerts a significant positive effect on the contribution of shift work to given operating hours, though there are strong differences: as already mentioned, the descriptive statistics suggested that being located in Spain is extraordinarily strongly associated with a high contribution of shift work to the given operating hours. The Spanish "location effect" is estimated to be twice as big as the German and the British, and three times bigger than the French, it yields to 15.91%. Still significant, the weakest association between location and the contribution of shift work to the duration of operating hours is found in Portugal. These results clearly point to the direction of nation-specific patterns in the utilisation of decoupling instruments, which necessarily have effects on the duration of operating hours. The country with the shortest operating hours, the Netherlands, also is the country with the smallest contribution of shift work to the constitution of operating hours.

Table 4.9 Regression results for the contribution of shift work, staggered working times and effective working times to the constitution of operating hours

	Shift	Staggered working time	Effective working time
Private establishment (yes=1)	-2.12***	-1.05	3.88***
Foreign control (yes=1)	9.59***	-2.30***	-7.32***
Single-establishment organisation (yes=1)	-0.77	-3.22***	3.81***
Collective agreement (yes=1)	4.13***	1.44***	-4.85***
Company size			
Micro	Ref.	Ref.	Ref.
Small	4.31***	2.18***	-5.23***
Medium	13.84***	1.59***	-14.49***
Large	32.58***	-1.47***	-30.93***
Country			
Netherlands	Ref.	Ref.	Ref.
Germany	7.93***	7.68***	-13.15***
Spain	15.91***	-9.54***	-0.74
France	5.04***	1.83**	-3.16***
UK	7.18***	0.07	-3.10**
Portugal	2.20***	0.39	2.35**
Sector			
Social services	Ref.	Ref.	Ref.
Primary	-5.01***	-5.73***	10.38***
Secondary	2.50***	-6.19***	3.86***
Construction	-17.86***	-7.60***	25.70***
Distributive services	-8.76***	1.78***	6.87***
Producer services	-14.42***	-3.02***	17.74***
Personal services	7.77***	4.92***	-12.79***
Constant	2.05	16.12***	74.84***
Number of observations	15,315	15,315	15,330
F	251.79***	104.37***	261.63***
R^2	0.2157	0.0999	0.1865

*** Significant at the 1%-level; ** Significant at the 5%-level; * Significant at the 10%-level.

Contribution of staggered working times to operating hours

Regarding the contribution of staggered working time to operating hours the regression model shows in concordance with the descriptive findings, that all the significant effects of the explanatory variables are clearly smaller than those concerning shift work (Table 4.9). With our explanatory variables, variances in the contribution of staggered working times to operating hours are explained less than in the contribution of shift work. Relative to the reference category of micro establishments we see a negative impact of large establishments (-1.47), but significant positive effects of small (2.18) and medium (1.59) units, so this type of operating hours extension is rather a small and medium establishment phenomenon.

Except for distributive and personal services all sectors of the economy are negatively associated with the contribution of staggered working times to the operating hours compared to social services. Thus the regression shows very clearly, that staggered working times as a means of decoupling working times and operating hours has separate service sector-specific importance; and within the service sector especially in personal, distributive and social services.

As the descriptive results indicate being located in Spain exerts a very strong negative effect on the contribution of staggered working time in contrast to being located in the Netherlands, relative to the reference of Germany. So again, there are significant nation-specific effects on the utilisation of decoupling instruments.

Contribution of effective working times to operating hours

A glance at the results for the estimations concerning the contribution of "regular working times" towards operating hours shows, that the smaller the establishment size class is, the bigger the contribution of this element in the constitution of operating hours (Table 4.9). Only in personal services is there a significant negative effect (relative to social services) in this respect; all the other sectors of the economy, especially construction, the primary sector, producer and distributive services show strong positive effects. The results of these estimations can be read like a sum of the two sections above, because shift work, staggered working times and effective working times are the three elements which constitute the total of the operating hours. The sector effects of personal and social services reflect that here, both, shift work and staggered working times are utilised to a greater extent.

Looking at the location effects demonstrates, that only being located in Portugal has a positive influence on the contribution of "regular working times" to operating hours relative to the Netherlands.

Furthermore the models show that private and single-enterprise establishments have significant negative associations with the contribution of shift and staggered working times, but a positive impact on regular working times. This necessarily results in shorter operating hours.

4.5 Conclusions

This chapter presented results on the duration and the constitution of operating hours in the service sector in a comparative way for the first time ever. Until the EUCOWE project European surveys on operating hours have been limited to establishments in the producing industries and excluded micro- and small units. Because we were exploring unknown territory here, it was necessary to theoretically reflect on special features and definitional problems work and work organisation in the service sector, first. An outstanding feature of the service sector is its heterogeneity. It contains establishments with extremely long and extremely short operating hours, there are sectors which are subject to processes of rationalisation and standardisation comparable to the traditional producing industries as well as sectors, where rationalisation is very restricted, since slack times are systematically included, just because the service has to be provided to potential customers, clients or patients, who actually are not present, but could be present soon. This mixture of principle provision and actual performance of a service affects work organisation and operating hours' management in the whole services sector, but is especially crucial in personal and social services. The provision of services has to cope with distinctive zones of uncertainty, coping with emergencies and crises, with controlling and monitoring requirements. All this makes it distinctively difficult to standardise and rationalise work in the service sector, which has ramifications for the make up of operating hours. Another characteristic of the services sector is that it contains establishments which are determined partly or wholly on social grounds. This holds especially true for establishments in social services.

Turning to the empirical results one has to conclude, that there are, indeed, several indicators for sector-specific operating hours and operating hours' management. Firstly the sector-specific heterogeneity in the duration of operating hours is far greater in social and personal services than in the rest of the service industry. Furthermore there are clear differences concerning the qualification of employees, the share of part-time employees and the share of enterprises, which belong to public body and non-government organisations within sub sectors of economy.

Multivariate analyses have shown that size effects exert the strongest influence on the duration of operating hours within the service industries (see also Smith, Zagelmeyer and Sieglen, Chapter 5, this volume). The sector itself also has distinctive separate effects on the operating hours. It is strongest in personal and social services, while operating in producer services leads to significantly shorter operating hours. Controlling for establishment-specific variables, nation-specific variations in operating hours are found to matter too: for establishments in Germany estimated operating hours are the longest among the surveyed countries and shortest in the Netherlands. In a comparative perspective which concentrates on separate sub-sector structures most of the findings of the aggregate view were even clearer. The size effect on operating hours duration is far stronger in social and personal services than in producer and distributive services, here even medium sized establishment exert a stronger impact on the duration in the former than large establishment in the latter. Furthermore there are sub-sector specific country effects. Being located in Portugal has a strong positive effect on operating hours in personal services, the UK location is strongly associated with long operating hours in producer services. Looking at social services being located in Germany and France exerts a positive impact on operation hours.

Naturally these differences reflect the working time organisation used to achieve the respective duration of operating hours. Staggered working times are a service-sector specific means to accomplish operating hours′ prolongation. Excluding producer services all service sub sectors have a positive impact on the share to which staggered working times contribute to operating hours. Staggered working times, as a modern form to decouple working times and operating hours, are thus a service phenomenon. This does not mean, in reverse, that shift work is less associated with the service sector. Personal and social services have a particularly strong shift effect, too. Furthermore the contribution of staggered working times to the constitution of operating hours is bigger in small and medium sized establishment than in micro and large establishments.

In the EUCOWE survey we do not have information about institutional rigidities and cultural differences at our disposal, so an analysis of country-specific effects on operating hours is not possible. However, we see very clearly that there are strong associations between the use of shift work and staggered working times and the respective countries. In the Netherlands – the country with the shortest operating hours on average – establishments also use shift work and staggered working times to a smaller extent than in other countries in the sample, while the countries with the longer operating hours show strong positive effects in this respect. Here one finds interesting country-specific differences. First and foremost the strongest positive location effect on the share of shift work on operating hours, as well as the most negative location effect on the share of staggered working times can be found in Spain. In contrast, for Portugal and the Netherlands, the lowest location effect for shift work and the highest location effect for staggered working can be observed. Portuguese personal services have comparatively long operating hours and the contribution of staggered working is high. We presume most of the country effects concerning the operating hours' duration are put down to country specific use of flexible working times.

The reasons for country-specific utilisation of decoupling instruments need to be looked in future research. Desiderata for future research can be regarded as the development of instruments to capture and measure the fine-tuning in the operating-hours management. The traditional instruments of the workstation and the employee concept can only be considered as a proxy for the measurement of the operating hours in services. Although they show distinctive differences between the service sector and the secondary sector as well as in between the sub sectors of the service sector, they are still open problems concerning, for example, the density of operating hours, the thinning out of shift systems and particularly the calculation of operating hours in non-continuous processes of production and provision of services. The theoretical debates show that these problems will also gain more importance for the producing industries since coping with uncertainties and a decrease of Tayloristic work organisation are diagnosed for the production model, too. Thus future research will have to look for even more detailed instruments to capture and measure operating hours in the dimension of duration and flexibility.

References

Amend, E. and F. Bauer (2006) Nordrhein-Westfalen – Standortkrise des Ruhrgebiets dominiert Beschäftigungsentwicklung, *Sozialer Fortschritt*, 11-12: 283- 287.

Anxo, D. and D. Storrie (eds.) (2001) *The job creation potential of the service sector in Europe*, Luxembourg: Office for Official Publications of the European Commision.

Anxo, D. and C. Fagan (2001) Service employment – A gender perspective, in: D. Anxo and D. Storrie (eds.) *The job creation potential of the service sector in Europe*, Luxembourg: Office for Official Publications of the European Commision, 89-113.

Baethge, M. and I. Wilkens (eds.) (2001) *Die große Hoffnung für das 21. Jahrhundert? Perspektiven und Strategien für die Entwicklung der Dienstleistungsbeschäftigung*, Opladen: Leske und Budrich.

Baethge, M. and I. Wilkens (2001) „Goldenes Zeitalter“ – „Tertiäre Krise“: Perspektiven von Dienstleistungsbeschäftigung zu Beginn des 21. Jahrhunderts (Einleitung), in: M. Baethge and I. Wilkens (eds.) *Die große Hoffnung für das 21. Jahrhundert? Perspektiven und Strategien für die Entwicklung der Dienstleistungsbeschäftigung*, Opladen: Leske und Budrich, 9-20.

Baethge, M. (2000) Der unendlich lange Abschied vom Industrialismus und die Zukunft der Dienstleistungsarbeit, *WSI-Mitteilungen*, 3: 149-156.

Bauer, F. (2001) Professionalisierungstheoretische Überlegungen zum Verhältnis von Forschung und Beratung, in: W. R. Heinz, H. Kotthoff and G. Peter (eds.) *Beratung ohne Forschung, Forschung ohne Beratung*, Münster: LIT Verlag, 57-71.

Bauer, F., H. Groß and G. Sieglen (2007) Methodology of the EUCOWE Project, in: L. Delsen, D. Bosworth, H. Groß, R. Muñoz de Bustillo y Llorente (eds.) *Operating Hours and Working Times. A Survey of Capacity Utilisation and Employment in the European Union*, Heidelberg: Physica Verlag, 21-40.

Bauer, F., H. Groß, R. Muñoz de Bustillo y Llorente, E. Fernández Macías and G. Sieglen (2007) Cross-country Comparison of Operating Hours, Capacity Utilisation, Working Times and Employment, in: L. Delsen, D. Bosworth, H. Groß and R. Muñoz de Bustillo y Llorente (eds.) *Operating Hours and Working Times. A Survey of Capacity Utilisation and Employment in the European Union*, Heidelberg: Physica Verlag, 41-72.

Bauer, F., H. Groß, S. Lehndorff, S. Schief and G. Sieglen (2007) Operating Hours, Working Times and Employment in Germany, in: L. Delsen, D. Bosworth, H. Groß and R. Muñoz de Bustillo y Llorente (eds.) *Operating Hours and Working Times. A Survey of Capacity Utilisation and Employment in the European Union*, Heidelberg: Physica Verlag, 95-120.

Bauer, F. and A. Otto (2006) Schrumpfung im Ruhrgebiet – Wachstum im Saarland. Eine komparative Analyse der Beschäftigungsentwicklung in zwei ehemaligen Montanregionen, *Zeitschrift für Wirtschaftsgeographie*, 50 (3-4): 147-161.

Bauer, F., H. Groß, G. Sieglen and M. Schwarz (2005) *Betriebszeit- und Arbeitszeitmanagement. Ergebnisse einer repräsentativen Betriebsbefragung in Europa,* Münster: LIT Verlag.

Bauer, F., H. Groß, E. Munz and S. Sayin (2002) *Neue Formen des betrieblichen Arbeits- und Betriebszeitmanagements 2001. Ergebnisse einer repräsentativen Betriebsbefragung,* ed. by Ministerium für Arbeit, und Soziales, Qualifikation und Technologie des Landes Nordrhein-Westfalen, Düsseldorf.

Baumol, W. J. (1967) Macroeconomics of unbalanced growth: The anatomy of urban crisis, *American Economic Review*, June, 741-755.

Bell, D. (1975) *Die nachindustrielle Gesellschaft*, Frankfurt am Main: Suhrkamp.

Berger, J. and C. Offe (1984) Die Entwicklungsdynamik des Dienstleistungssektors, in: C. Offe (ed.) (1984a) *Arbeitsgesellschaft. Strukturprobleme und Zukunftsperspektiven,* Frankfurt am Main, New York: Campus Verlag, 217- 270.

Berger, U (1984) *Wachstum und Rationalisierung der industriellen Dienstleistungsarbeit,* Frankfurt am Main, New York: Campus Verlag.

Berger, U. and C. Offe (1984) Das Rationalisierungsdilemma der Angestelltenarbeit, in: C. Offe (ed.) (1984a) *Arbeitsgesellschaft. Strukturprobleme und Zukunftsperspektiven*, Frankfurt am Main, New York: Campus, 271-290.

Bosch, G. (2001) Germany: A "Service Gap?", in: J. E. Dølvik (ed.) *At your service? Comparative perspectives on employment and labour relations in the European private sector services*, Brussels, *etc.*: P.I.E.-Peter Lang, 53-101.

Bosch, G. (ed.) (1998) *Zukunft der Erwerbsarbeit*, Frankfurt am Main, New York: Campus Verlag.

Bosch, G. and A. Wagner (2000) Dienstleistungsbeschäftigung in Europa. Ein Ländervergleich, in: *Institut Arbeit und Technik, Jahrbuch 1999/2000*, Gelsenkirchen, 82-102.

Brochier, C. (2001) Des jeunes corvéables, *Actes de la recherche en sciences sociales*, 138/2001, 73-83.

Combe, A. and W. Helsper (eds.) (1997) *Pädagogische Professionalität. Untersuchungen zum Typus pädagogischen Handelns*, Frankfurt am Main: Suhrkamp.

Clark, C. (1940) The *conditions of economic progress*, London. Sage.

Dathe, D. and M. Schmid (2001) Determinants of business and personal services: Evidences from the German regions, in: D. Anxo and D. Storrie (eds.) *The job creation potential of the service sector in Europe*, Luxembourg: Office for Official Publications of the European Commission, 181-208.

Delsen, L., D. Bosworth, H. Groß and R. Muñoz de Bustillo y Llorente (eds.) *Operating Hours and Working Times. A Survey of Capacity Utilisation and Employment in the European Union*, Heidelberg: Physica Verlag.

DIW (Deutsches Institut für Wirtschaftsforschung) (1996) Keine Dienstleistungslücke in Deutschland. Ein Vergleich mit den USA anhand von Haushaltsbefragungen, *DIW Wochenbericht*, 63 (14): 221-226.

DIW (Deutsches Institut für Wirtschaftsforschung) (1997) Rückstand beim Anteil der Dienstleistungstätigkeiten aufgeholt, *DIW Wochenbericht*, 64 (34): 613-617.

Dølvik, J. E. (ed.) (2001) *At your service? Comparative perspectives on employment and labour relations in the European private sector services*, Brussels, *etc.*: P.I.E.-Peter Lang.

Dølvik, J. E. (2001) Determinants of service employment, in: J. E Dølvik (ed.) *At your service? Comparative perspectives on employment and labour relations in the European private sector services*, Brussels, *etc.*: P.I.E.-Peter Lang, 17-52.

Einem, E. von (1986) Dienstleistungen und Beschäftigtenentwicklung, *WZB Discussion papers IIM/LMT 86-6*, Berlin: Social Science Research Center Berlin.

Elfring, T. (1988) *Service sector employment in advanced economies*, Aldershot, *etc.*: Gower.

Esping-Andersen, G. (1990) *The three worlds of welfare capitalism*, Cambridge: Polity Press.

Esping-Andersen, G. (1993) *Changing classes: Stratification and mobility in postindustrial societies*, London: Sage.

Esping-Andersen, G. (1999) *Social Foundations of postindustrial economies*, Oxford, New York: Oxford University Press.

Esping-Andersen, G. (2000) Two societies, one sociology, no theory, *British Journal of Sociology*, 51 (1): 59-77.

European Commission (1999a) *Dienstleistungen in Europa. Daten 1995-1997*, Luxembourg: Office for Official Publications of the European Commission.

European Commission (1999b) *Services in innovation – Innovations in services - Final report* (Haukness 1999), Luxembourg: Office for Official Publications of the European Commission.

European Commission (2000a) *Flexible work practices and communication technologies – Flexcot Final report* (Valenduc 2000), Luxembourg: Office for Official Publication of the European Commission.

European Commission (2000b) *Beschäftigung 2000*, Luxembourg: Office for Official Publication of the *European Commission.*

European Commission (2001) *Unterschiede beim Beschäftigungswachstum im Dienstleistungssektor: Deutschland und die USA in der comparable German American structural database* (Freemann/Schettkatt 2001) Luxembourg: Office for Official Publication of the European Commission.

Engfer, U. (1984) *Rationalisierungsstrategien im Einzelhandel*, Frankfurt am Main, New York: Campus Verlag.

Fisher, A. G. B. (1939) Production, primary, secondary and tertiary, *Economic Record*, 15 (June): 24-38.

Fourastié, J. (1954) *Die große Hoffnung des 20. Jahrhunderts*, Köln: Bund-Verlag.

Gershuny, J. (1983) *Social innovation and the division of labour*, Oxford: Oxford University Press.

Haukness, J. (1999) *Services in innovation – Innovations in services -Final report*, Luxembourg: Office for Official Publication of the European Commission.

Häußermann, H. and W. Siebel (1995) *Dienstleistungsgesellschaften*, Frankfurt am Main: Suhrkamp.

Gartner, A. and F. Riessman (1978) *Der aktive Konsument in der Dienstleistungsgesellschaft. Zur politischen Ökonomie des tertiären Sektors*, Frankfurt am Main: Suhrkamp.

Giarini, O. and W. R. Stahel (1993) *The limits to certainty. Facing risks in the new service economy*, Dordrecht: Springer Netherlands.

Katouzian, M. A. (1970) The development of the service sectors. A new approach, *Oxford Economic Papers*, 22 (3): 362-382.

Kaufmann, F. X. (1977) Zur Problematik der Effektivität und ihrer Erfassung im Bereich der sozialen Sicherung, in: B. Külp and H. D. Haas (eds.) *Soziale*

Probleme der modernen Industriegesellschaft, Berlin: Duncker und Humblot, 489-517.

Kern, H. and M. Schumann (1984) *Das Ende der Arbeitsteilung? Rationalisierung in der industriellen Produktion*, München: Beck.

Knuth, M. (1999) *The toll of change. Economic restructuring, worker displacement and unemployment in West Germany*, Gelsenkirchen: Institut Arbeit und Technik.

Mellano, M. (2001) *New employment opportunities in the third sector. An evaluation of innovative policies for social integration in Europe (Nets)*, Brussels: Office for Official Publications of the European Commission.

Muñoz de Bustillo y Llorente, R. and E. F. Fernández Macías (2007) Operating hours, working times and employment in Spain, in: L. Delsen, D. Bosworth, H. Groß and R. Muñoz de Bustillo y Llorente (eds.) *Operating Hours and Working Times. A Survey of Capacity Utilisation and Employment in the European Union*, Heidelberg: Physica Verlag, 169-195.

Nordhause-Janz, J. and U. Pekruhl (eds.) (2000) *Arbeiten in neuen Strukturen? Partizipation, Kooperation, Autonomie und Gruppenarbeit in Deutschland,* München und Mering: Rainer Hampp Verlag.

Nordhause-Janz, J. and U. Pekruhl (2000) Managementmethoden oder Zukunftskonzepte? Zur Entwicklung von Arbeitsstrukturen und Gruppenarbeit in Deutschland in: J. Nordhause-Janz and U. Pekruhl (eds.) *Arbeiten in neuen Strukturen? Partizipation, Kooperation, Autonomie und Gruppenarbeit in Deutschland*, München und Mering: Rainer Hampp Verlag, 13-68.

OECD (2000) *Employment Outlook*, Paris: Organisation for Economic Co-Operation and Development.

OECD (2001*) Services Statistics on value added and employment*, Paris: Organisation for Economic Co-Operation and Development.

Oevermann, U. (1996) Theoretische Skizze einer revidierten Theorie professionalisierten Handelns, in A. Combe and W. Helsper (eds.) *Pädagogische Professionalität. Untersuchungen zum Typus pädagogischen Handelns*, Frankfurt am Main: Suhrkamp, 70-182.

Offe, C. (ed.) (1984a) *Arbeitsgesellschaft. Strukturprobleme und Zukunftsperspektiven*, Frankfurt am Main, New York: Campus Verlag.

Offe, C. (1984b) Das Wachstum der Dienstleistungsarbeit. Vier soziologische Erklärungsansätze, in: C. Offe (ed.) (1984a) *Arbeitsgesellschaft. Strukturprobleme und Zukunftsperspektiven*, Frankfurt am Main, New York: Campus Verlag 291-319.

Piore, M. J. and C. Sable (1984) *The Second Industrial Divide. Possibilities for Prosperity*, New York: Basic Books.

Reichert, R. (2002) „Volunteering" und Bürgerarbeit in Gemeinwohlkonzepten, *Arbeit*, 11 (1): 33-47.

Scharpf, F. W. (1986) Strukturen der postindustriellen Gesellschaft, *Soziale Welt*, 37 (1): 4-24.

Scharpf, F. W. (1998) Die Zukunft der Arbeit im renovierten „Modell Deutschland", *Gewerkschaftliche Monatshefte*, 49 (6-7): 433-443.

Schmid, G. (2001) Beyond conventional service economics – utility services, service product chains and job services, in: D. Anxo and D. Storrie (eds.) *The job creation potential of the service sector in Europe*, Luxembourg: Office for Official Publications of the European Commission, 287-303.

Singelmann, J. (1978) *From Agriculture to Services. The Transformation of Industrial Employment*, London: Sage.

Storrie, D. (2001) Service Employment, productivity and growth, in D. Anxo and D. Storrie (eds.) *The job creation potential of the service sector in Europe*, Luxembourg: Office for Official Publications of the European Commission, 31-65.

Weinkopf, C. (1998) Möglichkeiten der Beschäftigungsförderung im Dienstleistungssektor, in: G. Bosch (ed.) *Zukunft der Erwerbsarbeit*, Frankfurt am Main, New York: Campus Verlag, 458-482.

Wernet, A. (1997) *Professioneller Habitus im Recht*, Berlin: Edition Sigma.

5 Small and Medium-sized Establishments in Europe: Operating Hours and Working-Time Patterns

Mark Smith, Stefan Zagelmeyer and Georg Sieglen

5.1 Introduction

Small and Medium-sized Enterprises have become an increasingly important component of policy at both the national and European level in recent years (Unger, 2003; Devins and Johnson, 2003). The importance of SMEs in terms of their share of employment is undeniable and Gray (2004) suggests that around 99% of EU firms are SMEs accounting for 122 million private sector jobs. Although SMEs are often promoted for their employment creation or innovation potential, less is known about their working-time patterns (Sieglen *et al.*, 2001). This chapter explores the relationship between operating hours and working patterns in establishments of different sizes in six European countries. We analyse the extent to which the operating times of small and medium sized establishments are explained by their different utilisation of working arrangements and the particular constraints or flexibilities that smaller organisations may face in relation to larger establishments. SMEs are often identified as a source of job growth and increased competitively in a European context but while SMEs may have inherent flexibilities their size may also create constraints when it comes to the development and implementation of complex working-time arrangements and compensation systems. Using the EUCOWE survey of more than 17,000 establishments based in Germany, France, the UK, the Netherlands, Portugal and Spain, we show how operating hours are positively related to establishment size and the use of various working-time patterns. However, at the same time, the operating hours of SMEs can benefit from the adoption of working time practices likely to extend operating hours.

L. Delsen et al., *Comparative Analyses of Operating Hours and Working Times in the European Union*,
DOI: 10.1007/978-3-7908-2185-7_5,

The chapter is divided into six sections. The next Section 5.2 reviews the links between working time and organisational size. Section 5.3 briefly considers some methodological issues relating to the use of the EUCOWE survey in this paper. Section 5.4 examines the operating hours by establishment size, establishment autonomy and country, and examines the working-time arrangements employed to meet operating time requirements. Section 5.5 uses multivariate analysis to examine the extent to which working patterns and other factors affect operating hours in SMEs. The final Section 5.6 draws on the empirical results and discusses the implications of the findings.

5.2 Small and medium sized establishments and working patterns

Like other organisations, SMEs will be subject to national and pan-national regulation of working time. Although all European Union countries are subject to the European Working Time Directive, its implementation and specific national legislation and collective regulation further shape working time practices at the workplace level. Limits on daily or weekly hours, annual leave and overtime will all affect the use of particular working practices to meet fluctuations or extend operating hours (Freyssinet and Michon, 2003). However, there are a number of factors and characteristics of SMEs that may act against strict compliance with national regulation. SMEs have been described as being governed by more "personal and arbitrary" forms of control, even though this may be ineffective (Woods and Joyce, 2003: 181). Indeed the exclusion of smaller firms from aspects of collective regulation in some European countries confirms the different status of regulation within an SME setting, for example firm size thresholds exist for Work Council regulations (Slomp, 1995). SMEs are also less likely to have working time collectively regulated as union membership and union activity tends to fall as firm size declines. The close involvement of owners in the management of SMEs may also be a factor that inhibits collective regulation (Bluhm, 2001: 163). Although there are some examples of firm-size thresholds for working time regulation (Freysinet and Michon, 2003), exemption from regulation around collective representation and low trade union representation may further encourage informality around, for example, the organisation of working time. SMEs are often controlled directly by an owner or close associate and this proximity of the owner/manger may also encourage informal arrangements that benefit both employee and employer. Informal working practices in SMEs may mean that employers feel less bound by regulation and employees are less aware of their rights (Bluhm, 2001). Personal and informal management style that can lead to the circumvention of collective regulations may also extend to the use of unpaid overtime or overtime at non-premia rates (Kodz *et al.*, 2003). On the other hand, for the employee in an SME, where wages are often lower than in larger firms (CEC, 2002), low pay can create an additional incentive to work long hours at a premia.

It is perhaps surprising that more is not known about the working-time patterns and operating times in SMEs given the centrality of SMEs to employment policy in Europe (CEC, 2002). In all workplaces there is a strong link between operating hours and working time and nowhere is this link stronger than in SMEs where size limitations have the potential to limit opportunities for extended operating times or place increased reliance on existing employees. Although SMEs have been described as being at the forefront of employment creation and more agile or adaptable than large bureaucratic organisations (see Parker, 2001) they may also face additional constraints in the organisation of working time when it comes to extending operating hours. Longer operating hours require the deeper or wider use of employees. For SMEs the use of a wider range of employees may be difficult given their size. Resource constraints may create an "aversion" to growth (Gray, 2004: 453) including increasing the numbers employed, a potential constraint in itself. On the other hand, more intensive use of a smaller range of employees can provide an immediate and potentially cheaper solution although it may place greater demands on just a few members of staff. Furthermore, the development and implementation of complex working-time arrangements may make considerable demands on management time and skills, resources which are often limited in SMEs (Atherton, 2003; Jones, 2004). These constraints may explain the greater use of less formal methods of extending working time among SMEs such as overtime and more limited use of more complex working-time arrangements such as working time accounts (Arthur, 2002), annualised hours (Hart and Bell, 2003) and shifts (IDS, 2001).

Other barriers to the extension of operating times may include the limited strategic orientation of management in SMEs (Gray, 2004). Extended operating hours may require a strategic approach to the use of labour and working time but SMEs are not known for this type of thinking and more regularly described as reactive and unplanned (Devins and Johnson, 2003). Atherton (2003) suggests resource scarcity in SMEs can lead to greater levels of uncertainty, and for example, the establishment of a shift system to extend operating times can involve considerable up front investment (see Hart and Bell, 2003). By contrast increasing the overtime of existing workers might be regarded as relatively risk free.

It is however important to note that the SME sector is heterogeneous both within and across countries (Bagnasco, 1995). Significant differences may exist in the use of technology, types of market and support from local institutions (Bagnasco and Sabel, 1995). Important differences also exist between micro, small and medium sized enterprises (Devins and Johnson, 2003). Similarly small establishments that are part of multi-site organisations may have access to greater resources, for example management skills and experience, and thus provide an important comparator for working practices in single site SMEs. For these reasons the results in this paper are disaggregated both for establishments of different sizes, autonomy and across different sectors.

5.3 The research

By using data from the European Capital Operating time and Work and Employment (EUCOWE) project we can explore the link between working-time patterns, employment and operating times of establishments. Since in the EUCOWE survey distinguished between the establishment, the survey unit, and the company it seems important also to consider this difference when analysing establishments of different sizes. The establishment is defined as a single physical location where business is conducted or where services or industrial operations are performed; meanwhile the company is defined as economic and legal entity that encompass one or more establishments or plants. Establishments that are part of multi-establishment companies or firms might be de jure independent, but are also de facto part of the large firm. However, firm size corresponds more closely to the notion of business size and patterns of government regulation and business access to financial markets is tied more closely to firm size than to plant size (Davis *et al.*, 1996: 301).

In the context of operating hours and working-time management we might expect small and medium-sized establishments that are part of a bigger enterprise to resemble large-scale enterprises more than single small and medium-sized establishments. For example, the operation and adaptation of complex working-time arrangements to lengthen operating hours may be less cost intensive in a small establishment that is part of a multi-site firm. Similarly work organisation matters might be expected to be regulated by the enterprise management, limiting the scope of managers at the establishment level. Therefore in the following analyses we distinguish between "stand-alone" small and medium establishments ("single SMEs*"), small and medium-sized establishments that are part of a multi-establishment enterprise ("multi SMEs*") and large-scale establishments (LSEs).[1]

The vast majority (99.4%) of the establishments in the surveyed countries are SMEs*, with 80.5% being single SMEs* and 18.9% multi SMEs*. While there are only very small between-country differences in the shares of SMEs* among all establishments, the share of single SMEs* differs significantly between countries; ranging from only 61.4% in the UK to 94.3% in Spain. A relatively high share of single SMEs* can also be found in Germany (85.3%), while there is considerable similarity in the proportions in the remaining three countries (73% to 75%). The distribution of SMEs* also has a sectoral dimension and, with the exception of the UK, single SMEs* tend to be found slightly more often in the producing sector than in the service sector. Overall the majority, three fifths (59.1%), of small and medium-sized establishments are single micro organisations (1 to 9 employees) but the proportion varies between countries, ranging from 35.5% in the UK to 80.9% in Spain. One fifth of the SMEs* are single small establishments (10 to 49 employees), 9.1% are multi micro establishments, 8% are multi small establishments and medium-sized establishments (50 to 249 employees) account for just under 4%.

5.4 Operating times and working-time patterns

Different operating time requirements of organisations will help determine the need to use various forms of flexible working and the relative reliance on some measures, for example those that are more complex or expensive. The pressures on SMEs* may be more acute as the capacity to extend or vary operating times may be limited by the personnel capacity of the or-

1 In contrast to the usual use of 'SMEs' as small and medium enterprises, here this abbreviation is used for establishments and marked with a "*". SMEs* are here defined as establishments with 1 to 249 employees with at least one employee who is subject to the health or unemployment insurance or who is participating in a pension scheme. Those establishments with more than 249 employees are defined as LSEs.

ganisation itself. Here we use the direct measure of operating times as our key indicator.[2]

The mean average operating hours per day of all organisations in the sample, irrespective of size, sector of economic activity, and country, is 9.8 hours. Differentiating between the different countries in the survey, the mean operating hours per day are highest in Germany with 10.5 hours, followed by the United Kingdom with 10.2 hours while Portuguese, French, and Dutch organisations operate for between 9.4 and 9.8 hours per day. Spanish organisations find themselves at the bottom of the league table with 8.6 hours. These differences in the mean operating hours per day may have several causes and the composition of firms by size is an important factor.

Our initial findings indicate that there is a direct relationship between mean operating hours per day and both establishment size and the unit's autonomy. Single/multi micro establishments, *i.e.* organisations of up to nine employees, operate on average 9.2/9.3 hours per day with daily operating hours increasing to 10.7/11.1 for establishments with 10-49 employees, and to 13.0/14.6 for medium-sized establishments (50-249 employees) (Figure 5.1). Large establishments, with 250 or more employees, operate on average 16.2 hours per day. Operating hours of large establishments differ only slightly between countries – only in the Netherlands are operating hours more than an hour below the six-country average. In contrast, there are considerable between-country differences in daily operating hours of SMEs*, exceeding eight hours, with the shortest hours in Spanish multi-micro establishments (7.9 hours) and longest hours in German multi medium-sized establishment (16.2 hours). In Spain the overall importance of micro establishments with short daily operating hours helps to explain the relatively low country mean.

The pattern observed for daily operating times is repeated for mean operating hours per week with single/multi micro establishments operating on average 51.3/52.7 hours per week, small establishments 61.8/65.9 hours, and medium-sized establishment 77.2/89.5 hours. Here a similar pattern of differences can be observed not only by country but also by

2 Operating times can be calculated by both the direct and indirect measures. The direct measure uses responses from the survey to the question "How many hours does your establishment operate on a typical day" with a similar question for weekly operating hours. By contrast, the indirect measure is calculated as the employee-proportional mean of contractual working hours, overtime hours, staggered working hours and shift work hours (see Delsen, Bauer, Cette and Smith, Chapter 1, this volume and Bauer et al., 2007).

different types of establishments (Figure 5.1): weekly operating hours in German multi medium-sized establishments (99.5 hours) are again more than twice as long as in Spanish multi micro establishments (45.5 hours).

Figure 5.1 Operating hours (direct measure) by type of establishment and country (a) daily (b) weekly (c) yearly

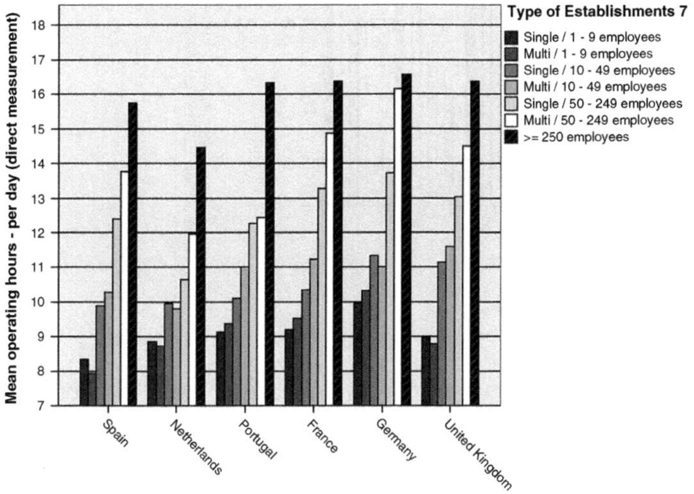

(a) Daily operating hours

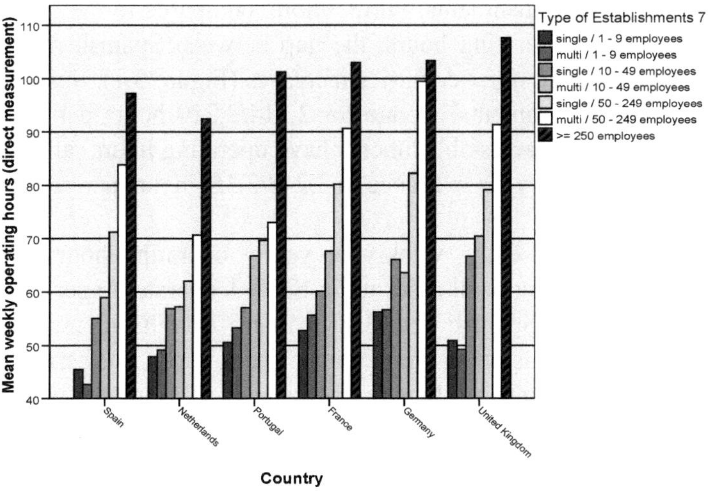

(b) Weekly operating hours

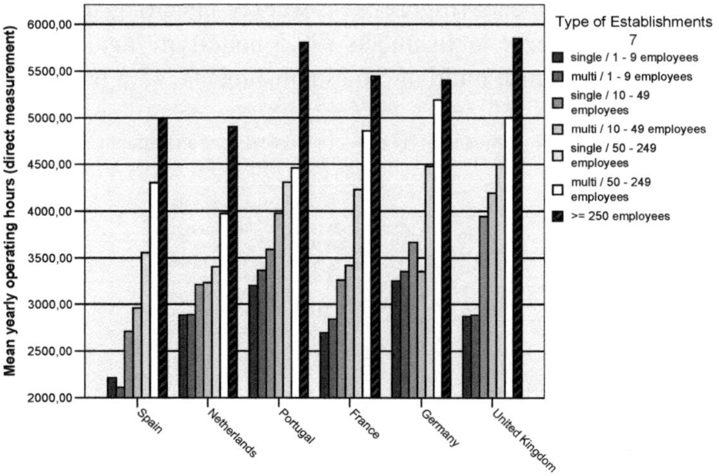

(c) Yearly operating hours

The mean operating hours per year[3], our third measure, are 3,054 hours for all organisations in the survey, with single/multi micro and small organisations operating at 2,785/2,945 hours and 3,408/3,520 hours respectively. However, the respective figures for medium-sized and large organisations rise dramatically to 4,172/4,822 hours and 5,373 hours respectively. The short daily and weekly operating hours in Spain are matched by short yearly operating times producing a mean of 2,314 hours compared to 2,981 hours in France and between 3,042 and 3,512 hours in German, Portuguese, Dutch and UK establishments. Furthermore, compared to the country differences in daily operating hours, the gap between Spanish micro establishments and those in other countries increases (Figure 5.1): Spanish single/multi micro establishments operate for 2,214/2,210 hours per year while in other countries these establishments have operating hours ranging from 2,696/2,873 hours per year in France to 3,248/3,351 hours per year in Germany.

Irrespective of whether daily, weekly or yearly operating hours are analysed we find that in almost all cases multi SMEs* operate longer than single SMEs* (with only Spanish and British micro establishments and German small establishments displaying an opposite pattern). Furthermore operating hours increase significantly with SME size in all countries while,

3 This measure is calculated by extrapolating the operating hours reported for a typical week in March or April 2003 to a whole year, taking into account the number of non-operating days reported.

once again, only moderate cross-country differences can be observed among larger establishments.

For any establishment, a prerequisite for extending operating time beyond working time of employees is the possibility to decouple daily and weekly operating hours from contractual weekly working time by using different working-time arrangements to meet the demands of certain operating hours. Relevant working time practices that can be used to achieve such extensions include overtime, staggered working hours, shift work, Saturday work and Sunday work. For smaller establishments the potential for such decoupling may be constrained and thus their utilisation of working-time arrangements may differ from those of larger establishments.

When we compare the shares of establishments in which operating hours are decoupled[4] from full-time working hours we find, unsurprisingly, similar distributions to those for operating hours. The average share of establishments with operating hours decoupled from working time is 40.3%; ranging from 35.6% among single establishments to 55.5% among multi SMEs* and 79.8% among large establishments. Here once again German SMEs* have the highest values (single/multi SMEs*: 52.5%/70.3%), followed by the United Kingdom and France. However, in contrast to the country-ranking of operating hours, where Dutch SMEs* were found to have operating hours only slightly longer than the short hours in Spanish SMEs*, the decoupling shares among Dutch SMEs* of 34.8%/62.1% for single/multi SMEs* are clearly higher than in both Spain (8.2%/12.7%) and Portugal (22.1%/34.3%). This result is at least partly explained by the higher share of part-time contracts (<35 hours per week) and the higher share of establishments with staggered working times in the Netherlands. Interestingly the share of Dutch establishments with "decoupled" operating hours has risen considerably in recent years (Delsen and Smits, 2007). By contrast, in Germany, with the exception of single micro establishments, at least 60% of establishments have decoupled operating hours. Even in single micro establishments we find just less than half (47.3%) with decoupled operating hours compared to only 5.4% among Spanish single micro establishments. The impact of establishment autonomy is significant, however to varying degree in the surveyed countries: while in the Netherlands decoupling shares vary strongly between single and multi establishments,

4 Establishments with decoupled operating hours are establishments where the average contractual weekly working hours of all fulltime employees is less than the indirect measure of operating hours.

these differences are relative small in Spain and especially in the United Kingdom.

As one of the simplest forms of working time flexibility, overtime is widely used across many organisations. A quarter of the sample establishments reported using overtime hours; ranging from 22.3% among single SMEs*, to 35.7% among multi SMEs* and 61.3% among large establishments. Here we observe strong differences between countries with Portugal and particularly Spain at the lower end of the shares using overtime hours. On the other hand, at the top end, 34.1% of the German single micro establishments use overtime and 77.6% of the UK multi medium-sized establishments (Figure 5.2). In Spain and Portugal formal overtime hours seem to be more of an exception among single/multi micro establishments (1.0%/2.4% and 3.1%/2.7% respectively), while the share of micro establishments with overtime hours is considerably higher in the Netherlands (23.6%/37.3%), Germany (34.1%/44.2%) and the United Kingdom (33.0%/45.4%).

Figure 5.2 Decoupling of operating hours by different working-time arrangements by type of establishment and country (a) operating hours (b) overtime hours (c) mean overtime hours per employee

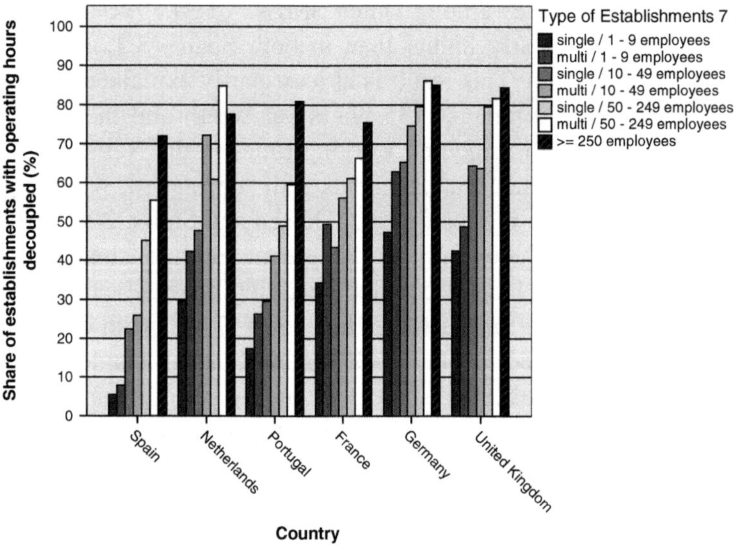

(a) Decoupled operating hours

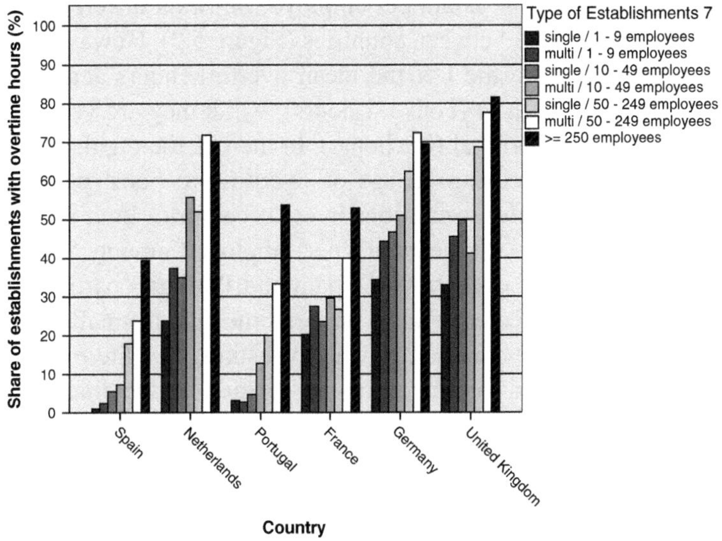

(b) Overtime hours

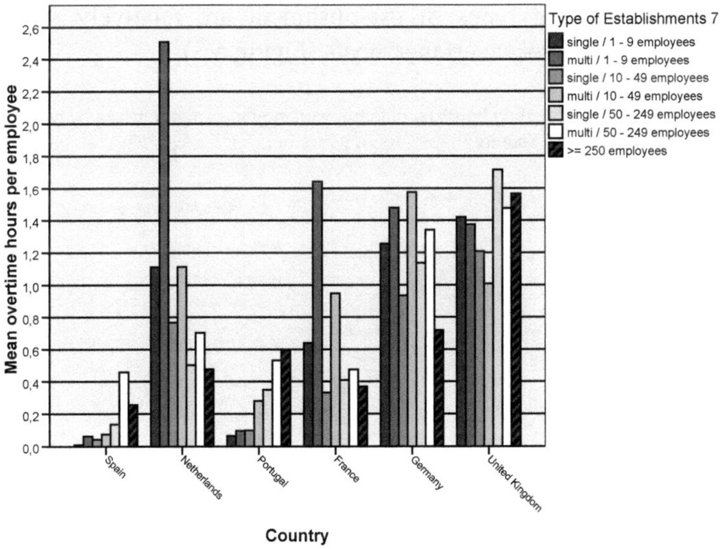

(c) Mean overtime hours

The mean number of overtime hours per employee shows a different picture with no clear similarities between countries (Figure 5.2). However, we do find that in Germany and the UK the mean overtime hours across all establishments are again highest (both 1.2 hours), while they are very low in Spain (0.02 hours) and Portugal (0.1 hours). In the UK the regulation of overtime permits the institutionalised use of overtime to boost pay and meet normal workloads, tighter restrictions in other countries limit its use. The relatively long mean overtime hours per employee among SMEs* compared to LSEs (with the exception of Spain and Portugal) partly supports our expectation of a greater reliance on overtime among small establishments compared to more complex staffing measures. In spite of these country-differences no clear pattern occurs in relation to the impact of establishment types.

Staggered working time is another means of decoupling operating hours from working time and a fifth of all establishments in the sample operated such schemes; ranging from almost zero in Spain to a third in Germany. Although staggered working time is used less than overtime hours the between-country differences follow a similar pattern. Furthermore the differences between different types of establishment are relatively small compared to other working-time arrangements (Figure 5.3).

Figure 5.3 Decoupling of operating hours by different working-time arrangements by type of establishment and country

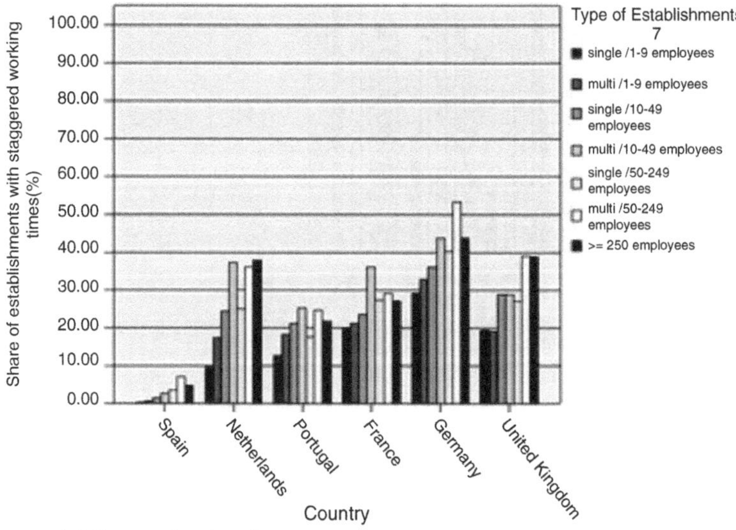

(a) Staggered working times

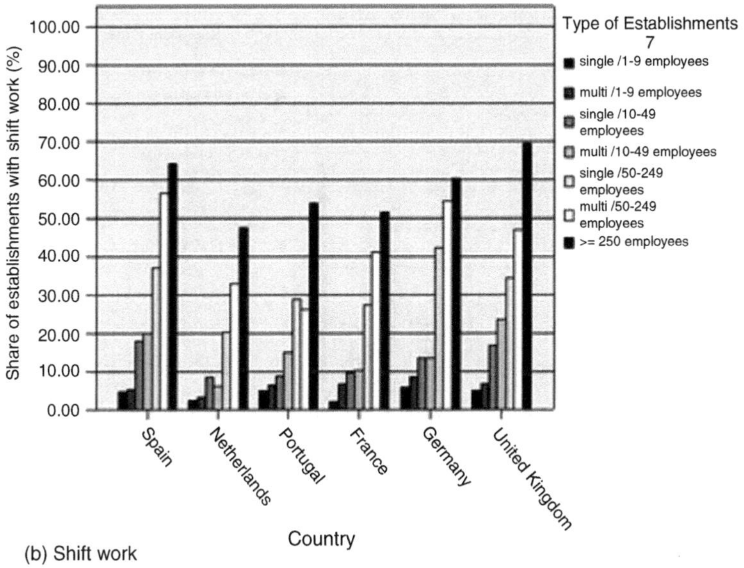

(b) Shift work

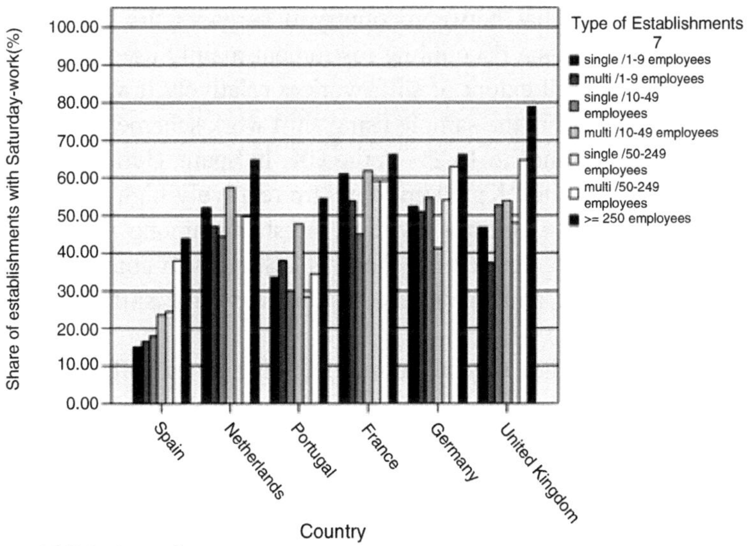

(c) Saturday work

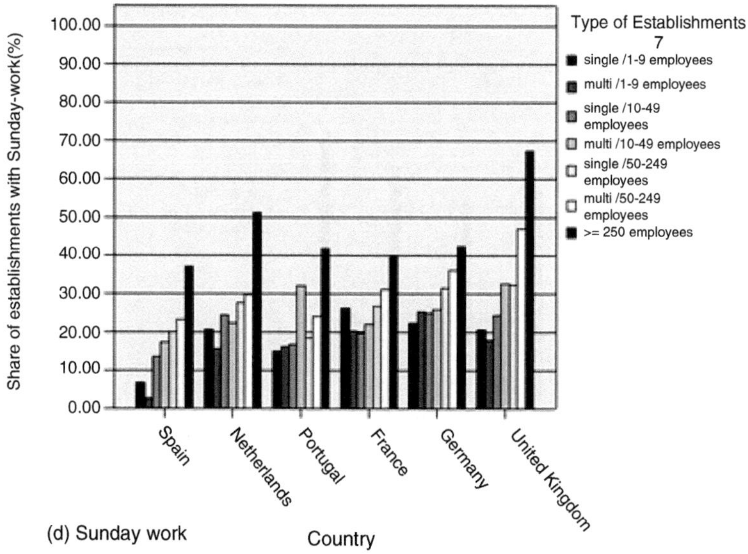

(d) Sunday work

By contrast, shift work is a more complicated form of working time arrangement and we find that between-country differences are relatively small and that shift work is a decoupling instrument mainly used by large establishments. The overall extent of shift work is relatively low with just 8.4% of all establishments in the sample using shift work schemes: ranging from 5.6% in the Netherlands to 14.2% in the UK. In Spain, Germany, and France along with the United Kingdom there are relatively high shares of establishments using shift work and we find the shares among multi medium-sized establishments are close to those of LSEs. Even among small establishments in the UK and Spain, the results show that shift work is used by around a fifth.

Weekend work is another way to extend operating times with just less than half (44.2%) of all organisations indicating that they operated on Saturdays (figure 5.3). Across countries, company coverage of Saturday work varies between 16% in Spain to close to half in France, Germany and the UK. Overall Saturday work is a little more widespread among large establishments (64.6%) than among multi SMEs* (50%) and single SMEs* (43.1%) but no clear trend can be observed. The relatively high share of single micro establishments that operate on Saturdays in all countries stands out (33% in Portugal to 61.0% in France) but again Spain is the exception (15.0%). On the other hand, Sunday work is less common, with just a fifth of the establishments operating, but here its use is relatively more frequent in the larger establishments compared to smaller establishments than it is the case for Saturday work. Overall 44.4% of all LSEs operated on a Sunday compared to 23.0% of the multi SMEs* and 19.1% of the single SMEs*.

An important factor in the use of different working-time patterns is the extent to which they are used to meet fluctuations in demand.[5] Given the limited resources available to SMEs* and their greater reliance on informal measures we might expect the number of measures to rise with establishment size. On the other hand, the more informal methods of managerial control in SMEs* may increase the scope to use multiple methods. The options to cope with fluctuations measured by the EUCOWE survey included the working time measures discussed above – overtime, Saturday work, Sunday work, shift work, staggered shifts – as well as part-time work, short-time work, working time accounts/flexitime/ annualised hours, subcontractors/agency/on-call-freelancers, hire and fire or 'other'. Table 5.1 shows the mean number of flexible measures used to meet fluctuations by establishment size and autonomy.

Overall we find that the information reported in Table 5.1 supports the other findings in our research namely that the use of different forms of working patterns rises with establishment size and with membership of a multi-establishment organisation. In both LSEs and multi-site small and medium size establishments there is a greater use of multiple workforce strategies to cope with fluctuations than in single SMEs*. However, we also find persistent country differences identified above. For example, establishments in the Netherlands and the UK seem to make use of a greater number of working-time arrangements than those in other countries, means of 2.4 and 2.6 measures compared to a five country average of 2.2 (no data for Spain). This country effect for the UK and Netherlands also holds when we look at single SMEs*. For multi-site SMEs* and larger establishments we find that Germany joins the Netherlands and the UK with a relatively high number of measures used to deal with fluctuations.

Thus we find overall that establishment size and autonomy play an important role in different operating hours and the use of different types of working pattern associated with extending operating times. Overall we find that larger establishments are more likely to use these different working arrangements. Furthermore, and perhaps unsurprisingly, we find that larger establishments are more likely to make use of more complex forms

5 Unfortunately these data are not available for Spain.

Table 5.1 Mean number of working-time measures used to meet fluctuations at the organisational level

	Primary sector	Secondary sector	Construction	Distributive services	Producer services	Social services	Personal services	Total
Germany								
single SME	2.0	2.3	2.4	2.2	2.4	1.6	1.8	2.1
multi SME	(2.5)	3.4	3.0	2.3	2.4	2.9	2.5	2.6
LSE	(4.0)	3.9	(3.6)	3.4	3.4	2.7	(2.7)	3.5
Total	2.1	2.4	2.4	2.2	2.4	1.8	1.9	2.2
France								
single SME	2.6	1.9	1.8	1.7	2.1	2.2	1.7	1.9
multi SME	2.4	2.8	2.3	1.8	1.9	2.2	1.9	2.0
LSE	(2.2)	3.2	(2.9)	2.7	3.3	2.5	(3.2)	3.0
Total	2.6	2.1	1.8	1.7	2.0	2.2	1.8	1.9
UK								
single SME	2.3	2.3	2.8	2.5	2.4	2.4	2.2	2.4
multi SME	(2.2)	2.2	1.7	2.8	1.9	2.5	2.3	2.3
LSE	(3.4)	4.0	(4.2)	3.4	4.1	3.8	(3.6)	3.9
Total	2.2	2.3	2.5	2.6	2.2	2.4	2.3	2.4
Netherlands								
single SME	3.4	2.9	2.5	2.3	2.3	1.8	3.3	2.6
multi SME	3.7	3.1	1.9	3.1	2.5	2.5	4.1	3.0
LSE	-	3.4	(4.1)	3.6	3.0	2.9	(3.5)	3.3
Total	3.4	3.0	2.4	2.5	2.4	2.1	3.5	2.7
Portugal								
single SME	1.8	1.3	1.4	1.2	1.3	2.0	1.7	1.4
multi SME	(1.0)	1.5	1.3	1.6	2.0	2.0	1.4	1.6
LSE	-	2.6	(3.0)	3.0	3.5	(1.0)	(2.0)	2.8
Total	1.8	1.4	1.4	1.4	1.5	2.0	1.6	1.5
EU5	2.3	2.3	2.3	2.2	2.2	2.0	2.0	2.2

Note: figures in parentheses where N < 30.
Source: establishment weighted EUCOWE data.

of working arrangement such as shifts. However, we also find only relatively small differences in the application of working-time arrangements such as staggered working times and weekend work between small and large establishments (particularly for Saturday work while for Sunday work differences are bigger). In relation to the utilisation of overtime we observe that its use rises in larger and in multi-site establishments but the intensity (overtime per employee) shows no such pattern; in countries such as the Netherlands, France, and Germany mean overtime hours per employee in SMEs* are clearly higher than in LSEs, as we expected. Larger establishments are not only making greater use of each form of working time arrangement but are also more likely to adopt a strategy of multiple forms of work arrangement to meet fluctuations in demand. Of the measures adopted by SMEs*, we find that Saturday work is most intensively used followed by overtime hours with staggered working times and Sunday work used less with only a minority of SMEs* utilising shift work. Spain, and to some extent Portugal, stand out with particularly low use of staggered working times, overtime hours and Sunday work in SMEs* (see Delsen and Smits, Chapter 3, this volume).

5.5 Multivariate analyses

While the earlier descriptive statistics indicate that all three indicators of operating time – operating hours per day, per week, and per year – are influenced by the size and autonomy of the establishment, there is no indication as to the importance of or the interaction between the different explanatory variables. In order to control for multiple influences and differentiate between them, the following section reports the results of multiple regression analyses of operating hours. Due to space restrictions, we only estimate different models that seek to explain (directly measured) operating hours per week and operating hours per year as dependent variables.

We estimated five regression models: one overall model and four models for micro, small, medium-sized and large establishments, in order to account overall effects and for size-interaction effects. In the models we include a range of dummy independent variables related to the character and thus implicitly goals of the organisations concerned. To begin with, we include measures of whether the enterprise was a profit or non-profit organisation and the extent of national/foreign control. Similarly, in order to identify the impact of being part of a larger organisation, we included a dummy variable for single-establishment organizations. Furthermore, the regression analyses include dummy variables that indicate whether the company is covered by a collective agreement on working time and/or operating hours, and the geographical scope of product markets. Labour costs as percentage of total costs is used as an indicator of the labour intensity of production.

Two different types of establishment size variables were included for the different types of estimations. The regression analyses with the full dataset include four banded dummy variables which relate to different size categories – micro establishments (1-9 employees), small establishments (10-49 employees), medium-sized establishments (50-249 employees), and LSEs (250+ employees). The size category of micro establishments was used as reference category. Using four size categories allowed us to control for non-linearities. The regression analyses within the different establishment size categories included a continuous variable for the total number of employees.

Since the descriptive statistics showed that Germany has the highest scores on two of the three indicators for operating time, Germany was chosen as the reference category for the six country dummies. In addition, the estimations include a set of industry dummy variables with thirteen categories relating to the sector of economic activity.[6] The reference category was the primary sector (agriculture, hunting and forestry plus mining and quarrying).

We also use a series of measures to explore the presence of various working-time arrangements and working patterns that may enhance operating hours. Continuous variables control for the proportion of part-time employees, the proportion of agency workers and working time average while dummies were used for Saturday work, Sunday work, staggered hours, shift work and overtime working. Here we report on the significant findings ($p<0.05$). As far as operating hours per week are concerned (see Table 5.2a), the regression with the total sample of all organisations in the dataset yields the following results.

Among the establishment attributes not related to working-time patterns, size-effects are clearly the strongest: weekly operating hours of micro establishments are estimated to be nearly 12 hours shorter than in large establishments, more than 6 hours shorter than in medium establishments and more than two hours shorter than in small sized establishments. However, our hypothesis that SMEs* that are part of a multi-site enterprise operate for longer than single-site SMEs* can not be affirmed, since effects are not significant.

6 Here we use seven sectors but then subdivide the secondary sector into seven subsectors: 1) Manufacture of food products, beverages and tobacco, 2) Manufacture of leather/leather products/textiles/textile products, 3) Manufacture of other non-metallic mineral products/rubber and plastic products/chemicals, chemical products and man-made fibers/coke, refined petroleum products and nuclear fuel/pulp, paper and paper products/publishing and printing/wood and wood products 4) Manufacture of basic metals and fabricated metal products, 5) Manufacture of machinery and equipment n.e.c., 6) Manufacture of electrical and optical equipment and 7) Electricity, gas and water supply/manufacturing n.e.c.

Table 5.2a Multivariate analysis of weekly operating hours

	All	Micro	Small	Medium	Large
Profit-orientation	0.45	1.78	0.74	-2.30	3.00
Foreign control	1.66	-2.38	2.50	2.03	0.39
Single-establishment	0.04	-2.09	0.51	-0.04	1.43
Collective agreement	2.89**	0.56	0.30	2.71	7.98**
Competition (ref: local)					
National	-1.51*	0.55	-1.60	-1.20	-6.40*
international	2.01*	2.88*	-0.56	2.54	-0.59
Labour costs (% total)	0.03*	0.02	-0.01	-0.01	0.08
No. employees		0.16	0.14**	0.02	0.00
Size (ref: micro)					
Small	2.50**				
Medium	6.39**				
Large	11.68**				
Country (ref: Germany)					
Spain	4.39**	-1.13	-0.10	7.75*	9.42
France	1.08	-4.62**	0.09	2.48	6.05*
UK	-0.68	-4.97**	1.41	-0.52	-1.80
Netherlands	-5.45**	-3.28*	-3.72*	-11.37**	-7.89*
Portugal	1.55	-3.69*	-0.32	3.61	8.50**
Sector (ref: primary)					
Construction	-1.43	-0.97	0.88	-2.54	-19.21**
Distributive services	-1.07	-2.89	0.98	0.57	-10.31*
Producer services	-2.15	-3.85*	1.62	-1.45	-14.15*
Social services	10.42**	4.34	9.24**	13.05**	7.79
Personal services	-1.98	2.39	2.34	4.73	-27.29**
Food manufacture	8.17*	12.34**	18.29**	13.36*	-7.85
Textile manufacture	1.82	-1.83	2.35	4.01	-5.53
Chemical/non-metals	3.56*	-1.46	1.23	6.72	2.11
Metal manufacture	7.33**	-2.81	6.93**	8.89*	2.01
Machinery manufacture	-0.82	-3.44*	0.22	-1.79	-6.68
Electrical manufacture	0.74	-3.87	-1.15	3.62	-6.68
Electricity/other manuf.	-2.78	-3.62	0.34	0.67	-18.76*
% part-time employees	-0.03*	-0.04*	-0.05	-0.01	0.00
% agency fixed-term	-0.05**	0.00	-0.03	-0.09**	-0.08
Saturday work	15.03**	9.93**	14.21**	19.87**	16.40**
Sunday work	32.24**	18.92**	30.08**	33.23**	38.12**
Working time average	0.19**	0.21**	0.05	0.34*	0.32*
Staggered working hours	5.32**	8.55**	7.34**	5.21**	2.31
Shift work	39.08**	27.46**	38.49**	38.96**	36.02**
Overtime	2.52**	0.11	-0.22	3.99*	2.76
Constant	2.92**	4.20**	36.67**	25.82**	35.71**
Number of observations	9,138	2,248	3,222	2,108	1,560
F	367.3**	35.1**	82.5**	115.5**	119.0**
R^2	0.66	0.46	0.63	0.62	0.57
MSE	25.45	16.55	21.04	29.02	34.44

Note: * p<0.05. ** p<0.01.

Country-effects are also relevant. Weekly operating hour effects in Germany are estimated to be five hours longer than in the Netherlands, and four hours shorter than in Spain. Micro and small establishments in Germany have operating hours up to five hours longer than in all other countries. However, operating hours of LSEs in Spain, Portugal and France are, on the other hand, significantly longer than in Germany. For all size categories, operating hours in Germany are significantly longer compared to the Netherlands.

Among the other establishment attributes not related to working-time patterns which were controlled for in the regressions we find collective bargaining coverage also has a significant effect, with operating times three hours longer in enterprises with a collective agreement. A wider scope of geographical competition seems to matter especially for micro establishments: competition on an international level (as compared to local level) has a significant positive effect on operating hours. National markets (as compared to local markets) have a significant negative effect, especially for large establishments. Foreign control has no significant effect on operating hours.

The share of labour costs on total costs has a significant, but relatively small positive effect on operating hours. Where significant, the sector effects are consistently negative for larger establishments while for other size classes we tend to find positive results from being located in certain sectors: social services, food manufacturing, and metal manufacture.

In order to explore the relevance of different working-time arrangements on operating hours we also included dummy-variables for several working-time patterns in the models. Shift work clearly has the strongest effect raising operating times by more than 39 hours with what comes close to the effect of a two-shift against a single-shift system. In the overall regression model we find a negative effect for high shares of agency and fixed-term employees.

There is a large impact from size-specific effects of Sunday and Saturday work on operating hours: here the larger establishments are, the more they seem to operate at weekends. In our descriptive analysis we found that the size-class differences for the share of establishments operating on Saturdays were relative moderate compared to those for operating on Sundays. The regression results show that if micro establishments operate on Sundays they operate only for about half of the time LSEs do, even when controlling for of other working-time patterns such as shift work.

Staggered working time systems are also a means to decouple operating hours from employee working time; however this seems to have only a relatively moderate effect on operating hours. The descriptive analysis showed that the share of SMEs applying staggered working times was only slightly below or, in some case, even above the share of LSEs. Confirming this, the regression result show, that staggered working times have a stronger positive effect on operating hours for micro and small establishments than for larger establishments.

A higher share of part-time employees has a significant negative effect on operating hours – particularly for micro establishments. This is may be the result of part-time employees not necessarily prolonging operating times, especially in small establishments.

In the analysis of mean operating hours per year (table 5.2b), the regression with the total sample of organisations produces similar effects to those found for weekly operating hours. We find that the effects of the different working-time patterns on yearly operating hours are similar to those found for weekly operating hours. Again there are negative sector effects on large establishment from construction, producer services, personal services and electricity/other manufacturing while, on the other hand, food and metal manufacture have more consistent positive effects across other size classes.

A strong difference between yearly and weekly analyses can be found in the country effects: while the maximum difference of nearly ten hours per week between Spain and the Netherlands accounts for around 34% of the constant, the maximum difference of about 800 hours per year between Portugal and the Netherlands accounts for around 47% of the constant. Thus we find that inter-county differences are stronger if we compare yearly operating hours and also that the country-effect ranking is somewhat different. If we compare the size-specific effects, it is clear that medium-sized and particularly LSEs establishments in Portugal tend to operate much longer than in the other countries in the survey.

These results highlight the clear direct relationship between company size on the one hand and either operating hours per week or operating hours per year on the other. Associated with this is the positive relationship between establishment size and the use of working-time patterns likely to raise operating hours, for example shift work and weekend work. Nevertheless SMEs* benefit from such working patterns differently. Somewhat surprisingly the single/multi establishment variable has no significant effect. The results suggest that shift work has the biggest effect on (directly measured) operating hours, followed by Sunday and Saturday work. Only for larger establishments does Sunday work have a bigger effect than shift work.

Table 5.2b Multivariate analysis of yearly operating hours

	All	Micro	Small	Medium	Large
Profit-orientation	44.3	65.7	40.8	-32.0	110.2
Foreign control	156.3*	16.6	123.0	103.5	159.6
Single-establishment	55.5	-80.0	86.8	16.5	85.1
Collective agreement	142.0**	26.9	19.4	150.3	408.3*
Competition (ref: local)					
National	-68.4	-9.4	-98.2	75.0	-278.1
International	56.8	98.9	-53.6	229.2	-125.8
Labour costs (% total)	1.9*	1.7	-0.4	0.1	4.3
Number of employees		20.7*	6.8**	1.0	0.0
Size (ref: micro)					
Small	197.0**				
Medium	434.8**				
Large	725.3**				
Country (ref: Germany)					
Spain	-144.4	-656.5**	-490.5**	82.4	285.8
France	-91.3	-555.6**	-239.4*	11.3	268.1
UK	-106.6	-455.1**	-88.3	-111.2	22.2
Netherlands	-209.8**	-158.1	-206.6*	-496.5*	-336.7
Portugal	599.8**	110.6	420.1**	806.3**	985.0**
Sector (ref: primary)					
Construction	-49.5	-65.1	39.7	-32.8	-1002.7*
Distributive services	5.3	-89.0	44.9	225.0	-490.1
Producer services	-36.3	-76.7	88.0	213.4	-840.6*
Social services	619.4**	264.7	489.1**	955.6**	438.9
Personal services	52.7	53.8	391.5*	534.4*	-1175.9*
Food manufacture	444.1*	686.0*	755.7*	881.4*	-323.5
Textile manufacture	120.6	-33.3	-21.7	265.5	-72.0
Chemical/non-metals	239.8*	77.7	2.4	494.2*	94.9
Metal manufacture	399.1**	-27.8	374.9**	483.8*	26.8
Machinery manuf.	-49.3	-32.0	32.4	-22.8	-568.8
Electrical manufacture	-52.3	-78.7	-152.5	239.1	-588.2
Electricity/other	-100.1	-57.7	-30.0	284.1	-999.8*
% part-time employees	0.8	-1.1	-0.3	3.2	2.2
% agency fixed-term	-2.2**	-0.4	-1.7	-3.1	-2.7
Saturday work	596.6**	384.3**	479.6**	833.7**	730.8**
Sunday work	1413.3**	850.8**	1240.1**	1373.2**	1649.4**
Working time average	8.0*	10.9*	-1.0	17.1*	12.4
Staggered working hrs	185.5**	348.0**	332.2**	210.9*	-35.9
Shift work	2114.7**	1307.1**	2136.9**	2155.3**	1940.9**
Overtime	65.1	-92.0	-28.9	183.9*	31.8
Number of holidays	-2.4	0.2	-2.1	-4.9	0.1
Constant	1699.5**	2213.5**	2397.6**	1294.8**	2304.9**
Number of observations	7,247	1,553	2,521	1,774	1,399
F	221.1**	19.0**	50.6**	69.2**	70.1**
R^2	0.60	0.43	0.57	0.54	0.49
MSE	1417.8	807.98	1147.5	1620.2	1903.5

Note: * $p<0.05$. ** $p<0.01$

5.6 Conclusions

In the empirical analyses of this chapter we explore the relationship between operating hours and working patterns in Small and Medium-Sized Establishments that are either single or part of a multi-site enterprise (SMEs*) in six European countries. Our study represents one of the first quantitative investigations into operating hours for single and multi-site establishments and the links with their working time practices. Our findings here confirm the limited potential of smaller establishments to adopt some more advanced forms of working time organisation that would allow them to extend operating hours. However, if they are applied, they have different effects than among Large Sized Establishments (LSEs): staggered working times have a positive and significant effect on operating hours only among micro and small establishments, shift work has a stronger effect for small and medium-sized establishment than for LSEs, but LSEs apply weekend work more intensively than SMEs*.

As far as smaller establishments are concerned, operating hours are considerably shorter than those for larger establishments: this relationship holds across countries and sectors. Nevertheless, the means of extending operating hours through overtime hours, staggered, shift and weekend work provide positive benefits to both small and large establishments. Correspondingly we find that in all countries the share of establishments decoupling operating hours from the working time of full-time employees is also considerably lower in smaller establishments than in larger establishments (LSEs). However, the link between decoupling and absolute operating times needs to be set in country context: operating hours in Dutch establishments are among the lowest in the studied countries yet the share of Dutch SMEs* with decoupled operating hours is not the lowest. The relatively short weekly operating hours of Spanish and Portuguese SMEs* also stand out and their utilisation of overtime hours, staggered hours and weekend work is lower than SMEs* in other countries, but it is unclear to what extent this is compensated for by informal working time measures.

We also show how being part of a multi-establishment organisation can have an impact on the variety of methods used to decouple and extend operating times. For almost all size-classes and countries the operating hours are longer and decoupling measures, particularly shift and Sunday work, are utilised more frequently by establishments that are part of a multi-site organisation (although our multivariate analyses found no significant effect of the status of autonomy). We also find that cross-country variations in mean operating hours of larger establishments are smaller than they are among SMEs* while, on the other hand, within country differences by size are relatively consistent.

The cross-country analysis of operating times also highlights significant country-specific differences which appear to influence operating hours whether measured on a weekly or yearly basis. Access to non-standard working-time arrangements may be shaped by the regulatory framework that the organisation is exposed to. The impact of these national regulatory frameworks can not be discounted here as we would expect limits on working-time patterns, as well as working time norms, to have a role. Interestingly, after controlling for size-, sector-, and other effects, the country-effects show that, in Portugal, Spain and France, especially large establishments operate relatively long hours. By contrast yearly operating hours in Portuguese establishments are the longest in all size-classes. German micro and small establishments have the longest weekly operating hours. Operating hours in the Netherlands are, in all size-classes, relatively short or the shortest compared to the other surveyed countries.

Finally it is also interesting that a collective agreement covering working time and/or operating hours did not have a negative impact on operating hours: instead collective agreements have a highly significant positive association for large establishments. Furthermore, our results suggest that limits on working time are not necessarily associated with operating hours since overtime had a relatively small impact on operating hours in the multivariate analyses (in only one instance). Overtime is one of the less complex working time measures available to SMEs and as such as our results highlight the challenges these establishments face in seeking to increase operating times.

References

Atherton, A. (2003) The Uncertainty of knowing: An analysis of the nature of knowledge in small business context." *Human Relations*. 56 (11): 1379-1398.

Arthur, L. (2002) *Work Life Balance: Britain and Germany Compared*, London: Anglo-German Foundation.

Bagnasco, A. (1995) An unexpected and Controversial return, in: A. Bagnasco and C. Sabel (eds.) *Small and Medium-Size Enterprises*, London: Pinter.

Bagnasco, A. and C. Sabel (1995) *Small and Medium-Size Enterprises*, London: Pinter.

Bauer, F., H. Groß and G. Sieglen (2007) Methodology of the EUCOWE Project, in: L. Delsen, D. Bosworth, H. Groß and R. Muñoz de Bustillo y Llorente (eds.) *Operating hours and working times: a survey of capacity utilisation and employment in the European Union*, Heidelberg: Physica-Verlag, 21-39.

Bauer, F., H. Groß and G. Sieglen (eds.) (2002) *Operating Hours in Europe*, Berichte des ISO 66, Köln: Institut zur Erforschung sozialer Chancen.

Bluhm, K. (2001) Exporting or Abandoning the 'German Model'? Labour Policies of German Manufacturing Firms in central Europe, *European Journal of Industrial Relations*, 7 (2): 153-173.

CEC (2002) *Council Recommendations of 18 February 2002 on the implementation of the Member States' employment policies*, I.60/70EN, Commission of the European Communities.

Davis, S. J., J. Haltiwanger and S. Schuh (1996) Small Business and Job Creation: Dissecting a Myth and Reassessing the Facts, *Small Business Economics*, 8 (4): 297-315.

Delsen, L., D. Bosworth, H. Groß and R. Muñoz de Bustillo y Llorente (2007) *Operating hours and working times: a survey of capacity utilisation and employment in the European Union*, Heidelberg: Physica-Verlag.

Delsen, L. and J. Smits (2007) Operating Hours, Working Times and Employment in the Netherlands, in: L. Delsen, D. Bosworth, H. Groß and R. Muñoz de Bustillo y Llorente (eds.) *Operating hours and working times: a survey of capacity utilisation and employment in the European Union*, Heidelberg: Physica-Verlag, 121-146.

Devins, D. and S. Johnson (2003) Training and development activities in SMEs: some findings from an Evaluation of the ESF Objective 4 Programme in Britain, *International Small Business Journal*, 21 (2): 231-228.

Freyssinet, J. and F. Michon (2003) *Overtime in Europe*, European Industrial Relations Observatory.

Gray, C. (2004) Management Development in European Small and Medium Enterprises, *Advances in Developing Human Resources*, 6 (4): 451-469.

Hart, D. and R. Bell (2003) Annualised Hours: the way forward in labour market flexibility?, *National Institute Economic Review*, July, 185-213.

Jones, J. (2004) Training and Development, and business growth: A study of Australian manufacturing small-medium sized firms, *Asia Pacific Journal of Human Resources*, 42 (1): 96-121.

Kodz, J., S. Davies, D. Lain, M. Strebler, J. Rick, P. Bates, J. Cummings and N. Meager (2003) *Working long hours: a review of the evidence Volume 2*, The Institute for Employment Studies DTi Employment Relations Research Series No 16.

Parker, R. (2001) The Myth of the Entrepreneurial Economy: Employment and in Small Firms, *Work Employment and Society*, 15 (4): 373-384.

Sieglen, G., H. Groß, and F. Bauer (2001) Employment policies of small and medium-sized enterprises (SMEs)", in: F. Bauer, H. Groß and G. Sieglen (eds.) *Operating Hours in Europe*, Berichte des ISO 66, Köln: Institut zur Erforschung sozialer Chancen.

Slomp, H. (1995) National variations in work participation, in: A-W Harzing and J. van Ruysseveldt (eds.) *International HRM*, London: Sage.

Unger, B. and K. Heitzmann (2003) The adjustment path of the Austrian Welfare state: back to Bismarck?, *Journal of European Social Policy*, 13 (4): 371-387.

Woods, A. and P. Joyce (2003) Owner Managers and the Practice of Strategic Management, *International Small Business Journal*, 21 (2): 181-195.

6 Patterns of Flexibility in Domestic and Foreign Enterprises[1]

Sebastian Schief

6.1 Introduction

This chapter tries to answer empirically the question whether the power of companies has reached a new level, as economic globalisation gathers pace, and, if so, what form this shift in the balance between the power of the local environment and that of companies takes. The decisive factor in this shift in the balance of power is said to be the threat to move production and hence jobs elsewhere, a threat that can be forestalled only if management's demands are met. According to this interpretation, this bargaining power places companies in the position to impose lower wages, longer working times and more flexible systems of work organisation.

Companies' power is determined by the tension between the local environment, *i.e.* the institutional setting at a given location, and the company itself and its particular organisational structures and culture. Companies will always try to obtain what they regard as the optimal conditions under which to produce goods or deliver services. However, local conditions, and in particular industrial relations and legal arrangements, may stand in the way of companies seeking a free hand to determine working and employment conditions. For some years now, there has been a wide-ranging academic debate on how to assess the strength of companies' position relative to the local environment (*e.g.* Bornschier, 1980; Chase-Dunn, 1990; Flecker, 2000; Hirsch, 1995; Hirst and Thompson, 1997; Krugman, 1994; Schief, 2003; 2008).

---

1 The author is grateful for the support of the Hans-Boeckler-Stiftung and the European Commission for this research.

L. Delsen et al., *Comparative Analyses of Operating Hours and Working Times in the European Union*,
DOI: 10.1007/978-3-7908-2185-7_6,

This chapter seeks to contribute to this debate by examining the influence of corporate organisation and institutional setting on companies' flexibility patterns. Flexibility patterns are defined as various combinations of personnel-related measures that are used to deal with short and long-term fluctuations in production or demand. The investigation focuses in particular on the impact of foreign compared to domestic companies on these flexibility patterns. The object of investigation would seem to be particularly well suited to our purpose, since both firms and the institutional setting can be assumed to exert considerable influence on the selection of measures intended to cope with fluctuations in production. However, this raises the question whether differences can be detected in the strength of these two influences and whether a hierarchy of influences can be established on the grounds of the strengths of the detected influences. To put it in a nutshell, our aim is to ascertain whether certain flexibility instruments are used more or less frequently by foreign compared to domestic companies and how the use of these instruments differs in the five EU countries under investigation. The differences between countries as well as domestic and foreign companies can be interpreted as a proxy for the influence of institutional setting and organisational structure.

The chapter is divided into four sections. In Section 6.2, a theoretical framework is outlined that can be used to examine the relationship between firms and their institutional setting under the influence of economic globalisation, that is the increasing interdependence of actors in the global economy. This is followed in Section 6.3 by a description of possible flexibility patterns, while in Section 6.4 the use of the dataset and methodology are explained. The subsequent empirical Section 6.5 of the chapter begins with an examination of differences in the flexibility patterns adopted by establishments in the five countries under investigation. This is followed by a comparison of the models used by domestic and foreign-owned establishments in the five countries and an investigation of establishments from Germany, the UK and USA abroad, three major countries of origin for establishments in the dataset. Finally, a multivariate analysis of the flexibility instrument "flexible working times" is carried out in order to check the correlations between the various types of influence. The chapter concludes in Section 6.6 with concluding remarks.

6.2 Globalisation, multinational companies and national institutional settings

In the academic debate on the extent and effects of an increasingly integrated global economy, two matters are heavily debated. The first is governance, *i.e.* the possibility of regulating processes through political action. The second is the role of companies – especially multinational companies – in a globalised economy (for a summary, see Schief, 2003: 33 *ff.*). One argument developed in the debate takes a largely globalised economy as a starting point and interprets developments since the beginning of the 1980s as a massive push towards globalisation. In this increasingly integrated global economy (*e.g.* Narr and Schubert, 1994), multinational companies are regarded as the principal actors (Hirsch-Kreinsen, 1997). The drive towards globalisation and the exposed position of multinationals have led, so it is argued, to a radical change in the relation between the state and the economy. From this point of view, the influence that can be exerted by nation states appears to be marginal compared to the rising influence of companies. The "competition state" (Hirsch, 1995) exists only as a service provider, regulating in order to optimise markets. However, both the impetus for and the objectives of state action are, in the view of authors like Narr, Schubert, Hirsch-Kreinsen or Hirsch dependent on capital in the shape of multinational companies. States' attempts to create favourable conditions for multinational companies lead to a "competing down" process (Chase-Dunn, 1990) between them.

The counterargument to this analysis, with its negative view of the influence that can be exerted by nation states, has been advanced by authors such as Krugman (1994) and Hirst and Thompson (1996), who take a fundamentally different view of both the extent and effects of globalisation. Drawing on historical analyses, Hirst and Thompson cast doubt on the uniqueness of the present rush towards globalisation, pointing to the significantly higher degree of integration in the global economy prior to 1914.

Krugman (1994) contests the existence of competition between nation states. In his view, it is national economic factors, in particular productivity, that determine a region's living standards rather than its position in global competitive markets. Nevertheless, he argues, the competitiveness argument occupies a position of hegemony in political discourse because it is admirably suited to "justify hard choices or to avoid it" (Krugman, 1994: 40).

Both Hirst and Thompson and Krugman also cast doubt on the notion that the increased mobility of capital is leading to a radical shift in investment and jobs from the developed to the less developed countries. They ground their argument on empirical findings showing that trade, production and financial relations are concentrated within the so-called triad of North America, Western Europe and Japan. Schief (2003) shows in his analysis that this is also true of direct investments by German companies.

Their well substantiated doubts about the existence and effects of a globalised economy lead the authors to speak of an internationalised economy (Hirst and Thompson, 1996), in which the influence that can be exerted by nation states is nowhere near as weak as is suggested by advocates of the "competition state" argument.

Assessment of the extent and effects of an integrated global economy leads logically to attempts to evaluate the opportunities open to multinational companies to influence national institutional settings, and *vice versa*. Thus Rubery and Grimshaw (2003), for example, see the rise of multinationals as a potential challenge to the continuation of national employment practices, since

> "some individual multinational corporations can now be considered more powerful than many nation states, and certainly have a value in excess of the GDP of many countries." (Rubery and Grimshaw, 2003: 198)

In their opinion, this economic power is combined with political power. Thus the great power of multinational corporations is reflected in the restricted possibilities available to nation states when it comes to regulation. The introduction of new management practices within subsidiaries can certainly exert an influence on national institutional settings; however, that influence can often spread much further:

> "More significantly, they can do what indigenous employers may feel unable to do – ignore custom and practice within the country and sector, and thereby introduce novel and different ways of working and new approaches to human resource management. (…) it is this influence of MNCs which may prevent or dissuade individual nation states or groups of nation states from pursuing their own system of social and economic organization." (Rubery and Grimshaw, 2003: 199)

Another aspect of the possible influence exerted by multinational corporations identified by Rubery and Grimshaw is the diffusion of so-called "best-practice" employment models, which in the long term could threaten the survival of alternative employment models.

Another proponent of this argument is Streeck (1993), who sees European integration of the mid-1980s as a basic agreement between the national political elites and large European companies, according to which business would support the Western European nation states in regaining control over foreign policy and receive, in return, an extensively deregulated economy ("a single market without a single state"). The social aspects of the single market were added later, but in Streeck's view they are limited to what is necessary to make the market politically and technically possible (*cf.* Streeck, 1993: 96).

The essence of the debate outlined above lies in the distribution of power between the two centres of influence – (multinational) companies, on the one hand, and the institutional setting, on the other. Is it the local environment that exerts the decisive influence on the organisation of employment and production or is it the corporate environment, that is specific to the companies in question? Schmidt and Dworschak (2002) break the question down further by identifying four kinds of influence that can impact on multinationals. The influence of the corporate environment can be divided into the effect exerted by the environment of origin, that is the country of origin effect, and the effect exerted by the company itself, that is the transnational effect. For its part, the influence of the local environment can be divided into the host country effect, that is the effect exerted by the host country's institutional and economic setting, and a discourse effect, that is the influence of assumptions and prejudices about the local environment. Since the analytical distinction between host country and discourse effect cannot be tested empirically, we will summarise these distinctions by referring in the rest of the chapter to the local environment effect.

The core question to be addressed in this chapter is which of these effects exerts what influence on companies' employment flexibility patterns. We start from the hypothesis that flexibility approaches are to a large extent shaped by the local environment to which companies are adjusting.[2]

2 Given the wide-ranging nature of the local environment versus company question, simply to investigate the "flexibility pattern" aspect may appear to be narrowing the focus too much. However, if general statements are to be examined empirically, there is no option but to concentrate on specific issues in order to permit operationalisation. This does not of course preclude the investigation of other questions.

6.3 Companies' flexibility patterns

Martinez-Lucio and Blyton (1995) describe flexibility as management's scope to vary or adjust the labour inputs, both quantitatively and qualitatively, in response to changes in demand. This labour input can be regulated in various ways. In the literature on companies' flexibility models, a distinction is usually made between the flexibility that is dependent on the internal labour market and the flexibility that can be achieved by recourse to the external labour market. The second dimension of the various flexibility models is the distinction between numerical and functional or quantitative and qualitative flexibility (see for example Atkinson, 1984; Delsen, 2002). On the basis of these different dimensions, four types of workforce flexibility can be identified, as shown in Table 6.1.

Table 6.1 Types of flexibility and their characteristics

	Numerical	Functional
Internal	Working time organisation Variation in working time Variation in work intensity	Retraining and redeployment Multiple skills and job rotation Delegation of responsibility
External	Recruitment and dismissal Fixed-term employment contracts Agency work	Outsourcing Networks of firms Contracts for services/freelancing

Sources: Atkinson (1984), Delsen (2002), Lehndorff and Voss-Dahm (2005).

Internal numerical flexibility can be achieved by use of the core workforce alone. Management can, for example, cut working time, arrange short-time working, use overtime or increase working time flexibility through the organisation of working time. A distinction should be made between a rigid increase or reduction in the volume of the labour input and a variable working time system that can absorb fluctuations in output.

However, management can also enhance and/or change the quality or function of its core workforce (internal functional flexibility). Some of the options here include job rotation, group work and multitasking. The basic idea is to extend the area within which employees can be deployed through further training, which tends of course to be a longer-term strategy for increasing flexibility.

External numerical flexibility is produced when companies have recourse to the external labour market in order to deal with fluctuations in production. This usually means the use of additional labour, for example through new hires, fixed-term appointments or the use of temporary agency staff.

External functional flexibility, on the other hand, is achieved when parts of the production process or certain services are outsourced or parts of companies are hived off. Freelancers should also be included here, since they may also take on certain tasks previously carried out by the company. In this way, employment contracts can be replaced by contracts for services (see Delsen, 2002: 255 *ff.*).

It should be noted that these four types of flexibility are not, in reality, mutually exclusive. Firms can, for example, make use simultaneously of elements of internal numerical flexibility and of external functional flexibility. Lehndorff and Voss-Dahm are thus quite right to point out that the internalisation of markets within companies and changes in labour market regulations are increasingly blurring the differences between the various flexibility models (see Lehndorff and Voss-Dahm, 2005: 14; Flecker, 1999: 20).

6.4 Data and methods

The empirical investigation draws on the data set from the EUCOWE[3] project on working times and operating hours in Europe. Since there are no Spanish data for certain parts of the investigation relevant to our present purpose, only France, Germany, the Netherlands, Portugal and the UK are included in our analysis. The observational unit is the establishment.

Part of this survey deals with fluctuations in production or service provision and the possible means of dealing with these fluctuations. Due to the increasing lack of differentiation between the four types of flexibility in Table 6.1, our analysis will be located one level lower and use a specific set of questions to operationalise the four flexibilisation instruments. Our focus will be on the actual instruments used to provide flexibility, since they can be more clearly distinguished from one another and are easy to operationalise. Among the many flexibility instruments that can be associated with one or other of the individual types of flexibility, we have se-

---

3 This project, entitled "A Comparative Study of Operating Hours, Working Time and Employment in France, Germany, the Netherlands, Portugal, Spain and the United Kingdom" (EUCOWE), was funded by the European Commission. For a detailed description of the study see Chapter 1 by Delsen et al. in this volume and Delsen et al. (2007).

lected for analysis the most common (see Bauer *et al.*, 2007). Thus the flexibilisation of production will be investigated by means of the following instruments:

- overtime (paid and unpaid);
- flexible working times (flexitime, working-time accounts);
- use of external workers (contract workers, agency and temporary workers, employees on-call) and
- recruitment and/or dismissal.

The first two flexibility instruments can be assigned to the internal numerical flexibility model, while the other two are external flexibility instruments. Whereas new hires and dismissals can be assigned unambiguously to numerical flexibility, the use of external workers cannot be unequivocally associated with the numerical or functional type. We are not concerned here with the exclusivity of flexibility instruments but rather with the frequency with which these instruments are used by various types of company.

The establishments were first asked whether they actually had to deal with variations in production (see the questionnaire in the annex of this volume). Each establishment that replied in the affirmative was then asked about the methods they used to do so.

The present investigation only includes establishments with 250 and more employees, since the comparison of foreign and domestic establishments are the main focus of our analysis. Small establishments would harm this comparison. Bodies incorporated under public law and non-profit-making organisations were also excluded, because the structure and strategy of this group of establishments differs from private establishments and is not our focus of interest. In total, 1,683 establishments fulfil these criteria. Of these, 884 (52.6%) stated that they have to deal with variations in production or service provision, and it is these establishments that are analysed here. Establishment proportional weighted data were used for the following bivariate analyses. Multivariate analysis was carried out with unweighted data to avoid distortions of the standard error.

6.5 The empirical investigation

Our analysis of establishment flexibility patterns is divided into three stages. In the first, the flexibility instruments, within the five countries for which data are available, are examined (local environment effect). This is followed by a comparison of domestic and foreign-owned establishments in these countries (transnational effect, country of origin effect). In the third stage of the analysis, the influence of three major countries of origin (Germany, UK and USA) on flexibility instruments is investigated (country of origin effect). The final stage comprises a multivariate analysis of flexible working times. By structuring the investigation in this way, we will be able to examine the three effects outlined above and the interactions between them.

6.5.1 Flexibility patterns within the countries under investigation

In this first part of the analysis, the influence of the local environment on establishment flexibility is investigated. The aim, therefore, is to ascertain whether there are statistically significant differences between different local environments in the use of particular flexibility instruments.

Table 6.2 Share of establishments with 250+ employees using particular flexibility instruments to cope with fluctuation in business activity, by country and sector

N= 884	Germany	France	UK	Netherlands	Portugal
		Overtime			
Manufacturing	67.6	64.7	88.1	84.7	62.5
Services	66.4	56.5	94.1	75.3	40.0
Total	67.1	60.5	91.3	78.8	54.3
		Flexible working times			
Manufacturing	83.1	42.8	18.2	15.6	20.2
Services	74.5	41.6	20.8	29.2	42.0
Total	79.6	42.2	19.5	24.1	27.9
		External labour supply			
Manufacturing	45.9	88.4	71.0	85.0	36.4
Services	31.2	73.4	49.9	68.1	9.8
Total	39.9	80.7	59.8	74.5	26.6
		Recruitment and dimisal			
Manufacturing	49.3	6.0	63.8	38.1	55.1
Services	42.8	15.7	41.9	44.0	68.6
Total	46.7	11.0	52.2	41.7	60.4

Note: All figures have significant differences (Cramer's V).
Source: EUCOWE, own calculations.

In general, significant differences are found for all types of flexibility, as can be seen from Table 6.2. Great Britain is the country that makes by far the greatest use of overtime to absorb fluctuations. More than nine out of ten establishments with at least 250 employees in the UK use this instrument to deal with variations in production or service provision. Thus overtime can be seen as *the* British flexibility instrument. An investigation by Wagner and Pannenberg (2001) confirms the high level of overtime use in the UK. Whereas almost 80% of establishments of this size in the Netherlands use this form of flexibility, the figure for Germany is only two thirds and for France about 60%. The lowest figure – about 54% – is observed for Portugal. The results of Bauer *et al.* (2007) are in line with these figures, too.

The result for the second flexibility instrument, flexible working times, is quite different. Flexible working times means the use of working-time accounts or flexitime in order to deal with fluctuations in demand. Establishments in Germany make by far the greatest use of this form of flexibility. Eight out of ten large establishments in Germany use this instrument, which can be seen as *the* German flexibility instrument. The widespread use of flexible working times in Germany is also confirmed by the ISO study on working and operating hours (Bauer *et al.*, 2002). German establishments are followed, at a considerable distance, by their French counterparts, where only slightly more than four out of ten establishments report using this form of flexibility. The shares in Portugal (27.9%), the Netherlands (24.1%) and the UK (19.5%) are even lower.

The use of external labour, such as temporary agency workers, is encountered most frequently in France and can be regarded as the predominant flexibility instrument in France. About eight out of ten French establishments state that they use this form of flexibility. The share of establishments in the Netherlands is only insignificantly smaller, at 74.5%. Six out of ten establishments in the UK have recourse to this instrument, while only about 40% of their counterparts in Germany use it. In Portugal, on the other hand, the share is even lower, at only 27%.

The recruitment or dismissal of workers as a means of coping with variations in production or service provision is used most frequently by establishments in Portugal (60.4%). In France, on the other hand, only slightly more than 11% of establishments with 250 or more employees report using this instrument. The UK, Germany and the Netherlands lie somewhere between these extremes, with figures of between 42 and 47%.

In some countries, there are bigger differences in the use of flexibility instruments between manufacturing and service establishments. Across all the countries in the investigation, considerably fewer service establishments make use of external labour than those in the manufacturing sector. This difference is most evident in Portugal (26.6%) and France (21.2%). In Portugal, moreover, considerably fewer service-sector establishments use overtime (about 20%) in order to deal with variations in demand; on the other hand, the share of establishments in the manufacturing sector that make use of flexible working time is only about half of that in the service sector. It is also interesting that recruitment and dismissal are used as flexibility instruments in about 63% of British manufacturing establishments but only in about 42% of service-sector establishments.

There are large differences between the flexibility instruments in use in the countries investigated. The UK can be characterised as the overtime country and Germany as the flexible working time country. In the Netherlands, on the other hand, just as many establishments use overtime as use external sources of labour. In France, establishments prefer to deal with variations in demand by calling on external sources of labour, while in Portugal overtime and recruitment or dismissal are the types of flexibility used by the greatest share of establishments.

6.5.2 Foreign versus domestic establishments: flexibility models compared

In this section, we test for the existence of influence exerted by establishments' environment, that is the transnational and country of origin effects. In concrete terms, this will involve testing whether there are significant differences in flexibility patterns between foreign-owned and domestic establishments.[4] The relatively small number of foreign-owned establishments in our sample does not allow us to make a further distinction between manufacturing and service establishments.

In Portugal, no significant differences were found between foreign and domestically owned establishments for any of the indicators. For the other four countries, on the other hand, such differences can be observed for at least three of the four indicators (see Table 6.3).

In Germany, fewer foreign ('F:') than domestically ('D:') owned establishments use overtime to deal with variations in demand (D: 69.2%; F: 62.7%). On the other hand, considerably more foreign-owned establishments than domestic establishments call on external labour sources (D:

4 A distinction will be made between wholly German-owned establishments and establishments that have at least one foreign part owner. Of course domestically owned establishments can also be transnational, but we regard this lack of clarity as tolerable, since we are dealing with establishments operating in their own national environment. On the other hand, the transnational effect makes itself felt primarily outside of the country of origin.

Table 6.3 Share of establishments with 250+ employees that use particular flexibility instruments, by country and domestic (D) or foreign ownership (F)

N=866	Germany		France		UK		Netherlands		Portugal	
	D	F	D	F	D	F	D	F	D	F
Overtime	**69.2**	**62.7**	**56.7**	**70.4**	**87.3**	**94.6**	80.8	78.9	53.2	55.9
Flexible working time	**79.1**	**81.9**	**44.0**	**37.9**	**11.8**	**26.0**	**22.1**	**24.3**	30.0	25.0
External labour	**35.9**	**49.5**	80.5	81.7	**46.8**	**70.8**	**82.2**	**67.1**	21.5	33.3
Recruitment/ dismissal	**44.6**	**50.6**	**13.0**	**6.1**	**55.5**	**47.7**	**48.9**	**38.1**	62.6	54.1

Note: figures in bold have significant differences (Cramer's V).
Source: EUCOWE, own calculations.

35.9%; F: 49.5%). The difference between the two groups of establishments with regard to flexible working time is small, but significant: an even greater share of foreign-owned establishments use this form of flexibility than establishments in German ownership (D: 79.1%; F: 81.9%). Recruitment and dismissal are reported significantly more frequently as a source of flexibility by foreign-owned firms than by domestic establishments (D: 44.6%; F: 50.6%). Thus three of the four flexibility instruments are used more by foreign-owned establishments than by those in German ownership.

In France, on the other hand, more foreign-owned establishments use overtime in order to deal with variations in demand than establishments in French ownership (D: 56.7%; F: 70.4%). However, fewer foreign-owned establishments rely on dismissals or recruitment (D: 13.0%; F: 6.1%) and flexible working time (D: 44.0%; F: 37.9%) than is the case with French-owned establishments. On the other hand, there are no differences between the two groups of establishments with regard to the most frequently used flexibility instrument in France, namely recourse to external labour.

In the UK as well, three of the four flexibility instruments are used by more foreign-owned establishments than by establishments in British ownership. The only one used more frequently by British-owned establishments is the recruitment or dismissal of workers. The differences in the use of external labour and of flexible working time are considerable. More than twice as many foreign-owned as British-owned establishments state that they use flexible working time in order to deal with fluctuations in production or the provision of services (D: 11.8%; F: 26.0%). The share of foreign-owned establishments that use external labour for this purpose is about 25 percentage points higher than that of British establishments with 250 or more employees (D: 46.8%; 70.8%). The use of overtime, the most frequently used form of flexibility in the UK, is even more widespread among foreign-owned establishments than among those in British ownership (D: 87.3%; F: 94.6%).

In the Netherlands, it is striking that there are no significant differences between foreign and Dutch-owned establishments in the use of overtime, the commonest flexibility instrument. Furthermore, considerably fewer foreign establishments make use of external labour (82.2%; 67.1%) and dismissals and/or recruitment (48.9%; 38.1%) in order to deal with variations in demand. On the other hand, flexible working times are used by a higher share of foreign-owned establishments (D: 22.1%; F: 27.3%).

In Germany, France and the UK, the flexibility instruments most frequently reported by domestic establishments are also those most frequently mentioned by foreign-owned establishments. In the case of the Netherlands, two main flexibility instruments were identified, one of which – overtime – is just as widely used in foreign-owned as in domestic establishments. However, there are considerable differences in the use of external labour, which can be observed much more frequently in Dutch establishments. No significant differences between foreign-owned and domestic establishments could be observed in Portugal, suggesting that no effects of the above-mentioned type could be detected. The key lesson to be drawn from this part of the analysis is that effects attributable to the establishments' environment were detected in four of the five countries investigated, but that there were no differences between foreign and domestically owned establishments with regard to the main flexibility instruments used.[5]

6.5.3 Flexibility models in British, German and American establishments abroad

As is evident from the previous subsection, foreign ownership does in some cases exert a clear influence on establishment flexibility models, albeit without fundamentally challenging the dominant national models. This influence has two components: the transnational effect, *i.e.* the effect of the company itself, and the country of origin effect. In order to be able to investigate these effects in greater depth, we will examine the flexibility models adopted by German, British and American establishments[6] with

5 One certainly has to take into account that a simple bivariate analysis like this may only be an indicator for the above mentioned reasoning. We therefore additionally carry out a multivariate analysis in Section 6.5.4.

6 Germany, the UK and the USA because these are three major countries of origin of companies operating abroad in the dataset.

250 or more employees in the countries under investigation. German establishments in Germany and British establishments in the UK are of course excluded. Table 6.4 presents the results for the three groups of establishments.

Significant differences can also be observed in the use of flexible working times. However, whereas an almost equal share of British and German establishments (47%) use this instrument, only about 39% of American ones do so. As with overtime, there is a very considerable difference between the share of German establishments abroad and that of establishments in Germany that use this instrument. The same is true of British establishments abroad and establishments in the UK.

Table 6.4 Share of establishments with 250 employees and more that use certain flexibility instruments, by selected countries of origin

	British establishments	German establishments	US establishments
Overtime	63.0	86.2	81.3
Flexible working times	47.0	46.8	39.0
External labour	54.5	64.7	67.0
Recruitment/dismissal	26.5	17.7	32.0

Note: All figures have significant differences (Cramer's V).
Source: EUCOWE, own calculations.

British establishments abroad make least use of external labour, with only 54.5% reporting that they do so, compared with about two thirds of German and American establishments abroad.

The use of recruitment and dismissals as a means of dealing with variations in demand is most frequent among American establishments abroad (32.0%). About one quarter of British establishments and just 18% of German establishments have recourse to this flexibility instrument. For this form of flexibility as well, there is an enormous difference between British establishments abroad and in the UK.

Essentially, these results can be interpreted as supporting the existence of a country of origin effect, since different flexibility patterns are associated with the various countries of origin. Finally, for all four types of flexibility investigated, significant differences were observed between the establishments from three different countries of origin. However, certain reservations arise when it comes to comparison of these results with those for establishments in Great Britain and Germany. Considerable differences were observed between establishments in Great Britain and British establishments abroad, and the same applies to establishments in Germany and German establishments abroad.[7]

6.5.4 Multivariate analysis of flexible working time

The results obtained to date make the presumption of a hierarchy of effects appear plausible. The local environment effect seems to exert a considerably stronger influence on establishments' flexibility patterns than the transnational and country of origin effects, *i.e.* the effects produced by the establishments' characteristics. In order to verify this hierarchy of effects, logistic regressions for one of the types of flexibility investigated, namely flexible working times, will be calculated by way of example (Table 6.5). This type of flexibility was selected because it was here that the greatest differences between the countries were observed in the descriptive analyses, as well as significant differences between the various types of establishment. Dummies for the countries are generated as independent variables for the local environment effects. The independent variable "existence of a foreign owner" is used to represent the transnational effect. In order also to be able to investigate the country of origin effect, the three nationalities of foreign owners used above (USA, UK and Germany) are introduced into the regression as dummies. In addition to these effect variables, dummies for age, sector and size of establishment are included in the logistic regression as control variables. Additionally, we test whether membership of a corporate group exerts any influence.

A step-wise procedure was adopted in order that we could check the influence of the three effects on each other. In model 1 (Table 6.5), the only variable included in addition to the control variables is "foreign owner". A negative effect on the probability of the use of flexible working times is observed for establishments in foreign ownership. Domestically owned establishments have a higher probability of using flexible working times in order to deal with variations in demand. This provides empirical confirmation of the existence of the transnational effect. In model 2, in addition to the control variables, the variables for the three countries of origin (Germany, the UK and the USA) are introduced in order to test for the country of origin effect.

---

7 Regrettably, because of the relatively small number of establishments in our sample, we are unable to analyse establishments from individual countries operating in individual host countries, in order to control for the effect of different host countries.

Table 6.5 Logistic regressions for establishments with 250+ employees for the dependent variable "flexible working times"

	Model 1	Model 2	Model 3	Model 4
Sector				
Services	-0.007	-0.010	-0.030	-0.104
Manufacturing	Ref.	Ref.	Ref.	Ref.
Size				
500+ employees	0.655***	0.636***	0.654***	0.111
250–499 employees	Ref.	Ref.	Ref.	Ref.
Age				
Between 5 and 10 years old	-0.464	-0.370	-0.373	-0.336
Older than 10 years	-0.651	-0.188	-0.362	-0.303
Less than 5 years	Ref.	Ref.	Ref.	Ref.
Individual company or group				
Individual. company	0.129	0.151	0.116	-0.415+
Group	Ref.	Ref.	Ref.	Ref.
Transnational effect				
Foreign owner	-0.385**	-	-0.132	-0.062
Domestic owner	Ref.	-	Ref.	Ref.
Country of origin effect				
German owner	-	-0.757+	-0.665	0.159
No German owner	-	Ref.	Ref.	Ref.
American owner	-	-0.740**	-0.657*	-0.687*
No American owner	-	Ref.	Ref.	Ref.
British owner	-	-0.474	-0.388	-0.289
No British owner	-	Ref.	Ref.	Ref.
Local environment effect				
France	-	-	-	-1.920***
Netherlands	-	-	-	-2.538***
UK	-	-	-	-2.709***
Portugal	-	-	-	-2.448***
Germany	-	-	Ref.	Ref.
Intercept	-0.032	-0.113	-0.048	1.882***
Pseudo-R^2	0.0257	0.0300	0.0316	0.1984
Chi^2	30.66***	36.07***	37.68***	236.32***
N	862	869	862	862

+ P<0.1; * P<0.05; ** P<0.01; *** p<0.001
Source: EUCOWE, own calculations.

Whereas no significant effect is found for British owners, establishments in both German[8] and American ownership have a significantly lower probability of using this type of flexibility than establishments not in German or American ownership. However, the value for German-owned establishments is only weakly significant. Overall, the existence of a country of

8 i.e. German-owned establishments operating abroad.

origin effect can be established by means of this model, even if it applies only to two out of three countries of origin and to varying extents.

In model 3, both the transnational and country of origin effects are included, in addition to the control variables. The results show that the most consistent effect is found in American-owned establishments. The already weak effect for German-owned establishments is no longer significant in model 3, which is also true of the foreign establishment effect overall. This combination of results can be interpreted by means of the hierarchy of effects posited in the descriptive analysis. The transnational effect (foreign establishments) and country of origin effects (German and American establishments) can be detected independently of each other, but as soon as both effects are tested for in the same model, only the country of origin effect for the USA remains. This latter effect is, therefore, stronger than the transnational effect. Thus the fact of being American in origin is of greater importance for the lower probability of using flexible working times than the mere fact of being a foreign establishment.

In the final stage of the multivariate analysis, the dummies for the countries under investigation, *i.e.* the establishments' locations, are added in order to test for the local environment effect. The addition of the country variables increases the pseudo-R^2, that is the measure of the explanatory power of logistic regressions[9], from 0.03 to about 0.2. In addition, all the country effects are highly significant. Thus the greatest contribution to explaining the use of flexible working times is made in this model by the establishment's local environment, which can be interpreted as further clear evidence of the hierarchy of effects. In all the other countries, the probability of using this flexibility instrument is considerably lower than in Germany. The greatest difference is between Germany and the UK, while the smallest is between France and Germany. However, the country of origin effect remains for American-owned establishments. Such establishments obviously have a lower probability of using flexible working times, regardless of location.

The significant effects of the size of establishment in models 1 to 3 and of individual company status in model 4 constitute a further interesting aspect. It is known from various studies that larger establishments also make more frequent use of flexible working times (Bauer *et al.*, 2004). This finding is confirmed in the first three models. However, this size effect disappears in favour of the influence of membership of a corporate

9 In contrast to the R^2 of linear regressions, pseudo-R^2 is only an approximate measure of the explained variance.

group when the country variables are incorporated into the model. Obviously the decisive effect that increases the probability of using flexible working times is this membership of a group, rather than sheer size.

6.6 Conclusions

The results obtained confirm with some certainty the existence of all the effects listed at the outset, namely the country of origin, transnational and local environment effects. The influence of an establishment's country of origin and that of the host country were both demonstrated unequivocally. On the basis of these differences in the use of the various types of flexibility, specific flexibility patterns for the five countries under investigation could be detected. The differences between these national flexibility patterns are very pronounced, and the local environment effect is accordingly very powerful.

The second stage of our analysis provided further confirmation of the existence of the transnational and country of origin effects, although their influence appears to be considerably reduced. Certainly there are statistically verified differences between the flexibility patterns adopted by domestic and foreign-owned establishments; however, the differences between the two groups are considerably smaller than those between the various countries. Another significant finding from this part of the analysis is that no differences were found within the various countries between domestic and foreign-owned establishments with regard to the main types of flexibility.

The specific investigation of the country of origin effect, carried out by comparing the flexibility patterns adopted by American, German and British establishments operating abroad, also revealed significant differences between these groups of establishments. German and American establishments operating abroad report considerably more frequent use of overtime than British establishments operating abroad. On the other hand, considerably more German and British establishments abroad, compared to their American counterparts, use flexible working time in order to deal with variations in demand. However, the strength of the country of origin effect has to be put into context, since the differences between German firms abroad and establishments in Germany as well as between British establishments abroad and establishments in the UK are very large, which is further evidence that establishments tend to adapt to a considerable degree to their local environments.

The question of whether the above-mentioned effects influence establishments' flexibility patterns, and if so what form that influence takes, can be answered with the aid of a hierarchy of effects. The local environment effect clearly emerges as having the strongest influence. The country of origin effect has significantly less influence, since it could be detected in all four models only for American establishments. No effect could be observed for British establishments, while for German-owned establishments the effect loses its significance when it is tested with the transnational effect. The weakest influence is that exerted by the transnational effect. To that extent, all the effects have a significant influence, but the basic shape of the flexibility pattern is determined by the local environment in which a company is embedded. Only then do the country of origin and transnational effects make themselves felt in the hierarchy of effects.

Some clear conclusions can be drawn with regard to the debate, outlined at the beginning of this chapter, on the power of the local environment, that is the extent to which national policies can influence companies in general and multinational companies in particular. We have been unable to find any empirical evidence to support the argument that the influence of (multinational) companies in a globalised economy is considerably greater than that of national institutional environments.

On the other hand, the massive influence of the local environment effect shows what opportunities for shaping companies' behaviour actually exist here. At this level, the basic conditions for companies are laid down; these are then modified in different ways by individual companies but are not fundamentally called into question. To that extent, it can indeed be argued that ownership does play a role and that a company's country of origin is also influential. However, the key factors determining work organisation still seem to be located in the local environment.

References

Atkinson, J. (1984) Manpower strategies for flexible organizations, *Personnel Management*, August: 28-31.

Bauer, F., H. Groß, E. Munz and S. Sayin (2002) *Arbeits- und Betriebszeiten 2001,* Berichte des ISO 67, Köln: Institut zur Erforschung sozialer Chancen.

Bauer, F., H. Groß, K. Lehmann and E. Munz (2004) *Arbeitszeit 2003. Arbeitszeitgestaltung, Arbeitsorganisation und Tätigkeitsprofile,* Berichte des ISO 70, Köln: Institut zur Erforschung sozialer Chancen.

Bauer, F., H. Groß, R. Muñoz de Bustillo y Llorente, E. Fernández Macias and G. Sieglen (2007) Cross-country Comparison of Operating Hours, Capacity

Utilisation, Working Times and Employment, in: L. Delsen, D. Bosworth, H. Groß and R. Muñoz de Bustillo y Llorente (eds.) *Operating Hours and Working Times. A Survey of Capacity Utilisation and Employment in the European Union,* Heidelberg: Physica-Verlag, 41-71.

Bornschier, V. (1980) *Multinationale Konzerne, Wirtschaftspolitik und nationale Entwicklung im Weltsystem,* Frankfurt/Main/New York: Campus-Verlag.

Chase-Dunn, C. (1990) *Global Formation: Structures of the World Economy,* Cambridge: Basil Blackwell.

Delsen, L. (2002) Flexibility Conflict?, in: F. Bauer, H. Groß, and G. Sieglen (eds.) *Operating hours in Europe*, Berichte des ISO 66, Köln: Institut zur Erforschung sozialer Chancen, 217-236.

Delsen, L., D. Bosworth, H. Groß, and R. Muñoz de Bustillo y Llorente (eds.) (2007) *Operating Hours and Working Times. A Survey of Capacity Utilisation and Employment in the European Union*, Heidelberg: Physica-Verlag.

Flecker, J. (1999) "Sachzwang Flexibilisierung"? Unternehmensreorganisation und flexible Beschäftigungsformen, *Forba-Schriftenreihe 2/99*, Wien: FORBA.

Flecker, J. (2000) Transnationale Unternehmen und die Macht des Ortes, in: C. Dörrenbächer and D. Plehwe (eds.) *Grenzenlose Kontrolle? Organisatorischer Wandel und politische Macht multinationaler Unternehmen,* Berlin: Edition Sigma, 45-70.

Hirsch, J. (1995) *Der nationale Wettbewerbsstaat*, Berlin: Edition ID-Archiv.

Hirsch-Kreinsen, H. (1997) Globalisierung der Industrie: ihre Grenzen und Folgen, *WSI Mitteilungen*, 7: 487-494.

Hirst, P. and G. Thompson (1996) *Globalization in Question: The International Economy and the Possibilities of Governance*, Cambridge: Polity Press.

Krugman, P. (1994) Competitiveness: A Dangerous Obsession, *Foreign Affairs*, 73 (2): 28-46.

Lehndorff, S. and D. Voss-Dahm (2005) The delegation of uncertainty. Flexibility of service work and the role of the market, in: G. Bosch and S. Lehndorff (eds.) *Working in the service sector – a tale from different worlds*, London, New York: Routledge, 89-115.

Martinez-Lucio, M. and P. Blyton (1995) Industrial relations and the management of flexibility: factors shaping developments in Spain and the United Kingdom, *International Journal of Human Resource Management*, 6 (2): 271-291.

Mason, M. and D. Encarnation (1994) *Does Ownership matter? Japanese Multinationals in Europe*, Oxford: Clarendon Press.

Narr, W.-D. and A. Schubert (1994) *Weltökonomie: die Misere der Politik,* Frankfurt am Main: Suhrkamp.

Pannenberg, M. and G. G. Wagner (2001) Overtime work, overtime compensation and the distribution of economic well-being: evidence for West Germany and Great Britain, *Discussion paper series Forschungsinstitut zur Zukunft der Arbeit 318*, Bonn: IZA Forschungsinstitut zur Zukunft der Arbeit.

Rubery, J. and D. Grimshaw (2003) *The Organization of Employment – An International Perspective*, Basingstoke, Hampshire: Palgrave Macmillan.

Schief, S. (2003) *Globalisierung. Entwicklungspfade der Internationalisierung deutscher Konzerne*, Frankfurt am Main: Peter Lang Verlag.

Schief, S. (2008) Does location matter? – An empirical investigation of flexibility patterns in foreign and domestic companies in five European countries, *International Journal of Human Resource Management* (in press)

Schmidt, W. and B. Dworschak (2002) Entgelt- und Arbeitszeitregime unter dem Einfluß von Internationalisierung und multinationalen Unternehmen: ein deutsch-britischer Vergleich, in: *Schlussbericht des Schwerpunktprogrammes "Regulierung und Restrukturierung der Arbeit in den Spannungsfeldern von Globalisierung und Dezentralisierung" der Deutschen Forschungsgemeinschaft*, Erlangen, 69-98.

Streeck, W. (1993) The rise and decline of neocorporatism, in: L. Ulman, B. Eichengreen and W. Dickens (eds.) *Labor and an Integrated Europe*, Washington: The Brookings Institution, 80-101.

7 Capacity Utilisation, Working Time and the Quality of Work

Enrique Fernández-Macías and Rafael Muñoz de Bustillo Llorente

7.1 Introduction

Human beings face a double restriction in relation to time and its use. Firstly, time is clearly the ultimate scarce resource; there are only 24 hours in a day, seven days in a week and 52 weeks in a year. Although there are activities that can be done simultaneously, such as listening to the radio and cooking, generally speaking the time we devote to something, to work for example, has to be taken out of other activities, such as raising a family, or enjoying a film. Each person faces, therefore, an opportunity cost in terms of time in every activity he or she does. Secondly, human beings are social animals and the use of time is socially modelled. Since history has been recorded, men and women have coordinated their activities in order to work during certain hours, and rest and amuse themselves at other times; for historical and cultural reasons, using the words of the Ecclesiastes, "to everything there is a season and a time for every purpose under heaven". Some of these patterns of time use are biologically determined (circadian cycle, night and day, *etc.*), while others are explained by cultural factors.

Throughout history, the amount of time used to perform productive activities has followed an inverted U shape, rising with the arrival of agriculture and husbandry and even further with the coming of the industrial age, reaching a maximum at the end of the 18th century, and diminishing since then. So generally speaking, we can say that nowadays workers in high income countries devote less time to work than a century ago. But along with this process of reduction of working time, according to many analysts the last few decades have witnessed a slow process of de-

L. Delsen et al., *Comparative Analyses of Operating Hours and Working Times in the European Union*,
DOI: 10.1007/978-3-7908-2185-7_7,

standardisation of working time.[1] The once dominant rigid distribution of time between work, leisure and rest, represented by the "9 to 5" job, has become less common.[2] If we assume that the old time system of coordination of activities, so as to have most people doing the same things (working, resting, amusing themselves) at the same time, had a rationality based on individual and social preferences, this change will have an impact on the work-life balance of workers.

There are two major causes behind such a change. First, the process of structural change in high income countries has transformed them into service economies, and services, to a great extent, have to be produced at the same time they are consuming (see Bauer and Groß, Chapter 4, this volume). So production time has had to change and synchronise with consumption time, a change that, coinciding with an increase in the labour force participation of women, has lead to an increase in the length of production times. Second, longer production hours, *ceteris paribus*, mean a higher rate of profit.[3] In a time of increasing competition owing to the growing globalisation of the economy, a move towards higher capital utilisation rates can be expected (see Schief, Chapter 6, this volume).

The purpose of this chapter is to study the impact of different levels of capacity utilisation by firms on the organisation of working time, and through this, on the quality of work. In order to do so, in Section 7.2 we will briefly develop an analytical framework to be used to study the relationship between the time-intensity of capacity utilisation and the quality of work. With this background, in Section 7.3 we will explore the impact on the quality of work of the level of capacity utilisation and the different systems of work organisation used to achieve a higher degree of utilisation of capital, using both the EUCOWE data set (see Delsen, Bauer, Cette and Smith, Chapter 1, this volume and Delsen *et al.* (2007)) and the European Working Conditions Survey (see Parent-Thirion, Fernández Macías, Hurley and Vermeylen, 2007). Finally, in Section 7.4 we will review the main results of our analysis.

1 For a detailed discussion, see Muñoz de Bustillo et al. (2003).

2 For example, according to Hogarth et al. (2001) in the UK only 35% of employees worked the standard week (Monday to Friday 8-10 am to 4-6 pm).

3 $r = (b/v).u$, where r is the profit rate, defined as profits in relation to total capital, b is the share of profits from production, v is the capital-output relation, and u the index of capacity utilisation, defined as used capital in relation to total capital.

7.2 Capacity utilisation, organisation of working time and the quality of work: analytical framework

Figure 7.1 reproduces the interrelations between capacity utilisation, organisation of working time and the quality of work. Capacity utilisation refers to the extent to which an organisation uses its installed productive capacity: in the context of this chapter, we use the *extension* of operating times as a proxy measure of capacity utilisation (see below). Working time refers to time spent in paid work (therefore, excluding unpaid work, such as domestic or voluntary work). Finally, quality of work in this chapter refers both to quality of work itself (that is, the aspects of work that have an impact on the well-being of the worker) and work-life balance (that is, the possibility to have a fulfilled life inside and outside paid work).

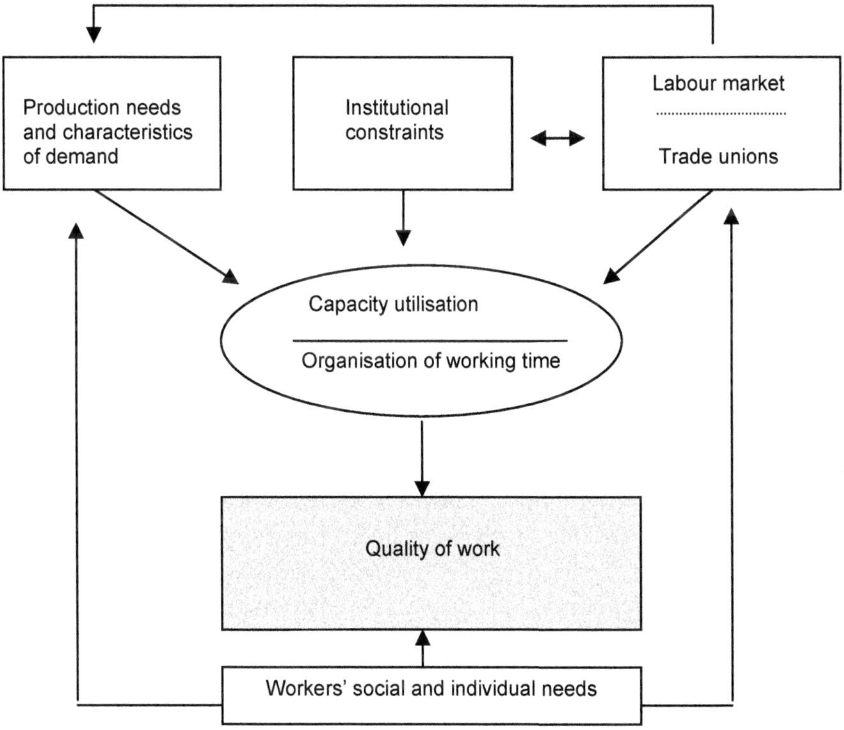

Figure 7.1 Capacity utilisation, organisation of working time and quality of work

Firms face a set of restrictions, related both to the type of demand and its temporal distribution (daily, weekly and yearly), and the technical characteristics of production (capital intensity, human capital needs, *etc.*): these factors shape the decisions taken by firms related to the level of utilisation of installed productive capacity. Furthermore, production takes place in a specific social environment, so firms also face institutional restraints that affect their capacity to organise production and working time according to their preferences. The social and institutional environment affects firm decisions either by changing the cost of specific working time organisation systems they would otherwise like to follow, or directly by forbidding certain practices – Sunday work, or night work for women, for example. Finally, the individual preferences of workers themselves, through the functioning of the labour market, will influence the final organisation of working time. Obviously, the importance of this last restriction will change with the situation on the labour market. In tight labour markets, it will be easier for workers to have their preferences heeded or otherwise to obtain compensation for not doing so, while in labour markets with excess supply the opposite will be the case. The existence of trade unions will also play a role in the process of meeting workers' preferences by amplifying their negotiating power.

A key element of Figure 7.1 is the potential conflict between the social and the individual needs of workers (in terms of their use of time, including duration of work, rest and other activities, and its distribution throughout the day, the week and the year) and the needs of the firm (also both in quantitative terms, *i.e.* duration of working time, and in terms of its distribution throughout the day, the week and the year). Generally speaking it is in the interest of the firm to prolong production time as much as possible, as longer hours of production mean a more extensive use of the existing capital, and therefore an increase in the rate of profit. There are two possible ways to meet this goal. The first is to have long working days. The second is to have successive workers substituting each other, decoupling operating and working times. The first system means working longer hours, the second working at different hours (or days). From the point of view of the worker, again generally speaking and *ceteris paribus*, shorter working hours are preferred to longer working hours, especially as income rises, in order to gain time to do other things outside of the realm of work. But it is not only the length of the working day/week/year that matters. Just as important as the duration of work is its schedule, *i.e.* its distribution throughout a given day/week/year. For biological reasons, night time is usually preferred to day for rest. For social reasons, people prefer spending their free time in time slots, where there is collective free time. The value of leisure time is often dependent on cultural patterns of time use. Similarly families face restrictions related to the school hours of their children, or the caring needs of their elders, leading to compatibility problems between working and other activities that also have fixed schedules. Thus the interests of companies and workers are likely to enter into conflict.

There is an abundant and growing literature on the implication of different working time arrangements on the quality of work. Earlier studies tended to focus on the impact of working time arrangements on the health and well-being of the worker, whereas more recent literature tends to focus much more on work-life balance issues (see Table 7.1). There is a reason for such a shift of concerns. Before the massive incorporation of women into the labour force, which took place progressively in the second half of the last century, the division of labour within the household solved many of the work-life incompatibility problems. Each partner had a full-time *job* – a market job usually performed by the man and a non-market job performed by the woman – with a specific timetable, and the synchronisation of the different obligations posed no major problems. The increasing participation of women in the labour force had a dramatic impact on the ability of households to meet simultaneously their labour market and household and social responsibilities, and the literature has echoed this change. The massive influx of women into the labour force led to changes in the temporal distribution of production in sectors of activity such as retailing and personal services, thus increasing the demand of the firms for non-standard working times.

Table 7.1 presents a summary of some of the results commonly found in this literature. As we can see, according to the literature, working time arrangements are not neutral in relation to the quality of work. Generally speaking there seems to be a negative relation between shift work and workers' well-being. This negative relationship explains the common existence of a night bonus premium to compensate workers for the working conditions associated with the night shift.[4] Johnson's (1997) analysis of the characteristics and implications of night shifts in Canada is illuminating in this respect. According to Johnson, one third of Canadian night-shift workers were working on night shifts as the only means to get a job in the firm, while another third mentioned higher wages as the main reason. The

4 In Spain, according to our analysis of the Ministry of Labour's National Collective Agreements Database, a 25% bonus is common in many activities, including cement, convenience stores, soft drinks, photography, animal feed or nursery homes. In others sectors, such as in the textile industries, the bonus is 28%, and in chemistry, it is 50%.

Table 7.1 Summary of previous findings on the impact of different working time arrangements on the quality of work

Type of working time arrangement	Potential advantages for the workers	Potential disadvantages for the workers	Sources
Shift work	Higher wages Increase choice of working time Reduction in day care cost Quieter and lower supervision during night shifts	Health (gastrointestinal, cardiovascular and sleep disorders), especially related to night shifts. Interference with social and family life Lower predictability in case of irregular shifts depending on the conditions of demand	Fudge (1980) Bosworth and Dawkins (1981) Wedderburn (1992) Rosa and Colligan (1997) Jansen (1987) Johnson (1997) Wallace (1998) Cullen *et al.* (2002) Rajaratnam and Arendt (2001)
Long hours	Long hours are often accompanied by more time autonomy Higher wages, often high positions	Health (cardiovascular, sleep problems, stress) Increased likelihood of occupational injury and illness Interference with social and family life	Harrington (2001) Dembe *et al.* (2005) Shields (1999) Liu and Tanaka (2002)
Part-time work	Better compatibility with other activities owing to low working hours	Underemployment in cases of involuntary part-time work. Higher work intensity and stress (the PT workers work mostly at peak time) Problems of communication and social interaction with other workers Concentration of PT work in low wage and low qualification sectors. Worse chances of promotion	ILO (1992) Corral and Susi (2004)
Compressed work	Increase in the length of rest periods Reduction in commuting time	Reduction of free time In working days Long working hours Increase of accidents at work and on route owing to longer working hours	Tepas (1985) Wedderburn (1996)
Flexible working time	Improvement of work-life balance	Longer working hours Increase in work intensity	MTAS (2000) Golden (2001)
Telework	No commuting Improvement of work life balance	Worse working conditions Intrusion of the firm in the private working life of the worker Isolation from other workers Longer working hours	European Telework Online Cullen *et al.* (2002)

rest were workers already employed in the firms when the firms decided to extend their operating hours to include a night shift as well. As we can see, there is not much room left for those without uncompensated preferences for working at night. The higher rate of labour turnover in firms with extended operating times, 10% versus 3.4% in U.S. companies (Circadian Technologies, 2004), points to a similar conclusion. Long working hours have also been found to have a negative impact on workers' health and general well-being, although the literature on this issue is scarcer and somewhat less conclusive. Part-time work has negative implications in terms of pay, career and development of the affected workers, but may lead to better possibilities for the reconciliation of work and life. Compressed work and flexible work schedules are arrangements that can increase the flexibility for the worker to determine his/her working hours, which may entail better work-life balance opportunities. However, paradoxically these working time arrangements are often correlated with longer working hours and therefore with negative health outcomes. This apparent paradox results from the fact that managers and professional workers tend to have more autonomy but work very long hours: in fact, working long hours may have become a sign of status for some categories of workers (see Gershuny, 2005).

In summary, the literature points to the existence of a trade-off between the quality of work and the extension of operating hours. This is the hypothesis we will test in the next section of the chapter.

7.3 Capacity utilisation, working time and quality of work from an empirical perspective

In this section, we will develop the model shown in Figure 7.1, using data from surveys on both capacity utilisation and working conditions. We will concentrate on the lower section of the model, trying to show empirically how capacity utilisation affects the quality of work and work-life balance through the organisation of working time, although we will also give some hints on the determinants of capacity utilisation itself (represented in the upper section of Figure 7.1). We use the findings from previous studies summarised in Table 7.1 as a guide for our own empirical analysis, based in two recent datasets: on the one hand, to study capacity utilisation and the working time systems used for extending operating hours we use the 2003 EUCOWE dataset (see Delsen, Bauer, Cette and Smith, Chapter 1, this volume); on the other, we draw on the 2005 edition of the European

Working Conditions Survey[5] (EWCS) to study how the different working time systems correlate with the quality of work and the capacities of workers to achieve a good work-life balance.

7.3.1 An overview of the determinants of capacity utilisation

Without claiming to carry out a detailed analysis of the determinants of capacity utilisation (other chapters of this volume deal specifically with that issue), we will briefly discuss the differences in patterns of capacity utilisation by sector and size of establishment in each of the six countries in the EUCOWE survey. This is important as general background to the rest of the analysis, as it gives us a deeper understanding of the concept which is at the core of the argument, the temporality of capacity utilisation. The indicator of capacity utilisation we will use is the weekly operating hours of the establishment as measured in the EUCOWE survey (based on the direct responses of managers). This simple indicator was chosen because it is directly comparable across countries, sectors and types of establishment, and its meaning is immediately comprehensible.

Table 7.2 shows the results of an ANOVA model with weekly operating hours as the dependent variable and sector, size of establishment and country as independent variables, with a separate ANOVA model for each one of the countries, to test for the existence of differences in the effects of size and sector across countries. In the model for all countries, construction and producer services display the lowest operating hours, and social services the highest (with the secondary sector as the reference category). There is a clear and consistent increase of capacity utilisation by size of establishment. And controlling by sector and size, the level of capacity utilisation is much lower in the Netherlands (Germany is the reference country), as well as Portugal and Spain; France and Germany occupy a very similar position in the middle of the EUCOWE countries and the UK display the longest operating hours.

5 The European Working Conditions Survey is a survey carried out every five years by the European Foundation for the Improvement of Living and Working Conditions, a European tripartite agency based in Dublin. It is based in a multi-stage stratified random sample, representative of the EU working population. For the wave that we will use in this paper, almost 30.000 workers were interviewed face-to-face in the last quarter of 2005. See the methodological annex of Parent-Thirion et al. (2007).

Looking at the ANOVA models for individual countries in Table 7.2, we can also see some interesting deviations from the general pattern. As explained in the ANOVA for all countries, construction and producer services have considerably lower operating hours than manufacturing; but there is a clear exception in the UK (where construction does not differ significantly from manufacturing). Distributive services have lower capacity utilisation than manufacturing in Germany, Spain and France, but not so in the UK, the Netherlands and Portugal. In all countries operating hours are considerably longer in social services than in manufacturing, except in the cases of France (where they do not differ substantially) and Germany (where they are actually lower, in part because operating hours in the manufacturing sector are extraordinarily long in Germany, as indicated by the intercept). By size there is, in all countries, a strong and consistent increase in capacity utilisation, but the impact differs: operating hours increase very steeply with size in the UK and Portugal, and at a much slower rate in the Netherlands.

Table 7.2 Determinants of capacity utilisation

	Model for all countries	ANOVA model for each individual country					
		Germany	Spain	France	UK	Netherlands	Portugal
Intercept	56.36**	64.58**	51.29**	58.18**	49.85**	47.73**	47.34**
Sector							
Primary sector	-2.23	4.62	-2.33	-11.48**	6.85	0.73	-6.59
Construction	-19.16**	-21.27**	-21.42**	-34.81**	2.44	-10.22**	-18.54**
Distributive serv.	-4.04**	-6.89**	-6.97**	-10.00**	1.79	3.26	1.09
Producer services	-15.04**	-25.21**	-18.05**	-20.50**	-0.21	-8.79**	-10.86**
Social services	6.54**	-6.20**	11.34**	0.91	9.82*	7.92**	24.50**
Personal services	19.91**	10.16**	18.37**	17.82**	5.08	22.29**	40.05**
Secondary sector	Ref.	Ref.	Ref.	Ref.	Ref.	Ref.	Ref.
Size							
10-19	6.50**	6.81*	6.70**	7.00*	10.93**	2.29	8.12**
20-99	17.38**	18.27**	17.07**	20.71**	28.36**	8.96**	14.36**
100-249	35.00**	23.84**	44.63**	41.65**	39.60**	20.01**	28.03**
250-499	46.78**	39.43**	48.92**	49.13**	51.71**	41.29**	53.65**
500+	56.31**	53.92**	56.71**	59.37**	63.25**	44.70**	69.40**
1-10 employees	Ref.	Ref.	Ref.	Ref.	Ref.	Ref.	Ref.
Country							
Spain	-4.69**						
France	-0.59						
UK	5.58**						
Netherlands	-11.17**						
Portugal	-5.48**						
Germany	Ref.						
R^2 of each model	0.256	0.237	0.285	0.282	0.153	0.228	0.259

Source: EUCOWE 2003 (data for establishments, unweighted).

Overall, this quick review of the determinants of capacity utilisation according to the EUCOWE survey serves as an empirical illustration of the top half of Figure 7.1. The strong influences of size and sector on the level of capacity utilisation across all countries suggest the importance of economic factors such as the organisation of production and characteristics on demand in determining capacity utilisation (see also Smith, Zagelmeyer and Sieglen, Chapter 6, and Bauer and Groß, Chapter 4, this volume). On the other hand, there are substantial differences between countries even when we control by sector and size of the establishment, indicating the importance of institutional factors such as cultural values, regulatory systems and industrial relations.

7.3.2 Capacity utilisation and the organisation of working time

The next logical step in the schematic diagram displayed in Figure 7.1 is the link between capacity utilisation and the organisation of working time. Both concepts are, in many ways, two sides of the same coin. From the perspective of the establishment, the operating hours of the establishment are the main and most direct determinant of the organisation of working time of employees. However, that does not mean that knowing the time intensity of capacity utilisation, or the extension of operating hours, allows us to determine how working times are organised in different establishments. The implementation of a specific extension of operating time can be achieved with different time organisation systems and arrangements, which imply different costs and benefits for companies and their employees. In this section we examine systems of working time organisation used by establishments in different countries to extend operating hours, by looking at the correlations between the different working time systems and operating hours, in a multivariate regression model (see Table 7.3).

Table 7.3 contains four different regression models: (A) an overall regression model with all data, controlling by sector, size and country, and using as independent variables the different working time systems for which the EUCOWE data provides information (see Delsen, Bauer, Cette and Smith, Chapter 1, this volume)[6]; (B) a model for each country, controlling for size and sector, with the same working time systems as independ-

6 There are indicators for shift work, staggered work, part-time work (in the three cases percentage of workers in the establishment), standard working hours (average per worker) and overtime (hours per worker).

Table 7.3 Operating hours and working time

	(A) Overall model	(B) Models for individual countries					
		Germany	Spain	France	UK	Netherlands	Portugal
Weekly operating hours	56.67	60.41	47.38	57.04	59.34	53.48	55.12
Decoupling rate	1.83	2.01	1.42	1.74	2.03	1.96	1.49
Regression results*							
% Shift workers	0.593	0.652	0.540	0.636	0.639	0.501	0.536
% Staggered workers	0.088			0.120		0.137	0.197
% Part-time workers			-0.111		0.165		
Average working hours	0.044	0.043		0.065	0.128		
Overtime hours per worker	0.045		0.114		0.094	0.050	0.088
Adjusted R Square	0.325	0.390	0.306	0.353	0.434	0.245	0.278

(C) Models for individual sectors	Primary sector	Secondary sector	Construction	Distributive services	Producer services	Social services	Personal services
Weekly operating hours	60.92	56.56	48.76	56.64	51.46	59.17	67.83
Decoupling rate	1.86	1.65	1.43	1.85	1.67	2.12	2.21
Regression results*							
% Shift workers	0.471	0.619	0.552	0.519	0.516	0.705	0.502
% Staggered workers	0.134	0.048	0.060	0.143	0.079	0.055	0.117
% Part-time workers	0.189						0.178
Average working hours	0.234					0.051	
Overtime hours per worker	0.318	0.055	0.133	0.076	0.085		
Adjusted R square	0.211	0.356	0.311	0.271	0.265	0.470	0.263

(D) Models for different establishment sizes	1-9 employees	10-19 employees	20-99 employees	100-249 employees	250-499 employees	500+ employees
Weekly operating hours	51.97	61.64	72.83	85.89	98.89	111.32
Decoupling rate	1.72	1.94	2.21	2.53	2.85	3.26
Regression results*						
% Shift workers	0.386	0.558	0.576	0.548	0.546	0.521
% Staggered workers	0.186	0.135	0.098	0.114	0.082	
% Part-time workers			0.050			
Average working hours	0.128					
Overtime hours per worker	0.083	0.075	0.052	0.077	0.082	0.041
Adjusted R square	0.194	0.294	0.307	0.261	0.240	0.238

Note: * standardised BETA coefficients.
All the coefficients significant at the 0.01 level (except overtime hours per worker in the Netherlands and in establishments with more than 500 employees, which are significant at the 0.05 level).
Source: EUCOWE 2003 (data for establishments, unweighted).

ent variables; (C) a similar model for each sector, controlling for country and size; and (D) a similar model for establishment size, controlling for sector and country. This combination of models allows us to account for the overall effect of each variable and also for any possible interactions. Since the independent variables have different measurement scales, in

Table 7.3 we show the standardised (beta) coefficients instead of the normal beta coefficients. The regressions all included the control variables (sector, size and country), but the variables referring to the different working time systems were introduced step-wise. All the coefficients shown are significant at the 0.01 level (except overtime hours per worker in the Netherlands and in establishments with more than 500 employees, which are significant at the 0.05 level). The R^2 shows the impact of the variables of working time discounting the variables used for controlling purposes (size, sector and country).[7]

Overall, the first impression we can draw from the table is that shift work is the most important tool used by establishments for extending operating hours, in all sectors, sizes of establishment and countries (see also Cette, Kocoglu and Sylvain, Chapter 2, and Delsen and Smits, Chapter 3, this volume). The overall model (A) shows that shift work has by far the strongest impact, and that staggered work patterns (which can be considered a more flexible type of shift work) also have a significant (though smaller) impact, as do average working hours and overtime (albeit quite marginally). The impact of part-time work is so limited that it is not even significant when controlling for all the other variables in the multivariate model, suggesting that part-time work is not significantly used as a tool for extending or varying operating hours.

In all countries, shift work is by far the most important working time arrangement used for extending operating hours (see panel B of Table 7.3). In Germany, only with shifts and average working time can we explain almost 40% of the variation of operating hours; in France and the UK shifts are also particularly important. Staggered working times are used significantly as a tool for extending operating hours in France, Netherlands and Portugal, but not so much in the other countries. The proportion of employees working part-time is only significantly related to the extension of operating hours in the UK (positively, which suggests that in the UK part-time work is used to extend operating hours) and Spain (but in this

7 This means that the actual R^2 for all cases is larger (so the models' fit is relatively high), but we wanted to eliminate the impact of the control variables so that the R^2 in the table can be used as an approximate indication of the importance of the working time tools in the determination of the operating hours in each case. In all the regression models in Table 7.3 only the contribution of the working time arrangements to the R^2 statistic is shown (subtracting from the total R^2 of the model the R^2 that results from controlling for sector, size and/or country). This means that the R^2 shown here is very conservative: most likely, it underestimates the real value.

case, the relation is negative, which suggests the opposite: part-time work in Spain is used in establishments with lower-than-average operating hours). Average working hours has a quite marginal correlation with the establishments' operating times everywhere except in the UK where the extension of individual working hours is a relatively important – but less so than shift work – tool for extending operating time). Overtime is used significantly for extending operating hours in Spain, the UK and Portugal (also in the Netherlands, but to a much lesser extent) (see also Delsen and Smits, Chapter 3, this volume).

The regression models in each of the sectors (panel C) show that again, shifts are the key working time system for extending operating hours everywhere, although it is particularly important in social services and manufacturing (where they explain most of the variance in operating hours). Staggered working times are significant in all sectors, but the standardised coefficient shows that its impact is relatively minor except in personal and distributive services, which seems to indicate that staggered working times are to some extent an adaptation of the traditional shift systems to the flexibility required by services (see also Bauer and Groß, Chapter 4, this volume). Part-time work is only important in personal services while overtime, has a significant impact in agriculture, industry, construction, distribution and producer services, and is most importantly in construction. On the other hand, average working times do not play a very significant role in any of the sectors (except agriculture).

Finally, in panel D of Table 7.3 we can see the same regression model for the different size classes of establishment while controlling by sector and country. Again, shift work appears everywhere, but in this case the importance of shift working, as indicated by the standardised coefficients, varies considerably. The use of shift work as a tool for extending operating hours is much less important in smaller establishments than elsewhere. By contrast, staggered working times are much more important in smaller establishments, and their importance diminishes with the size of the establishment. In smaller establishments, average working hours also have an important correlation with operating hours, something which does not happen in any of the other establishment sizes. This in part results from the fact that in smaller establishments the rate of decoupling – the ratio of operating hours and average working hours of employees – is lower. Finally, the use of overtime work does not depend significantly on the size of the establishment, as in all sizes it is significant, and the standardised coefficient shows only a marginal impact on operating hours.

To wrap up, we can summarise the main conclusions of this section as follows:

a Shift work is the main tool for extending operating hours everywhere, as illustrated by the strong correlation between the proportion of shift workers and operating hours in all sectors, sizes and countries.
b Staggered working times have a much weaker impact on the extension of operating hours. The countries which make most use of this working time arrangement for extending operating hours are Portugal, the Netherlands and France. It is most frequently used for extending operating hours in distributive and personal services, and in small establishments.
c Part-time work is used only marginally as a tool for determining operating hours, and has only very minor correlation with both indicators. Only in the UK (positively) and in Spain (negatively) is this correlation significant. The (positive) correlation is strongest in the personal services sector.
d Average working hours have a limited relationship with operating hours everywhere except in the UK (where it seems that simply extending the hours of employees is used as a tool for extending the hours of operation), and in the smaller establishments (mainly because in small establishments operating hours and average working hours are more similar and there is limited decoupling).
e Finally, overtime is significantly correlated with operating hours almost everywhere, but the strength of this correlation is not very important. This suggests that overtime is used as a tool for extending operating hours, but only to a limited extent. Overtime has a stronger correlation with operating times in Spain, the UK and Portugal, and in the construction sector.[8]

7.3.3 Working time and the quality of work

In the previous section, we identified the working time tools most used for extending operating hours in European companies: shift work was by far the most important, followed by staggered working times (which is in fact a form of shift work in which the successive shifts overlap), the extension

8 The fact that the use of overtime for varying operating times is highest in the sector with lowest operating hours supports the idea that it is a tool only for the marginal extension of operating times. Where operating times are short, but there is a need to extend them to a certain level, the easiest way to do it is probably through the use of overtime.

of normal working hours of employees and the use of overtime. With this information, we can now finally move to the last part of Figure 7.1 and look at the impact of these working time arrangements on the quality of work.

Unfortunately, the EUCOWE survey did not include any information on the conditions of work of individual employees. This means that for studying the impact of these working time arrangements on the quality of work we have to turn to another source, in this case the 2005 European Working Conditions Survey (EWCS). This survey, which is carried out every five years by the European Foundation for the Improvement of Living and Working Conditions – a European agency located in Dublin – is representative of the working population of all EU member states and includes very detailed information on conditions of work and employment, including of course working time arrangements. Therefore, in principle it suits our purposes: using an EWCS sub-sample of employees in the six countries covered in the EUCOWE study, we can look at the impact of the working time arrangements identified in the previous section on the quality of work.

But although the EWCS does cover the working time arrangements discussed in the previous section, the definitions are slightly different, making the link between EUCOWE and EWCS problematic in some cases:

- Shift work, which is the most important tool used in EU companies for extending operating hours, is very similarly defined in both surveys; in fact the overall estimations of the share of shift work in both surveys match almost perfectly[9], despite the big differences in methodology.
- On the other hand, in the EWCS there is no concept of staggered working times. As discussed earlier, the difference between shift work and staggered working times is small (staggered working times are basically overlapping shifts): in fact, from the perspective of the individual worker, there is no difference between traditional (non-overlapping) shift work and staggered working times, which is the main reason why there is no such a concept in the EWCS. However, this same reason makes the problem relatively unimportant since from the perspective of workers, the difference between shift work and staggered working times is very marginal, our discussion of the impact of shift work on quality of work broadly applies to staggered working times as well.

9 The difference in the estimation of the number of shift workers is less than two percentage points in all countries except France.

- Finally, in the EWCS only overall hours of work are measured, without differentiating contractual hours and overtime (paid or unpaid). So we will not be able to differentiate the impact on quality of work of the extension of contractual hours and overtime. Again, the problem is not so big because in the two cases the logic is the same, to extend the hours of work of the individual worker. Therefore, what we will study is the influence of long working hours on the quality of work.

Even though we think this section constitutes a relevant corollary of the previous analysis, the reader must be aware that this final element of the overall argument will be only an approximation. Ideally, we would like to have good measures of operating hours, working time arrangements and the quality of work from one single source: we would be entirely sure that the definitions are identical and we could even link the three elements directly (at the level of individual companies and within them, individual workers). But at present, this is not possible for lack of available data[10], so we have to use two different data sources (EUCOWE and EWCS) to be able to link capacity utilisation and quality of work. The link is through the organisation of working time, or more concretely through the specific working time arrangements used for extending operating hours.[11]

Analytic strategy

Quality of work is intrinsically a multivariate, multifaceted concept, which implies a considerable difficulty for the analysis. Put simply, we had two main options for studying the impact of working time arrangements on the quality of work: 1) we could try to develop some type of composite index of quality of work and then use it as the dependent variable; or 2) we could simultaneously use several different variables, that are arguably part of quality of work, as dependent variables. The first strategy would require an effort which is clearly beyond this chapter[12], so we opted for the second alternative, even though it has its problems as well. Showing many differ-

10 Some linked employer-employee surveys (such as the UK WERS survey) may in principle be used for this purpose but unfortunately, there is no international European survey with these characteristics at present.

11 The concepts are not identical, but they are broadly comparable so at least until more adequate international sources are available, it should serve as an approximation.

12 There is still no widely accepted notion of quality of work at the European level that could be used here.

ent indicators of quality of work at the same time makes it difficult to reach clear conclusions, as the different indicators may move in different directions. Furthermore the technical complexity of the analysis can increase considerably (especially if, as is the case here, we want to study the link between quality of work and several different independent variables).

Our strategy for the analysis of the link between the working time arrangements identified in the previous section and the quality of work is as follows:

- First, we selected a list of eighteen indicators of quality of work from the 2005 European Working Conditions Survey. We simply selected those indicators that in principle were related to the organisation of working time: the scheduling, variability and autonomy of work, five key indicators of health and safety, five indicators on remuneration, satisfaction with the conditions of work and perception of work-life conflict. Even though there is a certain degree of arbitrary decision in this list (as in any other), the fact that we cover several different aspects, all of them arguably central to the quality of work, means that the final results should be fairly balanced.
- Second, we specified the working time arrangements that we would use as independent variables in the analysis. As discussed before, there are two main issues that we can cover: shift work and long working hours. For shift work, we first identified all those working within any type of shift system. Then, we specified two further groups for those working *rotating shifts* and those working *night shifts* at least one week a month: these specific types of shifts, as we will see, have important implications for the conditions of work. For long working hours, we defined two types: *long weekly working hours* (those working 48 hours a week or more) and *long daily working hours* (working at least 10 hours a day more than 5 days a month).
- Finally, we tested, one by one, the relationship between our five independent variables and each of the eighteen quality of work indicators, using a multivariate logistic regression model with controls for country, sector, size of establishment and gender. These controls were introduced because we wanted to see the link between the working time arrangements and the quality of work clear of any compositional effect of the control variables.

The results of this analysis are shown in Table 7.4. Each one of the cells in the table shows the odds ratios (exponentiated coefficients) corresponding to a logistic regression model run for each specific combination of independent and dependent variable: for instance, the first cell in the top left of the table (8.639) shows that the odds that a shift worker works regularly in the evenings are 8.6 times higher than the odds of a non-shift worker. Each of these individual logistic regressions had controls for country, sector, size of the establishment and gender. The coefficients for these controls are, nevertheless, not shown in the table for obvious reasons of space.

Table 7.4 Working time and quality of work

	(A) Shift work			**(B) Long hours**	
		Specific shift systems			
	Working shifts	Rotating	Night	Long weekly working hours	Long daily working hours
1 Scheduling					
Work evenings	8.639***	17.81***	53.62***	3.993***	6.043***
Work nights	11.66***	17.98***		2.423***	3.236***
Work Saturdays	6.013***	6.406***	7.809***	4.578***	3.566***
Work Sundays	5.782***	6.927***	12.68***	3.352***	4.360***
2 Variability					
Unchanging schedules	0.286***	0.272***	0.257***	0.867	0.660***
Changing – long notice	2.953***	2.951***	3.050***	1.267	1.725***
Changing – short notice	3.984***	4.445***	5.070***	0.510	0.461*
3 Autonomy					
Working hours entirely set by establishment, no flex. for changes	1.418**	1.290	2.362***	0.481***	0.436***
Can choose between several fixed schedules	1.816***	2.066***	1.370	0.821	0.991
Can adapt working hours within certain limits	0.425***	0.443***	0.260***	1.260	1.588***
Working hours entirely set by employee	0.494**	0.557	0.381	5.271***	3.776***
4 Health and safety					
Perception of health and safety at risk because of work	1.627***	1.760***	1.810***	1.756***	1.369*
Perception that work affects health	1.575***	1.558**	1.784***	2.182***	1.719***
Reporting stress	1.391**	1.408*	1.576*	2.424***	2.048***
Reporting fatigue	1.478**	1.572**	1.758**	2.360***	1.884***
Reporting sleep problems	2.192***	2.611***	3.698***	2.391***	2.053***
5 Pay					
Low paid (in the 3 lower deciles)	1.001	0.839	0.441**	0.345***	0.325***
High paid (in the three higher deciles)	0.595***	0.639*	0.758	2.735***	2.662***
Receive extra pay for extra hours/overtime	2.083***	2.774***	2.517***	1.030	1.522***
Receive extra pay for bad working conditions	2.838***	3.844***	3.703***	1.326	1.156
Consider themselves well paid for the work they do	0.716**	0.731*	0.735	0.987	0.960
6 Unsatisfied with working conditions	1.788***	2.183***	2.147***	1.565*	1.263
7 Perceived work-life conflict (working hours do not fit life commit.)	2.713***	3.066***	3.713***	4.490***	3.199***

Source: EWS 2005 (subsample of approx. 5.000 employees in 6 EUCOWE countries).
* p<0.05; ** p<0.01; *** p<0.001

Shift work

Working shifts clearly increases the likelihood of having unsocial work schedules, as shown in panel A.1 of Table 7.4. The odds of shift workers working often at nights (at least five times a month) is almost 12 times higher than the odds of non-shift workers, and in the case of those with rotating shifts the odds are 18 times higher. Shift workers are also much more likely to have changing schedules (A.2), and when they have changing schedules they are more likely to be notified only a few days in advance (the odds ratio for changing schedules with short notice is almost 4). But do changing schedules mean more flexibility for shift workers to organise their working hours according to their needs? Not at all, as can be seen in the coefficients for autonomy in Table 7.4 (A.3). Shift workers tend to have considerably less autonomy in working hours than non-shift workers: the odds of shift workers being able to adapt their working hours with or without certain limits are below half those of the rest of workers, whereas they are between 1.5 and 2 times more likely to have schedule entirely set by their companies.

So the organisation of working time for shift workers is clearly disadvantageous. Shift workers are much more likely to work unsocial and changing schedules, with little autonomy to adapt their work schedules to their own needs. All these characteristics are clearly negative from a quality of work perspective, and especially in terms of work-life balance (see for instance Parnanen, Sutela and Mahler, 2005). Nevertheless, this was more or less to be expected: after all, shift work almost by definition entails a complicated organisation of working time. But what about other aspects of quality of work, such as health and well-being, pay or satisfaction?

As shown in Table 7.4 (A.4), shift work seems to have a clear negative impact (or at least, there is a clear correlation even after controlling for sector, size, country and gender) on the health and well-being on the worker. The odds of shift workers reporting that their job entails risks to their health and safety are almost twice those of other employees, and they are also more likely to perceive that their work directly affects their health. We have selected three specific indicators of impact of work on health from the 2005 EWCS that illustrate this issue: shift workers are considerably more likely to suffer from sleep problems caused by work (especially when they work at nights regularly, of course), from fatigue and also slightly more likely to suffer stress (although the effect of shift work on the latter is not so important, as indicated by the size of the odds ratio).

Pay can sometimes be used as a compensation for bad working conditions, but this is very difficult to capture in surveys such as the EWCS because such a compensation would only have a marginal effect on the distribution of pay, which is determined by much more important structural factors such as education or occupation (see Parent-Thirion *et al.*, 2007: 83-91). In the EWCS there is a direct question asking workers whether they receive special compensations for different working conditions, and this question shows that shift workers do receive compensation: the odds of shift workers receiving extra pay in compensation for bad working conditions is three times than those of other workers, and the odds of receiving extra pay for working extra hours twice (see A.5 in Table 7.4). However, this compensation does not make shift workers well-paid in comparative terms. The EWCS measures wages by deciles, and we could look at whether shift workers are significantly more likely than non-shift workers to fall into either low or high pay positions (defined as the lower and the higher three income deciles within each country). There is no difference between shift workers and the rest in the likelihood of falling into low-paid wages, but there is a significant difference in the odds of falling in the high pay categories: the odds of shift workers are almost half the odds of the rest. So even though shift workers tend to receive some compensation for their conditions of work, they are less likely to be in the higher-paid categories. In fact, shift workers are slightly less satisfied with their pay than non-shift workers, as shown also in Table 7.4.

The conditions of work of shift workers are clearly worse than those of other workers, and although there is compensation, it does not seem to be quite enough. Probably as a result, shift workers are twice as likely to be unsatisfied with their working conditions than non-shift workers, a clear and statistically significant relationship that is even stronger for rotating and night shifts. And they are even more unsatisfied with their work-life balance: shift workers are three times more likely to report a conflict between their professional and personal lives, four times more in the case of shift workers working regularly at nights.

Long working hours

In panel B of Table 7.4 we can see the relationship between the two forms of long working hours (as described above) and the different aspects of quality of work covered here. Long working hours, as shift work, implies a detrimental work scheduling, but is correlated with higher levels of autonomy at work. The negative impact of long hours on scheduling is nevertheless smaller than the negative impact of shift work: those working long weekly hours are four times more likely to work evenings and two and a half times more likely to work at nights than workers with standard working hours (whereas shift workers are almost nine times more likely to work evenings and 12 times more likely to work nights). In terms of the predictability of schedules, again long-hours workers are slightly disadvantaged, but much less so than shift workers: those working long daily hours are more likely to have changing schedules, but with a long period of notice. However, the largest difference between long hours and shift work is in terms of working time autonomy. Whereas shift workers had considerably less autonomy than non-shift workers in their working time organisation, those working long hours tend to have much more autonomy. The odds of those working long weekly hours having completely inflexible schedules is less than half the odds of the rest, whereas the odds of them having complete flexibility of schedules (under their own control) is five times higher.

Long working hours has a clear negative impact in terms of health at the workplace, according to the responses of workers to the EWCS. This negative impact is even stronger than that of shift work, as shown in panel A.4 of Table 7.4. The odds of reporting work-related health problems is around two and a half times larger for those working long weekly hours than for other workers (whereas shift work increased these odds by only around 50%). The negative impact of long hours is especially strong in the cases of stress, fatigue and sleep problems, in line with previous findings in the literature (as shown in Table 7.1). Even though the impact is negative in the two forms of long hours, working long daily hours does not increase heath problems at work so much as long weekly hours.

Clearly, long working hours are correlated with higher pay levels. Those working long weekly and daily hours are much more likely to be in the top three quintiles and much less likely to be in the bottom three quintiles (see panel B.5 of Table 7.4). This difference in pay levels do not seem to result from compensation mechanisms: the odds of receiving extra pay for overtime or bad working conditions is not significantly different for those working long weekly hours workers and the rest, and only slightly so in the case of long daily hours. Furthermore even though long-hours workers are considerably more likely to be in higher-paid jobs, they are not more satisfied with their pay than other workers (the difference in the odds ratio is very small and not statistically significant).

So the overall assessment of the conditions of work associated with working long hours is mixed. Long-hours workers are more likely to work unsocial and changing schedules, but they have more autonomy in their working time. Working long hours seems to have a clear negative impact on health and well being, but is associated with higher pay positions. This mixed balance may be reflected in the assessment made by long-hours workers themselves: they are only marginally less satisfied with their working conditions than other workers, and the difference is only marginally significant in statistical terms (see panel B.6 of Table 7.4). Certainly, the impact of long hours on satisfaction with working conditions is less negative than the impact of shift work. However, long hours does have a very strong negative impact in terms of satisfaction with work-life balance, even stronger than the impact of shift work (see panel B.7). Those working more than 48 hours a week are 4.5 times more likely to be unsatisfied with their work-life balance than workers with shorter schedules (those working long daily hours are around three times more likely to be unsatisfied with their work-life balance).

7.4 Conclusions

This chapter has attempted to clarify the links between two areas of socio-economic research that are clearly related, but not usually studied in an integrated fashion: the time intensity of firms' capacity utilisation and the quality of work of individual employees. We argued that the needs and preferences of workers as human beings and the rationale of firms as profit-driven market organisations tend to enter into conflict regarding time. The socially constructed norms around when each activity should take place are essentially in conflict with the underlying logic of capacity utilisation, which suggests that each activity (work) must take place when it is most profitable. Increasing the intensity of capacity utilisation means either extending the individual hours of work or re-scheduling working times to cover hours that were previously considered unsuitable (*i.e.* unsocial) for work. Because in modern market economies working time is the pivotal time for life, the time that determines the pace of living, the effects of this increasing time intensity of capacity utilisation tends to extend beyond the quality of work itself to all areas of social life.

A detailed analysis of the EUCOWE survey allowed us to determine what are the main ways in which companies organise the working times of their individual employees in order to utilise their productive capacity at the required level. In all the countries covered, the main tool used for increasing the time intensity of capacity utilisation is shift work. Other working time arrangements that are used significantly as tools for extending the operating hours of companies are (in decreasing order of importance): staggered working times (which is, in fact, a specific form of shift work), overtime, working hours (excluding overtime) and (only marginally) part-time work.

After identifying the main working time arrangements used for extending capacity utilisation, we studied their impact on the quality of work and work-life balance of individual employees. As a result of the characteristics of the data used, we restricted the analysis to two types of working time arrangements: shift work (which, from the perspective of the worker includes staggered working times) and long hours of work. From the perspective of the individual employee, these two main types of working time arrangements encapsulate the four forms of working time organisation that were previously identified as the main tools used for companies to extend operating times.

Our empirical analysis showed that shift work and long working hours clearly correlate with higher incidence of negative health outcomes such as stress, fatigue and sleep problems. Both types of working time arrangements imply having unsocial and/or exhausting work schedules. Shift work entails less time autonomy at work, whereas long working hours tends to be accompanied by more autonomy in the personal organisation of time. Both shift work and long working hours are very often economically compensated directly or indirectly, but this compensation does not seem to be considered sufficient for the workers affected. Finally, the levels of dissatisfaction with working conditions and especially work-life balance are considerably higher for shift workers and those working long hours than for the rest of employees.

The picture, therefore, is not very rosy. The time intensity of capacity utilisation (*i.e.* the extension of firms' operating hours) tends to have a negative impact on the quality of work and work-life balance. Of course, this does not mean that increasing the utilisation of productive capacity is not a legitimate aim, or one that it necessarily has negative implications for society as a whole or even for the workers affected. The main argument in favour of the increase in the intensity of capacity utilisation (that it implies increased output, which creates the possibilities for increasing the general levels of material well-being) is still valid in principle, although to the usual list of counter-arguments – equality, environmental, *etc.* – should be added the fact that it can certainly have negative implications for the quality of work and work-life balance of the employees affected and their families. On the other hand, the question is not only whether the extension of operating hours of companies has a negative impact on working conditions, but whether this impact is sufficiently and justly compensated. The identification of the situations where such compensation is not sufficient, and the reasons behind this, is the obvious next step of the research presented here.

References

Bosworth, D. and P. J. Dawkins (1981) *Work Patterns. An Economic Analysis*, Aldershot: Gower.

Circadian Technologies (2004) *Shiftwork Practices 2004*, Stoneham, MA: (http://circadian.com/practices).

Corral, A. and I. Susi (2004) *Part-time work in Europe*, European Observatory of Working Conditions Comparative Report, Dublin: European Foundation for the Improvement of Living and Working Conditions. (http://www.eurofound.eu.int/ewco/reports/TN0403TR01/TN0403TR01.pdf).

Cullen, K. (Coord.) (2002) *Results of a Family Survey*. FAMILIES project Deliverable No. 3, Dublin: Work Research Centre.

Delsen L., D. Bosworth, H. Groß and R. Muñoz de Bustillo (eds.) (2007) *Operating Hours and Working Times. A Survey of Capacity Utilization and Employment in the European Union*, Heidelberg: Physica-Verlag.

Dembe, A. E., J. B. Erickson, R. G. Delbos and S. M. Banks (2005) The impact of overtime and long work hours on occupational injuries and illnesses: new evidence from the United States, *Occupational and Environmental Medicine*, 62: 588-597.

European Telework Online (2004) *Teleworking: a Trade Union Perspective*, London: MSF Information Technology Professionals Association (http://eto.org.uk/faq/faq01.htm.).

Fernández Macías, E. (2006) *Construction of income bands for the 4th European Working Conditions Survey*, Research Paper, Dublin: European Foundation for the Improvement of Living and Working Conditions. (http://www.eurofound.eu.int/docs/ewco/4EWCS/4EWCSincomebands.pdf).

Gershuny, J. (2005) Busyness as the badge of honour for the new superordinate working class, *Social Research: An International Quarterly of Social Sciences*, 72: 287-314.

Golden, L. (2001) Flexible work schedules: what are we trading off to get them?, *Monthly Labour Review*, March: 50-67.

Harrington, J. M. (2001) Health effects of shift work and extended hours of work, *Occupational and Environmental Medicine*, 58: 68-72.

Hogarth, T., C. Hasluck and G. Pierre (2001) *Work-Life Balance 2000: Baseline study of work-life balance practices in Great Britain,* Warwick: Institute for Employment Research, University of Warwick.

Janssen, B. (1987) *Dagdienst en ploegendienst in vergelijkend perspectief (Daywork and shiftwork compared),* Lisse: Swets & Zeitlinger.

Johnson, K. L. (1997) *Shiftwork from a Work and Family Perspective*, R-98-2E, Toronto: Human Resources Development Canada.

ILO (1992) *Code of Practice on Working Time,* Geneva: International Labour Organisation.

Liu, Y. and H. Tanaka (2002) Overtime work, insufficient sleep, and risk of non-fatal acute myocardial infarction in Japanese men, *Occupational and Environmental Medicine*, 59: 447-451.

MTAS (2000) *Encuesta de Calidad de Vida en el Trabajo*, Madrid: Ministerio de Trabajo y Asuntos Sociales.

Muñoz de Bustillo, R., F. Esteve, E. Fernández Macías and A. García (2003) *Nuevos Tiempos de Actividad y Empleo,* Madrid: Ministerio de Trabajo y Asuntos Sociales.

Muñoz de Bustillo R. and E. Fernández Macías (2005) Job satisfaction as an indicator of the quality of work, *Journal of Socio-Economics*, 34: 656-673.

Parent-Thirion, A., E. Fernández Macías, J. Hurley and G. Vermeylen (2007) *Fourth European Working Conditions Survey*, Dublin: European Foundation for the Improvement of Living and Working Conditions.

Parnanen, A., H. Sutela and S. Mahler (2005) Combining family and full-time work, *European Working Conditions Observatory Comparative Report*, Dublin: European Foundation for the Improvement of Living and Working Conditions.

Ratjaratnam, S. M. W. and J. Arendt (2001) Health in a 24-h society, *Lancet*, 358, September 22: 999-1005.

Rosa, R. R. and M. J. Colligan (1997) *Plain Language about Shiftwork,* Cincinati, Ohio: U.S. Department of Health and Human Services.

Shields, M. (2000) Long working hours and health, *Perspectives*, Statistics Canada, Spring: 49-56.

Tepas, D. I. (1985) Flexitime, compressed workweeks and other alternative work schedules, in: S. Folkard and R. Monk (eds.) *Hours of work. Temporal factors in work-scheduling*, Chichester: John Wiley and Sons, 47-164.

Wallace, M. (1998) OHS Implications of Shiftwork and Irregular Hours, *National Occupation Health & Safety Development Grant,* Australia: National Occupation Health & Safety Commission.

Wedderburn, A. (1992) *Compensation for shiftwork*, Dublin: European Foundation for the Improvement of Living and Working Conditions.

Wedderburn, A. (1996) *Compressed Working Time*, BEST Bulletin, N° 10. Luxemburg: Office for Official Publications of the European Communities.

List of Tables

List of Figures

Author Index

Subject Index

Appendix EUCOWE Questionnaire

A Survey of Operating Hours, Working Time and Employment in France, Germany, the Netherlands, Portugal, Spain and the United Kingdom

Instructions

- Please ensure that all answers refer exclusively to the *addressed local unit* (*i.e.* your establishment)
- Please answer by ticking the relevant boxes or writing on the lines where indicated.
- The question relate to the situation at your establishment in a typical week in March or April 2003.
- All responses are completely *confidential*.
- Please return the questionnaire even if you are unable to complete it fully.
- Use the pre-paid reply envelope to return your questionnaire.
- Further information about this survey can be found at: www.iso-koeln.de/eucowe/

If you have any queries about the questionnaire please contact:
Name

Section 1: The local unit

1 What is your main product or service?

....

2 Is the establishment:

- ☐ An enterprise or part of an enterprise
- ☐ A public sector body (go to question 6)
- ☐ A non-profit organisation
- ☐ Other (please specify):

3 Is the establishment:

- ☐ The only establishment in the enterprise/organisation
- ☐ One of a number of establishments within an enterprise/organisation

4 Which of the following best describes the ownership or control of your organisation?

- ☐ (Country) owned or controlled (go to question 6)
- ☐ Jointly (country) and foreign owned or controlled (go to question 5)
- ☐ Foreign owned or controlled (go to question 5)

5 What is the nationality of the foreign main-owner or partner of your organisation?

....

6 How long has the establishment been in existence?

- ☐ More than 10 years
- ☐ 5-10 years
- ☐ Less than 5 years

7 Does your local unit negotiate or follow a collective agreement on the branch or firm level covering working times and/or operating hours?

- ☐ Yes
- ☐ No

8 At which levels does the local unit experience competition?
(tick as many as appropriate)

- ☐ Local
- ☐ National
- ☐ International
- ☐ Not applicable

Section 2: Employees, operating hours and contractual working times

The following questions refer to the number of employees, the operating hours and working times of employed persons in your establishment in a usual week in March or April 2003.

9 Please report the number of employees at your establishment in the following categories (please include agency workers, but exclude subcontractors, freelancers and honorary employees). *If exact values are not available, please estimate.*

Total number of employees ☐

Number of female employees ☐

10 What percentage of your employees fall into the administrative, technical or managerial category?

☐ %

11 Please report the number of agency workers and fixed-term employees at your establishment. (please exclude subcontractors, freelancers and honorary employees). *If exact figures are not available, please estimate.*

Number of agency workers and fixed-term employees ☐

12 Compared to 1998* has the number of employees decreased, remained about the same or increased?

☐ Employment decreased by about ☐ %

☐ Employment remained about the same

☐ Employment increased by about ☐ %

* or since establishment began operating, if later.

13 Contractual working hours
Please report the number of employees with the following *contractual weekly working hours* in a usual week in March or April 2003. *If exact figures are not available, please estimate.* If the reference period for working time is not a week, please state approximate weekly average.

Number of employees with contractual working hours between:

1-10 hours	11-12 hours	21-29 hours	30-34 hours	35-40 hours	41-48 hours	49-60 hours
☐	☐	☐	☐	☐	☐	☐

Number of employees without an agreed number of hours ☐ employees

Please estimate the average weekly working time of employees without an agreed number of hours ☐ hours

14 On average how many days holiday do your employees have in a year, excluding national holidays and working time reduction days? ☐ days

Section 3: Operating hours

Operating hours are the weekly business hours of your local unit including preparation times and times for maintenance. Operating hours can be just as long as the contractual working times of full time employees but they can also be longer. For local units in the service sector operating hours are not only the times of provision of services but also the times needed to enable the services to be provided.

15 How many hours does your establishment operate on a typical working day? ☐ hours

16 In a typical week in March or April 2003 on which days did your establishment operate? *(tick all that apply)*
□ Monday □ Tuesday □ Wednesday □ Thursday □ Friday □ Saturday □ Sunday

17 Over the last year how many days did your establishment not operate? ☐ days

18 How many hours did your establishment operate in a typical week in March or April 2003? ☐ hours

19 Compared to 1998* have the weekly operating hours decreased, remained about the same or increased?

☐ Weekly operating hours decreased by about ☐ %

☐ Weekly operating hours remained about the same

☐ Weekly operating hours increased by about ☐ %

* or since establishment began operating, if later

Section 4: Work organisation

Staggered working times

Staggered working time is a pattern of work where the hours of some workers overlap with those of others but is not shift work, for example one group of employees works from 7 a.m. to 2 p.m., another from 9 a.m. to 4 p.m. and a third group from 11 a.m. to 6 p.m. Thus operating hours stretch from 7 a.m. to 6 p.m.

20 In a typical week in March or April 2003 did your local unit utilise staggered working times?

☐ Yes

☐ No *(go to question 23)*

21 Does your local unit utilise staggered working times to: (tick all that apply)

☐ Lengthen operating hours

☐ Cope with peak periods

22 Please report how staggered working times were organised in a typical week in March or April 2003:

Number of days per week with staggered working ☐ days

Earliest possible start time ☐ :

Latest possible end time ☐ :

Total number of employees with staggered working times ☐ employees

Shift work

23 Did your local unit utilise shift work in a typical week in March or April 2003?

- ☐ Yes
- ☐ No *(go to question 27)*

24 How is your shift system organised? *(tick all that apply)*

- ☐ Continuous shift system (24 hours a day, 7 days a week)
- ☐ Semi-continuous shift system-model 1 (24 hours a day, 6 days a week)
- ☐ Semi-continuous shift system-model 2 (24 hours a day, 5 days a week)
- ☐ Intermittent shift system (less than 24 hours a day)

25 How many employees, on average, work in the respective shift systems?

Continuous shift system (24 hours a day, 7 days a week)	☐	employees
Semi-continuous shift system-model 1 (24 hours a day, 6 days a week)	☐	employees
Semi-continuous shift system-model 2 (24 hours a day, 5 days a week)	☐	employees
Intermittent shift system (less than 24 hours a day)	☐	employees

26 *For intermittent shifts only:*

On average, how many hours a day do you operate with intermittent shifts?	☐	hours
How many days per week do you operate with intermittent shifts?	☐	days

27 Did your establishment operate on a Saturday in a typical week in March or April 2003?

- ☐ Yes
- ☐ No *(go to question 28)*

Please report the number of employees working on a Saturday in a typical week in March or April 2003: ☐ employees

28 Did your establishment operate on a Sunday in a typical week in March or April 2003?

- ☐ Yes
- ☐ No (go to question 29)

Please report the number of employees working on a Sunday in a typical week in March or April 2003: ☐ employees

Section 5: Flexibility

29 Please indicate whether the establishment experienced considerable fluctuations in business activity in 2002.

- ☐ Experienced considerable fluctuations
- ☐ Did not experience considerable fluctuations *(go to question 32)*

Considerable fluctuations in 2002	Within a day		Within a week		Within a year	
	Fore-seeable fluctuations	Unfore-seeable fluctuations	Fore-seeable fluctuations	Unfore-seeable fluctuations	Fore-seeable fluctuations	Unfore-seeable fluctuations
Did the establishment experience any of the following fluctuations?	☐	☐	☐	☐	☐	☐

30 How do you cope with fluctuations?
Please tick the most important measures used (maximum 4).

- ☐ Overtime
- ☐ Short time
- ☐ Saturday work
- ☐ Sunday work
- ☐ Changes in shift patterns
- ☐ Staggered working times
- ☐ Working time accounts/Flexitime/Annualised working-time
- ☐ Subcontractors/agency workers/On-call workers/freelancers
- ☐ Hiring and firing
- ☐ Other

31 Is your establishment more or less able to cope with fluctuations in demand or activity compared to 1998*?

- ☐ Less able
- ☐ No change
- ☐ More able
- ☐ Don't know

* or since establishment began operating, if later.

32 Please report the number of overtime hours used in the establishment in a typical week in March or April 2003. *(If exact values are not available, please estimate.)* Enter zero if overtime not used.

Total overtime hours ☐ hours

33 Does your establishment pay premia for the following working time patterns? *Please tick as many as appropriate.*

	Financial premia	Time in lieu	
		"1 : 1"	More than "1 : 1"
Overtime	☐	☐	☐
Shift work	☐	☐	☐
Saturday work	☐	☐	☐
Sunday work	☐	☐	☐
Staggered working times	☐	☐	☐

34 Please estimate the share of labour costs in relation to total costs ☐ %

35 Compared to 1998*, has the share of labour costs in relation to total costs decreased, stayed constant or increased?

- ☐ Decreased
- ☐ Stayed constant
- ☐ Increased

* or since establishment began operating, if later.

Do you have any additional information or comments?

Thank you for completing the questionnaire.

Please use the pre-paid reply envelope to return your questionnaire.

About the Contributors

Frank Bauer is Senior Researcher in the Institute for Employment Research (IAB, Institut für Arbeitsmarkt- und Berufsforschung) in Germany and was co-ordinator (together with H. Groß) of the international project "A comparative study on operating hours, working times and employment in France, Germany, the Netherlands, Portugal, Spain and the United Kingdom – EUCOWE". Currently his research topics are regional labour markets, industrial agglomerations, regional clusters as well as the evaluation of active labour market policies. He published on topics like employment development on regional labour markets, flexibility and regulation of national and international patterns working times and operating hours, and on time use of families. Selected publications are: *Betriebszeit- und Arbeitszeitmanagement* (Münster, 2005) (with H. Groß, G. Sieglen and M. Schwarz); Betriebszeiten in Europa, in: H. Seifert (ed.) *Flexible Arbeitszeiten* (Frankfurt, 2005) (with H. Groß); *Arbeitszeit 2003. Arbeitszeitgestaltung, Arbeitsorganisation und Tätigkeitsprofile* (Köln, 2004) (with K. Lehmann, E. Munz and H. Groß); Operating hours, working times and employment in Germany, in: L. Delsen, D. Bosworth, H. Groß and R. Muñoz de Bustillo y Llorente) (eds.) *Operating Hours and Working Times. A Survey of Capacity Utilisation and Employment in the European Union*, Heidelberg: Physica Verlag, 2007); "Schrumpfung im Ruhrgebiet, Wachstum im Saarland. Eine komparative Analyse der Beschäftigungsentwicklung in zwei ehemaligen Montanregionen", *Zeitschrift für Wirtschaftsgeographie* (2006) (with A. Otte).
frank.bauer6@iab.de

Gilbert Cette is Director of the Macroeconomic Analysis and Forecasting Directorate of the Banque de France and Professor in Economics at the Université de la Méditerranée, Aix-Marseille, France. His main research topics are: productivity, growth, information and communication technology, labour market and working time. He has published a report *Productivity and Growth* for the French Council of Economics Advisers (2004) (with P. Artus). Recent articles include: "Investment in Information and

Communication Technologies: An Empirical Analysis", *Applied Economics Letters* (2005) (with Jimmy Lopez and P.-A. Noual); "ICT and Potential Output Growth", *Economics Letters* (2005) (with J. Mairesse and Yusuf Kocoglu); "Is Hourly Labour Productivity Structurally Higher in Some Major European Countries than it is in the United States?", *International Productivity Monitor* (2005); "Opportunity Costs of Having a Child, Financial Constraints and Fertility", *Applied Economics Letters* (2006) (with N. Dromel and D. Meda).
gilbert.cette@banque-France.fr

Lei Delsen is Associate Professor in the Department of Economics of the Radboud University Nijmegen, the Netherlands. His current research deals with a number of topical European labour market problems and issues, including new forms of work, retirement from work, employment policy and economic performance and labour market (related) institutions. He is author of *Exit polder model? Socioeconomic Changes in the Netherlands* (Westport: Praeger, 2002); Ins and outs of the Dutch life course savings scheme, in: A. D'Addio and P. Whiteford (eds.) *Modernising Social Policy for the New Life Course* (Paris: OECD, 2007). Articles include: "Corporatism and economic performance: does it still work?", *Acta Politica* (2008) (with J. Woldendorp); "Choices Within Collective Labour Agreements *à la Carte* in the Netherlands", *British Journal of Industrial Relations* (2006) (together with J. Benders and J. Smits) and "Labour Market Institutions and Economic Performance in the Netherlands", *International Economic Journal* (2005) (together with E. Poutsma).
l.delsen@fm.ru.nl

Hermann Groß is Senior Researcher at the Sozialforschungsstelle Dortmund, Germany and was co-ordinator (together with F. Bauer) of the international project "A comparative study on operating hours, working times and employment in France, Germany, the Netherlands, Portugal, Spain and the United Kingdom – EUCOWE". His current research is focused on time use issues, especially on the duration, flexibility and regulation of national and international patterns of working times and operating hours and on work-life-balance. He is author of numerous publications on working times and operating hours. Recent publications are: *Betriebszeit- und Arbeitszeitmanagement* (Münster, 2005) (with F. Bauer, G. Sieglen and M. Schwarz); Betriebszeiten in Europa, in: H. Seifert (ed.) *Flexible Arbeitszeiten* (Frankfurt, 2005) (with F. Bauer); *Arbeitszeit 2003. Arbeitszeitgestaltung, Arbeitsorganisation und Tätigkeitsprofile* (Köln, 2004)

(with F. Bauer, K. Lehmann and E. Munz); *Betriebs- und Arbeitszeiten 2005. Ergebnisse einer repräsentativen Betriebsbefragung* (Dortmund, 2007) (with M. Schwarz); *Operating Hours and Working Times. A Survey of Capacity Utilisation and Employment in the European Union* (Heidelberg: Physica Verlag, 2007) (edited with L. Delsen, D. Bosworth and R. Muñoz de Bustillo y Llorente).
gross@sfs-dortmund.de

Yusuf Kocoglu is Lecturer at the Université du Sud Toulon-Var, Toulon, France. He is researcher at Laboratoire d'économie appliqué (LEAD), Toulon, France and associate researcher at Centre d'étude de l'emploi (CEE), Noisy-le-Grand, Paris. His research interests are: economic growth, new economy, ICT diffusion, innovation and R & D, capital measurement and capital operating time and labour market and employment policies. He published numerous articles on ICT and economic growth. Recent publications include: "ICT and Potential Output Growth", *Economics Letters* (2005) (with G. Cette and J. Mairesse).
kocoglu@univ-aix.fr

Enrique Fernández Macías is Research Manager at the European Foundation for the Improvement of Living and Working Conditions, in Dublin. From 2001 to 2005 he was a researcher at the University of Salamanca, working in different European research projects. His main research interests lies in the field of labour studies. Some of his most recent publications in English are "Job Instability and Political Attitudes Towards Work: Some Lessons from the Spanish Case", *European Journal of Industrial Relations* (2003) and "Job Satisfaction as Indicator of the Quality of Work", *The Journal of Socioeconomics* (2005) (with R. Muñoz de Bustillo).
efe@eurofound.eu.int

Rafael Muñoz de Bustillo Llorente is Professor of Applied Economics at the University of Salamanca, Spain. He has written extensively on issues related with the economics of the welfare state, pension reforms, income distribution and labour market. Among his recent work in English we can highlight his critical analysis of the Spanish employment crisis of the 1980s and 1990s: "Employment Performance and Labor Market Institutions: The Case of Spain", in: D. R. Howell (ed.) *Fighting Unemployment: The Limits of Free Market Orthodoxy,* (Oxford: Oxford University Press,

2005) and "Job Satisfaction as Indicator of the Quality of Work", *The Journal of Socioeconomics* (2005) (with E. Fernández Macías).
bustillo@usal.es

Sebastian Schief is Senior Lecturer in the Department of Social Work and Social Policy at the University of Fribourg, Switzerland. His current research addresses an international comparative analysis of labour markets, industrial relations, working time, work organisation and globalization. Recent publications include various articles on older employees in Europe, patterns of flexibility of enterprises in European countries, working time policy trends, configurations of working time and employment rate as well as working time measurement.
sebastian.schief@unifr.ch

Georg Sieglen is Researcher in the Institute for Employment Research (IAB, Institut für Arbeitsmarkt- und Berufsforschung), Germany. Currently his research topics are regional labour markets and labour mobility in regional clusters. He published on national and international working time and operating hours research (together with F. Bauer and H. Groß 2002).
georg.sieglen@iab.de

Mark Smith is Associate Professor at Grenoble Ecole de Management, France. He previously worked at Manchester Business School and has carried out research work for a wide range of European and National institutions. He has research interests that focus on labour market outcomes on individuals and organisations including working conditions, working-time, and work-life balance. Recent publications include "Job Quality in Europe", *Industrial Relations Journal* (2008) (together with B. Burchell. C. Fagan and C. O'Brien) and "La prise en compte de la vie familiale des salariés par les enterprises: une comparaison européenne", *Recherches et Prévisions* (2008) (together with M-T. Letablier, C. Perraudin, D. Anxo, and C. Fagan). He is co-author (together with J. Rubery and C. Fagan) of *Women's Employment in Europe: Trends and Prospects* (London: Routledge, 1999). He has also co-authored a number of other book chapters and journal articles.
mark.smith@grenoble-em.com

Jeroen Smits is Senior Researcher in the Department of Economics of Radboud University Nijmegen, the Netherlands. He published on intermar-

riage (educational and ethnic homogamy), health inequality, gender and language issues, the relationship between social and geographic mobility, labour market issues, and education. Recent publications include "Effects of Socio-economic Status on Mortality: Separating the Nearby from the Farther Away", *Health Economics* (2005) (together with I. Keij and G. Westert), "Length of life inequality around the globe", *Social Science & Medicine* (forthcoming) (together with C. Monden), and "Five decades of educational assortative mating in ten East-Asian countries", *Social Forces* (forthcoming) (together with H. Park). His current research is focused on educational participation in developing countries, gender and development issues, and fertility.
j.smits@fm.ru.nl

Arnaud Sylvain is Statistician in the Civil Service Pension Department (Service des Pensions, French Ministry for the Budget, Public Accounts and the Civil Service). Previously he was in charge of the Survey of Capital Operating Time in Industry in Banque de France (2000-2003).
arnaud.sylvain@sp.finances.gouv.fr

Stefan Zagelmeyer is Professor of Economics and Human Resource Management at the International University of Applied Sciences Bad Honnef-Bonn, Germany. He has research interests in personnel economics, collective bargaining, comparative employment relations, and comparative human resource management. He has published book chapters and journal articles on collective bargaining, employee participation, job satisfaction, and employment pacts.
s.zagelmeyer@cbs-edu.de

GPSR Compliance

The European Union's (EU) General Product Safety Regulation (GPSR) is a set of rules that requires consumer products to be safe and our obligations to ensure this.

If you have any concerns about our products, you can contact us on ProductSafety@springernature.com

In case Publisher is established outside the EU, the EU authorized representative is:

Springer Nature Customer Service Center GmbH
Europaplatz 3
69115 Heidelberg, Germany

Batch number: 10725802

Printed by Printforce, the Netherlands